JUSTICE DEFEATED

Victims: OJ Simpson and The American Legal System

Steven H. Adler

authorHOUSE®

AuthorHouse™
1663 Liberty Drive, Suite 200
Bloomington, IN 47403
www.authorhouse.com
Phone: 1-800-839-8640

First published by AuthorHouse 12/3/2007

ISBN: 978-1-4343-1662-2 (sc)

Library of Congress Control Number: 2007904437

Printed in the United States of America
Bloomington, Indiana

This book is printed on acid-free paper.

CONTENTS

PREFACE

The O.J. Simpson trial was long, tedious, informative, titillating, confusing, captivating, annoying, provocative, revealing, sometimes humorous, embarrassing, and ultimately provided a controversial decision. It became the reality show for over a year. After the criminal trial those who believed they deserved O.J.'s money brought a legal action in a wrongful death suit. This trial did not have the spectacular attraction of the criminal trial. Eleven years after the trials O.J. stirred up the media again by offering a book and interviews that would explain how he would have committed the crimes. Outrage over such a book snuffed out this publicity circus. The level of protest emphasized how deeply people felt regarding O.J.'s guilt. The rumor was that the book offered a **confession**. This didn't make any sense and without resolving who was the killer this crime remains a mystery to the American public. What strikes me most is how strongly people feel about this case. My book will be disturbing to most people because they will discover no matter which side they took, they did it for mostly wrong reasons, exposing lazy thinking and a tendency to come to conclusions without examining the facts closely.

Many books have been written about the murders and O.J. Christopher Darden, Marcia Clark, Vincent Bugliosi, former famed prosecutor, Mark Furhman, Faye Resnick, and on have cashed in as authors. They all will tell you that O.J. is absolutely the killer and should have been found guilty. I read their books and didn't find anything that contradicts what is to follow. I could have done the same writings with the other books. So, I come to you as a voice against all these intelligent and informed people.

The trial will go down in history as a special event, but not important in the grand scheme of affecting the justice system in the U.S. Yet, after reading the book, _Triumph of Justice, The Final Judgment on the Simpson Saga,_ written by Daniel Petrocelli, Attorney, who represented Fred Goldman in the civil suit I find that the Simpson trial may have brought to light many of the deeper issues facing the justice system today. I decided to analyze why Mr. Petrocelli was successful in winning when the LA prosecutors had failed. The journey through his book took me on an unexpected path of revealing the conduct of a lawyer intent on winning in behalf of his client. The book's course could be a powerful weapon in bringing needed awareness of serious problems to the public. It points out what is undermining the foundations of our freedoms and forcing us to pay for the abuse. If citizens feel injured and taxed they might complain and cause change. In this respect, indirectly, O.J. and Mr. Petrocelli will make a long-term contribution to restoring our legal system to one based on the finding of _Truth and Justice._ I am making this point because if you see that this whole matter went wrong, the cause can be put at the feet of the lawyers who were more intent on benefiting from the celebrity and the money rather than the truth.

I will take you through a very careful analysis of how people involved in this case might have been thinking to allow this all to take place. I try to get into the minds of the police, prosecutors, lawyers, judges, witnesses, jurors, experts, spectators, and the innocent people caught up in this mystifying murder case. This case included spousal abuse, accusations of premeditated murder, rage, poor police work, good police work, media coverage, racism, lying, evidence and the planting of evidence, the conduct of guilty and innocent people, those seeking to financially benefit from this high profile double homicide, and the interesting tactics used to win in the court room today touch us in important ways. Mr. Petrocelli has us examine all these areas in a way I've never seen. He has many theories, employs many experts, has many witnesses, and the best legal representation money can buy. All this is examined in detail, respecting each word in his book used to describe events and premises.

Unless you read Mr. Petrocelli's book, you will have to rely on my interpretations of what he is saying. My writings may cause more book sales for Mr. Petrocelli just to check out what I'm saying. It would be ironic if my writing brings him back on the *New York Times* Best Seller list. Either way, I hope to touch your curiosity to the point of taking a hard look at what this unique and tragic event and examining how you came to your opinion of whether or not O.J. was the killer.

FORWARD

Perversion of Justice at Your Expense

It is certain that Mr. Petrocelli will not like this book. Many lawyers will not like this book. O.J. Simpson may not like his book even though I show that Mr. Petrocelli leads one to believe he received a fair verdict.

The jacket cover of the book promises _Triumph of Justice, The Final Judgment on the Simpson Saga proves conclusively, that O.J. Simpson told lie after lie and that he did indeed kill his ex-wife and an innocent man._ That was an attention-grabber for me. I had come away from the trial of the century confused.

After reading _Triumph of Justice_, I felt deceived by Mr. Petrocelli. All he offered were old theories, bad logic, and erroneous conclusions. He convinced me he had bag of full of legal magic tricks. I then read the book again, but this time started to take notes regarding the important issues being raised. Now that I was making a careful analysis I found the book is filled with gross manipulations, blatant disregard for the truth, tedious strategies, breaking down the witnesses, loading the juries, attempts to prejudice the public, working the press, and using the money card with righteousness. This was a contradiction of the promise to reveal Truth. I was looking for answers but after reading over 636 pages I had more questions.

Mr. Petrocelli avoids alternative reasonable explanations for the murders. His silence on these important questions made me suspicious of his motives and conclusions. What did find was an egotistic lawyer flapping his wings over the great job he did bringing O.J. down. He shows a lawyer's game plan for victory, no matter what the cost. I found this despicable every step of the way. It is clear that it isn't just Mr. Petrocelli, but also the dream of every materialistic lawyer. Lawyer jokes come about for good reasons. They are laughing along with us, all the way to their bank.

Let me be *very, very clear*, I am not including all lawyers with the criticisms I launch at Mr. Petrocelli. I have actively worked with lawyers and most take their profession for the special trust it possesses as the necessary provider of settling disputes, resolving estates, making laws, protecting the innocent and advocating justice and fairness. Those attorneys are not being accused with this scornful group passing the bar to use as a means to an end; giving them the license to move money around, possess power, and win at all cost. This group is clearly damaging the intent of the law. It is not just Mr. Petrocelli. Otherwise, there would be no need to be critical. The system would root him out.

My critique is filled with sarcasm because it is the way I react to being insulted intellectually. I'm pointing out that this type of legal maneuvering has become a very expensive part of our lives. The result is we are being heavily taxed at all ends, to support lawyer's mischief. It is a big tax that is hidden in the cost of the things we buy and the services we purchase. The price is found in our medical insurance, auto policies, doctor bills, cars, and food. Any kind of business that we do includes legal expenses. The cost of everything we buy is raised by the amount of money lawyers skim off the good efforts of American industry.

Think about the class action suits, the malpractice suits, and the lawsuits against American companies. At the end of the day, the lawyers get outrageous fees and the plaintiffs a few cents on the dollar. No one is spared this tax. The legal profession is corrupting the sacred principles that make America great under the guise of protection. This litigious society violates our sense of right and wrong. Greedy lawyers of America are stealing your money, value system, and pride in the Red, White, and Blue. Mr. Petrocelli and those like you are a stain on our flag. This book makes you a defendant in a court of professional misconduct. As prosecutor, judge, and jury, I have come in with evidence that you have violated your public's trust.

I was hoping to find the answers for many of the questions the criminal trial didn't cover. I was an O.J. Simpson trial junky. I was all over it. The T.V. presentations, radio talk shows, newspaper and magazine articles, examinations with friends and family, and daily conversations. When I watched O.J. take his ride on the L.A. freeways with his friend, Al Cowlings, there were already many indications of his involvement with the murders. There was incriminating information regarding the battering of his ex-wife, Nicole. A storeowner reported that he bought knives at a local mall. He had just finished a movie about Navy Seals, which implied he was trained in combat and the use of a knife.

After experiencing the intensity of the trial and all the surrounding commentary I was left with an empty feeling when O.J. was acquitted. Something spoke to me that he was guilty, but the government was unable to prove their case. There were too many unanswered questions in the criminal trial. Where were the dripping knife and the bloody murder clothes? I'm troubled by the small amount of blood evidence considering the nature of the murders. It didn't seem possible for O.J. to commit the crimes in such a short amount of time. One would think that the violence would have caused some noise to be heard. There were too many questions and too few answers. Was the result of good lawyering, bungling prosecutors, media hype or just plain confusion, I don't know, but twelve jurors labored through an enormous amount of testimony and evidence and couldn't find O.J. guilty. Their efforts should be respected. They were closer to the case than I. They had reasonable doubt.

After the verdict, lines were drawn. It appeared most of those who considered O.J. guilty were white and those happy to see him acquitted were black. Lines were drawn by some who felt especially offended by the spousal abuse, loyal believers that the U.S. doesn't go around prosecuting innocent people, hero worshippers who refused to believe that O.J. could commit such a heinous crime, and others. This trial created emotionally charged opinions, the facts and circumstances seemed less important.

I admit I had several biases before reading the book. I questioned the motives of some of the plaintiffs and was suspicious of legal manipulations, with the aim to step wherever they will to win. I needed compelling reasons to be convinced that O.J. committed the double homicide. The jacket said, *proves conclusively.* This is exactly what I was looking for. Like the rest of the spectators, I have some theories. There are several that stand out in my mind as likely possibilities. I was curious to see them revealed and if so, how the lawyers handled them.

Mr. Petrocelli states the physical evidence was conclusive proof that O.J. murdered Nicole and Ronald. Conclusive means putting an end to doubt. He offers several aspects of this conclusive proof. I submit, counselor and reader, there are other plausible alternative explanations to each of the supposed proofs of O.J.'s guilt laid down by Mr. Petrocelli. You can decide for yourself whether or not Mr. Petrocelli lives up to his claim of conclusively proving guilt. The jury in the criminal trial was shown all of the evidence yet they could not convict. It was *not* obvious to them. I will take you through this list and propose very likely alternatives to all the theories. The omission of investigation on several points yells FOUL to me.

It is obvious there was no way Mr. Petrocelli wanted to take the risk of establishing logical doubt about this case. A million two in fees to you was involved and possible defeat. Don't open any Pandora's boxes. Don't let the jury know that you aren't interested in any other explanation, but just a moment, if justice were the important mission in this case, as you state, not the money, why would you omit the tough questions that might exonerate O.J.? Mr. P., what I am not confused about after reading your book are the motives of the plaintiffs and the lawyers in this case. What you proved beyond a shadow of a doubt was that it was all about the money and only the money. What highly irritated me is your attempt to dress yourself and Fred Goldman in holy outfits. Your confessions throughout the book show us a different story, the true story! A lawyer and a plaintiff doing all they can to *move money around* to line their own pockets.

ABOUT THE ENDING

Unlike most readings you will decide the ending of this book. You are now a member of the fourth trial of O.J. Simpson. Your vote will count. You may have come with preconceived ideas about the guilt or innocence of O.J. Simpson. This book may change your mind. You will not only have a chance to cast your ballot as though you were a juror, but you will discover an opportunity to be part of fixing a serious problem affecting you personally. The rush that I got in writing this book is all about that. Fixing an American problem that is seriously out of control and using simple logic to answer a puzzle that has divided the American public.

The most important conclusion, after examining the circumstances carefully, is that there are compelling reasons to believe more than one killer committed this crime. This is not an original theory, but I believe I nail it. You will also see in the last chapter, Mr. Petrocelli reduced to a lying, bigoted, money-hungry lawyer that will stop at nothing and say anything to win a case. In some circles this may be considered good, but you would not want to be caught up in this evil aspect of the legal system.

There is a temptation to read the end of a book and get to the conclusion. That's okay, you own it, but if you read through you will be saving the best for last. You will be fully armed to defend whatever position you wish to take. You will also be able to give your ideas on how this terrible crime was committed. There was a lot involved in this case. Evidence, witnesses, high-powered lawyers, an enormous amount of money spent both on prosecuting and defending, issues of race, police foul play, poor handling of evidence, spousal abuse and more. Since we weren't at the crime scene we will never know what really happened. Yet, this case can be the launching pad for improving the legal system if you want to speak out. I give you that chance at the end of the book. I look forward to hearing from you.

ONE

Rushing To Judgment

One on One

"*He was a killer. That was never in doubt. The physical evidence was conclusive:*"[1] Fred Goldman and Daniel Petrocelli, his lawyer, say this with conviction. In *Triumph of Justice*, the reader is promised to be convinced that O.J. Simpson was the killer of Nicole Simpson and Ronald Goldman. At best, until now, all we have had is circumstantial evidence to help us form an opinion as to whether O.J. Simpson committed these murders. No eyewitnesses have come forth and not enough evidence was presented at the criminal trial to convince a jury that O.J. was the murderer. Mr. Petrocelli claims that his book contains the *convincing proof* O.J. is *absolutely* the killer.

Early in his book, Mr. Petrocelli confesses that he didn't watch the criminal trial, investigate the evidence, or has experience defending accused murders, yet he takes on the case because he is convinced that O.J. is the killer. This type of thinking puts my commonsense on alert. If one starts out with a conclusion before examining the facts and circumstances it causes me to suspect an agenda other than dealing with your proclaimed objective, finding truth and justice. Could this be another attorney's ploy in search of fees and fame? You have promised me that they are not your reasons and you will convince me that you have solved this terrible crime. I start giving you the benefit of the doubt you are telling the truth; after all you are a lawyer committed

1

to truth and justice. Mr. Petrocelli submits the following evidence to persuade the reader O.J. is the killer:

> *"1. A cap with hairs matching O.J.'s was found next to the Ron's and Nicole's dead bodies.*
>
> 2. *One of Simpson's large leather gloves was lying between them; and the matching glove; still holding strands of the victim's hair and was stained with their blood and Simpson's was found outside his house.*
>
> 3. *Size twelve shoe prints, slightly pigeon-toed, were clearly stamped in the victim's blood, at the murder scene. Simpson is one of the 9% of the population who wears size twelve shoe, and he is pigeon-toed.*
>
> 4. *Those shoe prints made an impression that matched only one sole in the whole world – Silga sole, manufactured at the Silga factory in Civitinova Marche, Italy, for the upscale shoemaker, Bruno Magli. (You) had photographs of Simpson wearing Bruno Magli shoes with the identical sole.*
>
> 5. *Simpson's white Ford, parked outside his house, contained not only Simpson's blood but Ron's and Nicole's, and a shoe impression consistent with the Bruno Magli stained the carpet on the driver's side.*
>
> 6. *A trail of Simpson's blood was dripped up his driveway, into his house, and up to his bedroom and bathroom.*
>
> 7. *His socks were lying on his bedroom floor, spattered with his blood and Nicole's.*
>
> 8. *Blue-black cotton fibers consistent with a dark sweat suit.*
>
> 9. *Rare carpet fibers of the type used in his Bronco were found at the murder scene.*
>
> 10. *His blood, his cuts, his clothing, his gloves, his shoes, his car, his house, his ex-wife's blood, Ron Goldman's blood...all painted to O.J. Simpson – and to no one else."*[2]

This is an impressive list of circumstantial evidence. Those of us who have been fooled with more compelling evidence have learned to be cautious before coming to conclusions without more information.

Before, accepting each of these as proof of O.J.'s guilt, I will look to how you present the evidence in your book.

There are many facets to analyzing and evaluating this trial and Mr. Petrocelli's observations: the evidence, motives, forensics, legal tactics, criminal profiling, jury biases, and psychological suppositions regarding relationships, greed and desire, the connection between spousal abuse and murder, hero worship, why people lie, protection of families and children and on. I will follow Daniel Petrocelli as he takes us on his detailed journey through the litigation of the civil trial.

I took all of Mr. Petrocelli's writings seriously. Throughout the book when he exaggerates unnecessarily or offers unsupported speculation, I react, usually with a firm critique or a question. For example, when Mr. Petrocelli says, *"I had to control a man who never once in his life let anyone control him."* [3] Please, Mr. P. how do you know that is to be the case? Why do you have to control him? Isn't seeking the truth an exercise of finding the facts, not manipulation and whatever *the need to control* carries?

I'm expecting a book revealing justice to be extremely careful in word choices and not giving the appearance of coloring the story for a manipulated conclusion. Yet, Mr. Petrocelli you let us into your world of ultimate control. You continually lead me to believe that you don't intend to live up to the to his promise of seeking justice but, rather money is really what is being sought after. You tell us that, *"This was my client's last chance for justice".* [4] We'll see.

You believed that if you couldn't remove the O.J. image you would not win the case. Did you doubt that your evidence was convincing enough to persuade a jury that he was guilty? For you to be concerned that a jury would not believe your evidence because O.J. was a smiling football hero is an insult to the jury system. A jury system has imperfections, but for you to reduce it to a popularity contest takes away from the meaning of the process. Considering the high profile of this case it would seem that a jury would take the evidence seriously. This attitude says to me that you lacked confidence in the evidence you had in your case. How could you be so convinced O.J. was clearly guilty and at the same time be so concerned that a jury wouldn't get it?

You believe calling him "O.J." on the stand seriously jeopardized your chances of winning. Again, you seem to have very little confidence in either the system or your ability to make a convincing case. Did you tell Fred Goldman that the case was so weak that merely by uttering "O.J." during the trial could cause you to lose?

You needed to show that "...*Simpson would lie to them. About everything...If he lied, he was guilty. An innocent man would not lie.*"[5] That sounds good, but would a father lie to protect a son from a murder charge? If O.J. believed that his son, Jason, or someone else he needed to protect, committed the murders would it be unreasonable for him to lie? The generalities you are applying to a murder trial give off a contradictory message since you believe it is obvious O.J. is the murderer. It doesn't seem that the obvious would be so difficult for you to prove.

You also go to lengths explaining that Simpson is *clever and calculating*. This begs a serious question. Would a clever and calculating man select a knife as a murder weapon? This seems to be a key point in this case. Wouldn't a clever and calculating person consider that using a knife to commit a murder is a very risky choice? A knife can drop, the killer can miss the target, blood produces possibly incriminating evidence and it is likely that an assault will provoke unwanted noise. There are so many dangerous variables that the choice of a knife in a premeditated murder that make it a poor choice. Aren't there far less risky ways to premeditate a murder? Aren't you giving us a contradiction regarding O.J.'s intelligence without an explanation? You want us to believe a clever and calculating man would make a poor choice of weapons in a circumstance where mistakes could lead to a lethal injection at the hand of the State of California. There is also little information that a person of means, adored and with great future possibilities uses a knife in a murder. Certainly, it is possible, but is it probable, or better, isn't there reasonable doubt that this would be the choice of a murder weapon of a clever and calculating man? You also tell us that O.J. is the kind of evil man that would kill the mother of his children while they were in the house. He would be putting himself in a position to possibly being forced to kill his children if they became eyewitnesses of the murder of their mother. This appears to be highly unlikely and needs you to help us understand what you found in O.J.'s

4

background that brings you to believe this is possible. Mr. Petrocelli, you are contradicting what I believe is commonsense by describing O.J. as clever and calculating, and at the same time accuse him of premeditating murders in such a risky way. The cost of bad planning here is rather fatal. You are getting off to a bad start on the journey to find the truth, counselor.

You accuse O.J. for managing his trial from his jail cell and being instrumental in winning his freedom. Aren't you overlooking the *Dream Team* of lawyers? You must have forgotten Mr. Cochran's dramatic presentations. What evidence do you have that establishes how influential O.J. was in putting this case together? Without telling us how you came to this conclusion you want us to accept your theory that O.J. is a powerfully controlling person and took charge of his defense. I can't go there without better information. Even if you are right, what is incriminating about O.J. being an active part of his defense? Considering what is at stake, I would expect him to be very involved with the process. I'm feeling you are trying to manipulate me here, Mr. P.

"If the jury believed that he never struck Nicole, they would believe anything Simpson told them."[6] The criminal trial showed Nicole with all the nasty bruises. They were shown repeatedly on television. Most of the television population in the world saw the terrible picture of Nicole's battered face.

"'Well, Nicole hit me a few times, and I didn't consider that too physical'". *"Here was the pride and ego of a professional athlete and a very narcissistic man. No mere woman could hurt him. And I let hem run with that ball"*[7]

You try to show that he is narcissistic: another gratuitous derogatory psychological analysis. I don't know how anyone would attempt to convince a jury that no beating took place given the exposure in the criminal trial. With all the information already shown to the public I'm troubled that you are troubled that the jury would be confused on this issue.

"I strongly believed our jury—any jury—would struggle to accept the physical evidence no matter how incriminating, unless they were convinced that O.J. Simpson was a man capable of committing these murders."[8]

For this to be true you want us to believe the criminal trial jury was deaf during those months and through all the dramatic presentations. Why would you expect another jury to be different or less defective unless you could somehow load the jury with people that had a bias? The criminal jury heard all about O.J.'s beatings of Nicole and his episodes of temper. I winced at the pictures of Nicole's face after her beating. This was a clear display of spousal abuse. It was a call to all watching that something should be done to protect victims of spousal abuse. Even if the jury at the criminal trial were deaf, they would also have to be blind to miss the point that Nicole was abused.

You portray the outcome of this second trial resting on how the jury takes to O.J.'s description of beating Nicole in 1989. *"Simpson would deny everything. The jury would decide in the next few minutes if Simpson was a liar and, in all likelihood, if he was a killer. The case could easily rest on this."*[9] All throughout your book you have a problem believing anything O.J. says, yet you can't accept that Nicole would lie. I am going to be less kind to the deceased based on information you provide in your writings. You pointed out that the judge ruled, in 1989, that if O.J. would in anyway assault Nicole again, *he would forfeit his prenuptial agreement.* This means abusing Nicole had a $15 million price tag. This judge was doing his share to discourage O.J. from losing his temper. Maybe he felt a clever and calculating man wouldn't give up this amount of money because he couldn't control his rage. Is it not possible that Nicole tried to plant the impression of spousal abuse to get help in petitioning the courts for the prenuptial to be rescinded? You point out she was desperate for financial security. You tell us that she cheated the IRS of money in connection with the sale of real estate that O.J. gave her a few years earlier. If she would lie to the IRS to avoid paying taxes, doesn't it create the suspicion that she is capable of lying to get $15 million from O.J.? Can't you picture her giving it a good try to get that prenuptial repealed? You let us know that Nicole talked to many people about how O.J. abused her. Isn't it reasonable that Nicole would have a restraining order issued if she really felt threatened by O.J.? Isn't it possible that Nicole wanted it both ways? She could have been building a case for the rescinding of the prenuptial while still having O.J. around to feed family and friends. It seems like you and Nicole are in the same league of master manipulation. You open the doors behind which there are many simple and important questions for which you offer no explanations or answers. The fact that so many alternative explanations exists to your theories that you are obviously avoiding, cause me to question how you are going to convince the reader that O.J. was *absolutely* the killer. I'm trying to keep an open mind despite these contradictions.

When O.J. attempted to clarify his role in beating Nicole he took full responsibility, and you dismissed this as a staged answer. His mantra you called it. *"That was a mantra, not an answer. It was also an old refrain. He had said it in deposition, he had said it on television, every time I saw Simpson he was saying the same thing. It got to be a joke in the office; I would pace our conference room, mocking Simpson's deep baritone,"*[10] You and your office felt his answer was a joke. Doesn't sound like a joke to me. He was taking full responsibility for causing the injuries on her face.

After deposing O.J. for eleven days again you state, *"Simpson is very clever; he's a shrewd guy, and he had a prepared response."*[11] Again, do shrewd men sacrifice $15 million because they don't get invited to a family reception after a dance recital for their daughter? Do shrewd men threaten their wife with a knife with $15 million at stake? You are asking us to believe that he left his home on Rockingham, within a very tight time frame in order to return to meet his driver, went to his children's home, with a knife, in a premeditated attempt to kill his wife. Is this a shrewd, clever, or calculated murder plan? No counselor, this is a flawed plan if the killer didn't want to get caught. Any motive less than killing Nicole would cost Mr. Simpson 15 million dollars. The history of how O.J. handled rejection from Nicole reveals a bad temper, but not that he is capable of killing.

In a premeditated crime, which is what you believe happened that night a clever, shrewd, and calculating man, even if in a state of rage, would have passed for a better opportunity not to get caught. Premeditating a murder means to me at least: 1. The perpetrator believes that murder is the only way to resolve the current anger and, 2. There is no interest in getting caught and paying for the crime. Your theories of why and how O.J. committed these crimes must convince me that both of these aspects fit the man and what evidence reveals.

The time that had passed between the end of the dance recital of his daughter and when the   murders took place seems too long to cause a spontaneous rage. He had burgers with Kato in between the recitals and the murders. The murder described by you and confirmed by the condition of the victims was exceptionally violent. Rage might be one of the explanations for the terrible way they were killed, but it also speaks to the work of highly professional killers not taking any chances. What in all the descriptions of O.J. suggests he is capable of this kind of behavior?   Football players are in the business of controlled rage. Is there any evidence that football players have a history of murder? These are guys are in a violent business. They settle their differences with violence. They are trained to seriously hurt people. Has this training sponsored murder, or the opposite? We are given evidence of O.J.'s temper, but nothing that rises to the level that suggests being a murderer. I was expecting you to give us convincing proof that O.J. is the kind of beast that would murder in the fashion that took place at Nicole's. I was looking for something that you found in his history that would suggest that he was the type of man capable of out-of-control rage.   I was looking for you to produce some person to testify they witnessed this kind of rage behavior. If you could have come up with a police report indicating over the top violence then your theory would make sense. Dan, please give us something to back up your profile of an evil and violent killer. To the contrary, you tell us he lost his temper the time he walked in on his promiscuous ex-wife having oral sex in the light of day while the children were in the house. He kicked in a door and made a scene. He didn't hit anyone. He didn't throw any dangerous object. Dan, isn't the incident that afternoon more likely the kind of situation to create a motive to bring rage at the murder level? But, it didn't happen. How many men capable of killing would pass under those circumstances? You make a point of infidelity being a lie. I couldn't agree more. Nicole was having relationships with several men while seeking to reunite with O.J. Aren't you accusing Nicole of being a liar? You have planted another contradiction, counselor.

You are concerned that the judge would not let you attack the witness. Your game plan on attacking the witness was crucial to winning the trial.

"In the criminal trial, Judge Lance Ito had given the defense lawyers an astonishing amount of leeway. It is my opinion that Ito did so because he believed, beyond any doubt, that O.J. Simpson had murdered two people." [12]

You believe Judge Ito thought that O.J. was guilty. You accuse him of being too liberal with the defense lawyers, yet you want him to give you a lot of room to attack. You are now a lawyer with no game plan and clairvoyant to boot. Why would you question Judge Ito's concern that the case wouldn't be reversed on appeal because he failed to give the defendant every opportunity to defend? Your criticism makes no sense to me. I would think you would agree that anyone defending his life should be given every opportunity to clear himself?

You will not accept the possibility that Nicole started the incident that caused her the bruises. Why not? Why automatically blame O.J.? Isn't it possible for a woman to be the provocateur? This is not to say that the violence is ever justified. We can't just dismiss the possibility that the argument began with Nicole. We weren't there. This is another case of speculation that is unnecessary. It wouldn't be the first time a women instigated a violent response. Nicole knew her enemy. You dedicate several pages to the details of Nicole being beaten. This is old information to anyone who followed the trial. You are not adding to the evidence of his guilt. Spouses have murdered without history of spousal abuse. Abusing spouses do murder, but not all abusing spouses murder. You try to make it sound like all abusers kill. You want us to believe all abusers are liars and therefore, all lying abusers are killers. Making out O.J. as a liar and an abuser, following your theory, you want the reader to conclude he must be the murderer. My questioning this logic is not a defense of liars or abusers, or that it is not possible for lying abusers to murder, but in analyzing who committed a murder, I need more than generalities to convict a person and cause a jury to order the death penalty.

Notes:

[1] Daniel Petrocelli, *Triumph of Justice*, (Crown, 1998), pg. 1

[2] Ibid, pg. 1

[3] Ibid, pg. 3

[4] Ibid, pg. 3

[5] Ibid, pg. 3

[6] Ibid, pg. 4

[7] Ibid, pg. 5

[8] Ibid, pg. 2

[9] Ibid, pg. 7

[10] Ibid, pg. 9

[11] Ibid, pg. 9

[12] Ibid, pg. 10

TWO
Good Question, Mr. P.

What Have I Gotten Myself Into?

Mr. Petrocelli, the first sentence of the second chapter of your book reveals how you bring a case to trial. You inform us that you had no involvement with the O.J. criminal case other than watching the Bronco chase? What chase? Are referring to the below speed limit drive on the L.A. freeway with a procession of police cars? It mesmerized you. Well, we were watching the same scene, but saw two different events. The pace was too slow for a killer wanting to avoid capture. The word *chase* means something else to me. Is O.J. acting like a shrewd and clever killer during this spectacle? Isn't he acting more like a man who is confused? If he was aware of who killed Nicole and Ron and if it was someone close to him, wouldn't it probably cause a great deal of stress that could make him act irrationally? All the psychological theories aside, what happened on the Los Angles Freeway was definitely not a *chase*. Using the word chase does imply guilt, but does it confirm guilt? Your characterization of this act as evidence of guilt in this case does not ring true. *"He must be guilty."* [1] Each time you present a conclusion I am looking for supporting logic, evidence or reasoning. You're not helping me here. Mr. P. these tactics cause me to question your motives. So far, all I can come up with are attempts to manipulate the reader with a volume of misdirection to cause a preconceived conclusion. After all, you collected one million two hundred thousand dollars in advance fees to litigate and you won.

Mr. Petrocelli you tell us with utmost conviction, from the start, that O.J. is the killer. This is so obvious to you that you can't understand how the jury in the criminal trial could have missed this one so badly. We know that can happen, but the criminal jury listened and saw evidence for a year and made their considered decision. You are in a hurry to conclude the first jury was wrong before you become familiar with the evidence of the murders. It seems that this is a flawed way to begin. Even despite that breach of logic, your guess could be correct for other reasons. Many people gave you over a million dollars to spend seeking the truth. Maybe your intuition is correct and there is no financial risk on your part should you be wrong. Good maneuvering, counselor. At least you are a sure winner in this case.

Despite the clarity of the evidence, you repeat that it is going to be difficult for you to win this case unless you can use maximum strategy and pose highly speculative theories.

"It was a textbook case of what is taught in law school as 'consciousness of guilt.' Fleeing was tantamount to a confession; nobody of his stature would run from the police unless he was guilty." [2]

O.J. was a hero on the football field and impressive in TV commercials, but insult the American public by suggesting that this gives him a free pass to kill two people. Quite the opposite, it's not uncommon that when a hero betrays the public the reaction is to give out more punishment. Remember Pete Rose, Tyson, and Martha Stewart?

You told us that you paid little attention to the criminal trial. You describe yourself as a busy litigating attorney *"I had little time or desire to tune into the Simpson case."* [3] Is that why you question whether or not you should take this case in the first place? You did notice, however, that the attorneys involved in the criminal trial received unprecedented international exposure. Along with criticizing the prosecution's closing arguments; you criticize the judges handling of the case.

"Aided greatly by Lance Ito's ruling throughout the trial, they pounded home their twin themes of police corruption and incompetence." [4]

Just a moment, only a page ago you confessed you didn't have time to watch the case. By concluding that O.J. was guilty without carefully observing the trial, unless you are in possession of new information coming to conclusions at this stage of your involvement, causes me to

question your motives. You admit how little you knew at the time, mostly hearsay, yet you are able to come to a definite conclusion. The testimony went on for days about the suspicious nature of the blood evidence. According to you it is not reasonable or plausible that police can or will plant evidence. Even though you didn't watch the criminal trial it's hard to believe that you missed the Furhman debacle. Is it not possible for a policeman, committing perjury and invoking the 5th Amendment over and over, to plant evidence? You want us to believe that a lying spouse abuser would definitely kill his wife. Isn't there an inconsistency here, Mr. Petrocelli? Liars are capable of some crimes, but all crimes. You offer no explanation as to why a policeman who committed perjury in this case would not also plant evidence. You dismiss this possibility as foolish, yet it is a critical element of the case. There are too many instances where the evidence used in this case doesn't make sense other than that it was planted. When Fuhrman used the 5th Amendment to avoid answering questions regarding planting, did you allow that there was a possibility planting took place. Don't you agree that if a detective uses the 5th
Amendment regarding evidence because he doesn't want to incriminate himself, the public should be concerned with his honesty. Fuhrman discovered the bloody glove on Simpson's property that night. The same glove that you want to use to incriminate O.J.

You criticize Johnnie Cochran and Barry Scheck for ranting and raving. I watched a great deal of the trial and followed much of the daily news coverage. I must have missed the ranting and ravings. It would have been good if you could have given an example. Oh, I'm sorry, you didn't watch the trial and you haven't gone over the evidence yet. Silly of me. Now that you are on stage you want the freedom to use the same lawyer theatrics you are now criticizing. You planned to be in O.J.'s face, control him, and be aggressive. Why is this strategy good for you, but not for them? Ok, the picture is getting clearer here.

In addition to applying my logic to this murder case, an important reason I wrote this critique is to speak to the problem I have with cesspool of lawyers that come to a conclusion and then artfully, manipulatively, strategically work their case to meet the desired result. This is serious and has corrupted our judicial system with prosecutors doing anything necessary to prevail and a litigious society filled with hired guns trained to triumph at all costs. You confess you are envious of the lawyers that got the spotlight in this trial. That seems natural. You were also upset that justice did not prevail. Again, Mr. P., let me remind you that you didn't pay attention to this long and complicated case and yet, you were upset that justice wasn't served. Sounds like a rush to judgment. You were profoundly upset when you heard the verdict and felt for Fred Goldman and the Brown family. You were not the only one upset over the trial. You are adept at understatement. Again, at the early days of accepting to represent Fred Goldman what was the basis of you feeling so strongly that you had an obligation to right this wrong?

After the trial there were many who were upset with the verdict. They were mostly white. And there were many pleased with the verdict, mostly black. This revealed a rather sad condition still existing in America. The way you are approaching solving the crime, says that the white folks are the smart ones and are interested in justice and those black folk, they just wanted to protect their hero. Wait a moment; O.J. was a hero for both black and white folk. Even you were an O.J. fan. How could you not be? He played honestly and brilliantly. He took his hits, worked hard for his team, and became an attractive folk hero. Someone everyone would like. He worked hard for all of these achievements. The white folk wanted us to believe that the only reason that the blacks supported O.J. was for race reasons. WOW! As a white person this is an embarrassingly bigoted conclusion. You want us to believe the only reason O.J. won was because Johnnie played the race card. As you will demonstrate, that card has two sides. The other side says that whites are the only ones who can be rational, just, and capable of administering justice. How many blacks contributed to the plaintiff's defense fund?

When presented with the opportunity to represent the Goldmans you thought it was a crazy idea because you weren't a logical candidate and didn't have the credentials for such a case so outside of your field of expertise. *"It was too farfetched."* [5] Isn't this like an eye doctor agreeing to do knee surgery, if the price was right? When, where and how was this taught in law school? You were concerned you would not be paid enough to take the case. One of your partners, Tom Lambert, encouraged you to pursue getting the case anyway. He reminded you it would be great for the firm (an economic evaluation, I suppose), it will be a huge case (repeat for emphasis, economic value), and great fun. That is an interesting use of words for the land of wordsmiths. The lawyers should consider the entertainment currency from this case. Priceless. This was a great case for your ego and your pocketbook. Your partner, Tom, was really selling you. He must have known how to push your hot buttons.

When you shared the possibility of getting the case with one of your clients, Paul Marciano of Guess Jeans, he encouraged you and added,

"*...you ought to do this. I am outraged that Simpson got away with these murders! Everyone else is, too. Goldman needs a good law firm and a good lawyer, otherwise he is going to get crushed. You must do this!*"[6]

Did you bother to ask your friend how he came to the conclusion that O.J. was the killer? Did he, like you, spend very little time watching the trial and yet made a judgment anyway? Considering his business and reputation, was he unlikely to have taken the hundreds of hours to watch this case and put his business on hold. You didn't seem to care how he came to his conclusion? How did he get the statistic that everyone else is outraged? Certainly not everyone; there were twelve jurors who were there every day and didn't fit into the pool of *everyone*. Did he show you survey results that brought him to this conclusion? Perhaps these everyone's were also mostly white folks.

"*Fred said he was in the process of interviewing a number of lawyers and asked if I would meet with him. I told him I wasn't sure I was the kind of lawyer he was looking for, but I would be willing to sit down with it discuss the situation.*"[7] What is changing your mind? Paul implores,

"'*Dan,' he interrupted, 'you must take this case. It's more important than you. It is important to this country that there is justice. All the cases are coming out the wrong way: the Rodney King trial, the Simpson trial, the Menendez brother's trial. This case needs a big law firm like yours, and it needs a lawyer like you*'".[8]

In addition to the appeal of public duty, you show us your mental exercise regarding the economic value of this case, measuring it against the promptings that justice is served. The temptation of going down in legal history had its currency. The money devil can be rather eloquent.

This is a chance for fame, even though you never conducted one of these operations before. A little OJT, pardon the pun. Even though you are being given an extra-ordinary chance to be in the national spotlight you might have passed since as you point out in your book there were many other lawyers with a track record that would be more logical candidates. Your motives are not a surprise. I understand the business of being a lawyer demands billable hours and drives many a decision. Since clients rarely know how to evaluate an attorney qualifications you would think the high road calls for an admission that you believe you are not the best qualified for the job? But, here we are and you did get the jury to agree with you. But, more on that later.

Your law firm, Mitchell, Silberberg, & Knupp has more than a hundred lawyers with sixty in the litigation group. They are one of the oldest and most respected law firms in Los Angeles. That is impressive. You are an important member of a firm that is in the business of

"...moving money from one rich man's pocket to another rich man's pocket." [9]

Sounds like a good business especially since you rarely went to trial. I guess you didn't trust jury verdicts. You became very good at boiling down the adversaries to make the best economic deals. As lawyer who avoids the legal system because he doesn't trust juries is now considering taking a case that may have to use the very jury system he faults. Are you hoping this will be another boiling down process of moving money around? This concept made an important impression on me. I'm looking to see how you find the truth even at the expense of losing a big payday. You keep insisting your motive was justice, yet you throw out these concepts that seem like contradictions. I guess if you can get money and justice it is a perfect world. We'll see.

You paint a sympathetic picture of Fred Goldman. Parents that lose a child to murder don't need help from you in attracting sympathy. The Fred Goldman that I observed on television was obnoxious. He took rage to another level and would grab the microphone and get in front of the camera, over and over again. He had all the answers. He wanted to be the judge, jury, prosecution, and commentator of the trial. It is one thing to grieve for a son; it's another to proclaim someone his murderer without either being a witness to the crime or waiting for the trial to end. Would it have shut him up to have O.J. convicted? I think not. He, too, felt he was owed something and wanted to make sure that he was financially compensated for this loss. Yet you say that Fred was not interested in the money. I don't know why you put such a good spin on Fred considering the way he deceived you.

Your firm rarely took cases on contingency and you did not want the case on this basis. This appears as a serious contradiction to your belief that it was obvious that O.J. was the killer and wrongful death suits are normally taken on contingency. On one hand you couldn't see how the jury missed that in the criminal case; you blame it on the prosecution's mishandling and on the other you are willing to give up millions of dollars in fees because of a risk in losing the case. The contingency payment to you would have been as much as nine times the one million two hundred thousand in fees. That begs a question as to why you would pass up such easy money. You said the evidence was compelling. *"…it just needed to be tried better, to a more receptive jury, and to a different result."*[10] Both you and Fred felt you had a winner. The only wild card was convincing the jury. Millions of tax dollars had been spent developing the case. All the mistakes of Clark and Darden could be avoided. With such a clear victory at hand, the depositions would be easy. How could O.J. hide from all of this clear-cut evidence? Your friends all told you he was guilty, so you were convinced without even having to study the case. Even with all of this, you needed to be guaranteed more than a million dollars to try the case. *"This was personal."*[11] Yet you say you were being motivated to help a father undo an injustice against his murdered son. Please!

You speak again regarding whether or not you the right lawyer for this case? You tell us you were not; better than Fred could understand.

"Many other attorneys, particularly personal injury lawyers, had vast amounts more experience than I did handling this kind of case. I had none. Many litigation attorneys had far more trial experience. My cases had made it…only once to conclusion in front of a jury. All the rest had settled. I was not a natural for this case."[12]

You had only one jury trial under your belt, though you are a successful lawyer. What is more revealing is the fact that Fred didn't have the money or didn't want to spend the money to finance the legal fees and didn't want to help find the money. He thought he deserved money. Isn't this is an odd attitude for an enraged father fighting for

17

justice? Fred will do the talking, but not the walking. Shame on him. Not a penny sacrificed to help find justice. Fred wanted someone else to pay the way.

"We decided that, on balance, if funds could be raised, taking this case was a good thing... Assuming we could work out acceptable economic arrangements, if I got the call from the Goldman's we would take it." [13]

Considering all the virtues presented by this case, why wasn't per bono an option by your firm? Considering that you would be part of legal history and the public relations value alone, it seems a pro bono would have been the noble gesture. But you and your firm decided that only if you could be assured payment of your legal fees, you would take the case. What happened to patriotism? A no-risk case for you, based on your view of the evidence, a chance to right an injustice, the fame of being a part of one of the highest profile cases of modern times and no financial risk. *"There was also the simple fact that it was the right thing to do."* [14] I guess you and Fred Goldman would agree to that. No risk, even though O.J. would have to pay his way. Remember in the criminal trial he paid his way, was found not guilty and didn't get any of that money back. Now you want him to pay again and you are not willing to step up. I guess Mr. P. this case isn't really that important enough to take financial risks. I am perplexed about the financial arrangement you did make. All his life, O.J. has been quite a money machine. A contingency case victory would have paid you much more. The verdict you received was $33.5 million. Based on O.J. assets you would have earned from 10 to 12 million dollars. Yet you preferred a guaranteed, paid in advance $1.2 million. From a business standpoint, not accepting this case on a contingent basis contradicts your conviction about O.J.'s guilt and your ability to win. Unless there is something else you are not telling Mr. Goldman and us.

Fred calls you and says he wants you to be his attorney. You would love to represent him, but you need to talk further about the details before you can accept. Perfectly reasonable, since you were both concerned about the money. One hour later, without your permission, he tells the press that you are his lawyer and you find out lying in bed as it is announced on TV. After being deceived, how come you didn't tell Fred to get lost? You have discovered he is a wild card. He manipulated you into being his attorney. I guess he sensed your appetite for fame.

After seeing your name on TV, there is no way you could go back. Your new client has started off showing you he is a manipulator. The insult of being manipulated apparently isn't enough to ignore the money and fame.

The next morning you face the media feeding frenzy. You remark how smooth Fred was and how scared you were. He certainly knows how to play the press and you. Now you are making all the arrangements to deal with the media, organizing your legal team, selling the case to the partners, getting information about the case to your office all before Fred Goldman has officially engaged you and solved the money problem. Professional prostitution is taking place and you want your money up front. Glory, Glory.

Notes:

[1] Daniel Petrocelli, *Triumph of Justice*, (Crown, 1998), pg. 19

[2] Ibid, pg. 19

[3] Ibid, pg. 20

[4] Ibid, pg. 20

[5] Ibid, pg. 23

[6] Ibid, pg. 24

[7] Ibid, pg. 25

[8] Ibid, pg. 25

[9] Ibid, pg. 30

[10] Ibid, pg. 37

[11] Ibid, pg. 34

[12] Ibid, pg. 35

[13] Ibid, pg. 37

[14] Ibid, pg. 37

THREE

Making Lots of Rain, Daniel?

The "Big Unit"

"The question in this case was how to pay for it. People had pledged money, I just didn't know whether they would come through and whether it would be enough." [1]

You wonder where all this money was going to come from. One would think this was Fred Goldman's problem, but since he had already hooked you into taking the job, he left it to you to figure out how to fund it. Not very clever on your part, Dan. You came up with the idea of fund raising, radio talk show pleas, advertisements, and celebrity donations. You've got a good marketing awareness. Just what course in law school did they cover raising money to pay for lawsuits? However, The initial results were meager. You raised only about $100,000. I guess all those committed to the cause of justice felt someone else should pay for the process.

You asked Fred to be the spokesman for fund raising campaign, but he didn't want to have anything to do with raising money. He didn't want to make any sacrifices, financial or otherwise. He wanted others to do the dirty work. He even has the gall to come to you and criticize your concern for the money. It appears he wasn't truthful with you in the first place. He should have made it clear that the lawyer that took this case also had to take full financial responsibility. He got you to take your time to speak at fundraisers. Good salesman, Fred.

He finally consented to speak at certain dignified events, after being pressured by both you and your colleagues. At the $500 a plate Drai's, a high end restaurant, you refer to this civil suit as especially important because the justice system in L.A. had gone amuck and this would do more then bring O.J. to justice.

"Events like these underscored how deeply this case extended beyond the Goldmans and Browns, beyond the victims, beyond O.J. Simpson, to the community itself.... So there was a lot riding on our civil case. People wanted to right a wrong. People wanted to know that their legal system worked. People wanted justice."[2]

You pitched that a victory in the civil suit would make a clear statement that things were better in L.A. and the legal system was working, as it should. That is a big statement, Dan. Considering the public relations value of this case and according to you the chance to right an extreme injustice, you would also be setting a new legal standard straight in L.A. Yet, your large firm, one who had fed off of the system in L.A. for many years, couldn't reach out to help by taking poor Fred Goldman's case on contingency or pro bono. Were there were other motives for the fundraising? Maybe you needed to be sure you had the public support. Since the first round of $600,000 wasn't enough, you hire a professional direct-mail fund-raising firm to plead for more money. Great idea, institutionalize the process and make sure that everyone in L.A. knows that you and Fred Goldman are going to get justice. One problem, though, Fred doesn't want to put his name on the letter. So you show up at his house and demand that he both signs your fee agreement and participates in the fundraising campaign or you can't continue. After you let the horse out of the barn, you are threatening Fred. Good start.

Ron DiNicola took charge of the direct-mail effort, and produced another $700,000. All tolled, the Ron Goldman Justice Fund received $1.2 million in contributions.

"These funds made a huge difference, giving us the financial wherewithal to compete with the defense on a level playing field."[3]

Good selling Dan, another $700,000 in the bank for a total of $1,200,000. Now that you are officially his lawyer it's time to tell the press. You have covered your wallet with a lot of money for a case you are convinced is so clearly decided before going to trial. Good business strategy Dan. According to you, the defense had nothing, but incriminating evidence, obvious liars, and everyone was sure that O.J. was the killer. You didn't detail it at the end of your book, but let me guess exactly how when it was all over how much did you bill the defense fund. How about $1,200,000 to the penny as a good guess? Did you send Fred a bill after his windfall? Did Fred pay taxes on this money? Or did you cover that some other way? You are very quiet about the money end of this case.

Now how about those parties to the lawsuit that makes up such an interesting line-up. There was Ron Goldman, who would be represented by his father Fred, Sharon Rufo, the estranged mother, the Browns, Nicole's parents, and Fred Goldman. Sharon had filed a suit very early and even brought a lawyer to the funeral. Now she stands to split half of the award. Where was her share of the attorney fees? The Brown's decided not to claim a wrongful death suit due to the children, but will join in for battery charges. It seems the children are the most worthy candidates for O.J.'s money. This is another instance proving that the squeaky wheel gets the grease. You still insist it is not for the money, but for justice. Where is the justice in putting the children and these families through one more trial when you are acting like a lawyer that knows that the clients are not going to benefit financially? You have covered your financial end, but what about your clients?

You go into detail that you wanted to be the lead attorney on the case, primarily because of the strength of your firm and the amount of money you and your client raised. There would be natural redundancies that had to be worked out in such a complicated case. If Fred hadn't launched a civil suit, there would still be two civil suits striving for the same result. Since the case was so obvious, from the credentials of the other lawyers, it seems that even if Fred hadn't become a plaintiff there were other lawsuits designed to arrive at the same result. Fred's concern was that this case was about justice and bringing in O.J. to pay for his crimes so you think his concern naturally would have to be the quality of legal expertise. Did Fred know if you were a better lawyer than those representing the Browns or Rufo? Over and over you and Fred proclaim it was clear that O.J. was the killer and everyone felt there was a miscarriage of justice. Why was Mr. Goldman, without being willing to sacrifice financially and reluctant to help in fundraising, so intent on being part of this case? After all, you admit this case didn't take rocket science since the evidence was obvious that O.J. was the killer.

All the evidence, other than supposedly nailing O.J. on the Bruno Magli shoes matter, is a just a rehash of what was covered in the criminal trial. I will be reviewing with you distinctions that I take exception to, which speak to the re-characterizations of facts and circumstances that make me question the whole validity of your position in this case.

The description of Michael Piuse, the counsel for the Browns, indicates he was quite capable of handling this case. He was a former prosecutor with familiarity of criminal cases and, *"...routinely got big damage awards for his clients in wrongful death cases..."* [4] According to you Brewer counsel for Rufo, was also qualified to handle this case. Apparently you outbid or out-fundraised them. You make it clear to the other lawyers that you felt you were the better lawyer for this case. Dan, is your ego working overtime here? Remember this is not going to be a tough case. O.J. is guilty, what's the problem?

Fred signs your fee agreement so the legal wars can begin. You take us through the machinations of the many legal maneuverings. Attorneys working the rules to gain advantage, they maneuver to frustrate the opponents, delaying tactics for more frustration, positioning strategies to put the other side off-balance, and many other tactics that provide the most benefit. They set the rules and try to shape the personality of the conflict to tilt of the story in the best light for the client. This masterful gamesmanship of building up billable hours and driving the opponent crazy must have been a fascinating class in law school. Was it called Moving Money Around 101?

It's not my concern about how you practice law in pursuit of victory, but since you steadfastly maintain that it is not the money but the justice that is your mission, as a citizen, I applaud that objective. But, after hearing your speech I expect to see you follow-through and conduct yourself accordingly. When you then describe how you employ tactics to take advantage of situations, I question your sincerity.

You make a point of telling us that Baker, O.J.'s attorney, had a problem accepting that O.J. was the killer. Isn't it a little early for that criticism, Mr. P? You insist that you have the right to address O.J. as though he were the murderer. At the beginning of this trial this was not definitely established. What ever happened to the principle that a person is innocent until proven guilty? At all times, you show us that you want to be the judge and the jury, counselor. All you have are guesses and a lot of posturing. Even today it is still a guess, but you insist on treating this serious accusation as a fact. Good aggressive lawyering, but unprincipled and appalling logic. You are emphatic that you and Fred want the whole world to know about this case -- as if they didn't. You want it tried in the world of public opinion.

"I wanted the public to be aware of what was going on and to be in a position to give us as much help as possible." [5]

This of course, would make it more difficult to find an unbiased jury. You also believe there are missing witnesses out there. Did you really mean to say that *there might be* additional witnesses? Saying that you know something that is just a guess seems to be a habit. Let's not forget the distinction between knowing and guessing is very important in a murder trial.

You have a problem with O.J. producing a video telling his side of the story. You can't imagine anything more prejudicial. What ever happened to his right to free speech? You concede that a video produced by O.J. would give you an opportunity to pick apart any flaws or lies in his story. Since this publicity might contaminate a jury pool, you offer a solution. The judge can ask prospective jurors if the press influenced them. You make it appear that a primary goal is to tell the whole world O.J. is the killer before the trial begins. You insist on the right to bias the public. You want O.J. videotaped during the depositions so you can study his mannerisms and be in a better position to control him during the trial. Isn't there a possibility that information discovered during the depositions could be misunderstood when presented out of context? Does your sort of justice include a manipulated verdict and moving money around? You are arguing that the victory will go to the shrewdest, most controlling, son-of-a-bitch attorney who successfully broke down the witnesses and managed the press.

I just can't resist reminding you that the public knows of the sorry state of the legal profession these days. Lawyers are routinely the butt of critical jokes and contempt for how they have polluted our legal system. They know that the legal system today is a financial feeding frenzy for lawyers at the expense of the integrity of our society. Much of what lawyers do is transparently self-serving and has nothing to do with truth and justice. For you to believe that the public does not question verdicts contradicts the whole basis of your endeavor. Why should your trial be more respected than the criminal trial? I guess with $1.2 million in the bank you don't care much about this argument.

"Of course, Bob Baker would not want to admit he was representing a killer. This was Los Angeles, and in many circles O.J. Simpson was a pariah, along with those who continued to associate with him." [6]

Again, you criticize Mr. Baker, O.J.'s attorney, for not wanting to admit he was representing a killer. Dan, isn't this what it's all about? Did you really think he would tell you his client was the killer? Even if O.J. were the killer, it is highly unlikely he would confess to his lawyer or that his lawyer would want to know. You insist, again, early in the process that O.J. is the killer. You keep repeating this over and over, like a mantra. *O.J. is the killer. O.J. is the killer.* I have the feeling that your publisher is paying you for the amount of words you use. Your protestations can be considered ranting to prejudice the reader. There are several major questions that need to be resolved before the judicial observer can feel O.J. got a fair trial. You conveniently avoid these issues. Perhaps because you were concerned that it could scuttle your case. Or, perhaps you refused to open any new doors fearing O.J.'s innocence would be revealed. Mr. P. your legal strategy map that gives you the road to get to the victory line clearly avoids any high roads. Apparently the low road is better, akin to sewer dwelling. I see the trap you are in. It goes back to the despicable condition of your profession in the U.S. You said that in many circles O.J. was a pariah along with his friends. I guess he must know what feels like being a lawyer.

"In late November I started hearing rumblings that Baker's firm might withdraw from the case because they weren't getting paid. A long article on the speculation appeared in the Los Angeles Times. *Simpson's scheduled deposition was approaching, and I was concerned that the defense would use this as a tactic to delay it."* [7]

You say you were concerned that Baker's firm might withdraw because they weren't getting paid. You are repeating an unfounded rumor. O.J. was able to pay for his counsel. He didn't have to resort to a direct mail campaign to have others pay his fee. Maybe Mr. Baker did the work pro bono because he knew his client was innocent. Can you tell I am picking on you again because you insist on throwing out speculations that are superficial and prejudicial? If you had a good case you wouldn't sound so desperate to prejudice. You are making me suspicious of your motives.

"I was. We all were. We were vocal, we were in his face, we were in his client's face. We called his client a killer over and over again. We put it right out in the open and were not going to let him hide. I explained to the judge how Simpson was conducting his own publicity campaign, including the behavior of this entourage and the spin they were putting on the case." [8]

You admit that you were employing tactics to appeal to the media, a euphemism for influencing the public. Calling O.J. *killer, killer* over and over again may be good public relations for your client, but clearly a strategy to create bias in potential jurors. Still, at this stage, you don't have enough information to make an educated guess about O.J.'s guilt. Remember the depositions hadn't started and you hadn't had a chance to consult with any of the key players or experts. Is this how you work, come to a conclusion and build a story that gets you there? When you looked at the task of disseminating all the information you tell us

"...I couldn't begin to fathom how we could possibly make a dent in it, let alone read review and master all of it." [9]

It really shouldn't have been that difficult. Just draw on what fit your conclusion and leave the rest out. You were never expecting to find more evidence that would prove O.J.'s guilt. With this scenario, what do we have? One jury saying "not guilty" and your jury saying "guilty." Sounds like a tie. The only benefit to anyone is the chance for you to move money around. Observers would have to be confused by your statement that you were looking for justice. If your motive was money, more power to you and the legal industry. You can't even be honest about that. What a pathetic situation. Fight it out in court once in awhile and take your chance on a jury. Let's not forget you are in a win/win situation, $1.2 million in your firm's bank account. Besides you are *"...having the time of your life."* [10] I guess this was the fun part of the case.

Notes:

[1] Daniel Petrocelli, *Triumph of Justice*, (Crown, 1998), pg. 50

[2] Ibid, pg. 52

[3] Ibid, pg. 53

[4] Ibid, pg. 56

[5] Ibid, pg. 59

[6] Ibid, pg. 63

[7] Ibid, pg. 63

[8] Ibid, pg. 64

[9] Ibid, pg. 47

[10] Ibid, pg. 65

FOUR

On the Job Training is More Accurate

On the Job

"Learning on the job was our task" [1] for mastering the mountain of information accumulated during the criminal trial. Yet you *"...didn't know where to begin."* [2] Now, for effect it seems, you confess that you are *"...overwhelmed with the work ahead of us."* [3] You felt *"...clueless. I thought to myself. "What am I doing here? What did I expect to find?"* [4] This is as bad as a surgeon looking at his patient on the operating table and admitting he didn't know where to begin with this procedure. But. Dan, what is the problem? You believe O.J. is guilty, and you only have to get those things that brought you to that conclusion and nail it. I hope Fred knew you had so much self-doubt about succeeding.

You admit *"...this was the first time I had ever been inside Parker Center. In fact this was the first time I'd ever been inside any police station."* [5] You begin to analyze the LA Police Department and explain how the police were criticized for being soft when O.J. voluntarily came in to speak to them. Wouldn't it be bad form for the police to grill him when he comes in under his own steam without an attorney? O.J. could have walked out at anytime. Doesn't it strike you as unusual that after killing two people, O.J. would volunteer to sit with the police without a lawyer? He was free to attempt to make his escape from Chicago or when he returned to L.A.

Further, you and the police were both upset when the prosecution didn't use the *chase* as additional evidence that O.J. was acting like a guilty person. Again, you call it fleeing, giving it a consciousness of guilt. O.J. has plenty of experience running away from pursuers. The speed of this chase would have caught him way behind the line of scrimmage. This contradiction should have caused you to look for another explanation. Both you and the police are locked into believing he is guilty and are not willing to look for other possibilities. Are you afraid that asking the serious questions might subvert your mission of moving those dollars around? You speak of how the police second-guessed the prosecution regarding the evidence submitted in the case. Isn't it the job of the police to collect evidence, not be the lawyers or the judge? Was it their job to decide if O.J. was guilty? Isn't that the juror's job? In the pursuit of justice the police should not have an agenda, just find the evidence. You show us the police also wanted to be the judge and the jury. They are upset with the verdict as though they have a stake in this case. This was a big mistake and may have caused them to get into trouble. When the police believe in the guilt of the offender they run the risk of appearing to step over the line. With this attitude, they don't help the prosecution. Doesn't it make sense that Mr. Fuhrman lied because he was trying to tilt the case against O.J.? The public is especially sensitive to this conduct. We know that being framed for a crime is not that unusual; ask some blacks. The L.A. police, even though only a small percentage of the force behaved badly, have been under a high amount of scrutiny because of this groups sorry history of abuse. Whenever the public smells smoke they assume fire. Your idealistic notion of police work is surprises me. I'd rather think you just don't want to concede that some of the evidence could have been planted.

It is a shame Marcia Clark would not meet with you. *"I felt Clark was trying to return to her own life and didn't need to be dragged back in by me."* [6] Marcia has quite a bit at stake in O.J. losing the civil trial. It would be vindication of sorts. Or did she learn the truth during the trial that O.J. was not the killer and it was best to leave the whole matter alone?

Hodgeman, another assistant prosecutor, did meet with you. He was profoundly disturbed that O.J. walked. The only advice he gave you was to have a strong leader organize your legal team better and make sure the lawyers worked together. He didn't give you any helpful insight into proving O.J. was the killer. I see that the little he said spoke volumes. After a trial that is lost wouldn't there be some significant "should have, could have, would haves. Big points missed or poorly presented. Perhaps, there was some evidence that was not properly presented. Something. Otherwise it is a silent admission that they gave it their best shot with the evidence. What does that leave you other than be a stronger organized lawyer? Where is the evidence to convict. Unless Hodgeman is also saying the jury didn't get it. Then he should have told you so.

You also met with Chris Darden for a half hour. He blamed the judge for being too liberal and allowing the defense too much latitude. This is the same meager help from someone who was so close to the subject matter. All he could advise was to get a tougher judge. With your claim of such clear evidence and all the spectators of the case convinced about O.J.'s guilt, how could it come down to the prosecution bungling the case? This trial took place in slow motion. There was every opportunity for all the Monday, Tuesday, Wednesday quarterbacks to adjust their game plans and correct their legal efforts. Did everyone in the D.A.'s office miss the mistakes that were so clear after the *not guilty* verdict? That means you have to be better than the collective population of the L.A. prosecution team. This is a big assignment for a lawyer that has never done this before.

It is easy to say that the case was lost because of poor lawyers and a jury that just didn't get it. Even if it were true, how would one more trial change that? Should you have lost the civil trial would the Monday morning quarterbacks make the same excuses of observations of poor lawyers and jury bias? Whatever the verdict, you managed to change the composition of the jury to no blacks. That would be obvious.

Finally, you get to some of your theories as to why O.J. was the killer. You visit the crime scene at Bundy and present and important theory. You state the murders happened in "...*no time*".[7] I have serious problem with this conclusion. Later you use this to make your point and at that time I'll go into a deeper analysis of why I believe your logic is not reasonable and undermines your claims of O.J. being the killer.

You hire a jury selection consulting firm, DecisionQuest, founded by Donald Vinson. They give advice as to how to position your client to get the best approval ratings. It is important to select the jury when the approval ratings are high. *"Vinson also agreed we should maintain a very public posture."*[8] "As he put it, *'Dan, this case will be litigated in the public eye..'."* [9] A good packaging strategy was necessary to create as much bias as possible in the discovery of justice. (a bit of sarcasm, sorry.) You believe it is important to work with the media to keep your client's image positive for as long as possible. Why couldn't trust the media to get it right without your help? Not only did you have to manipulate the witnesses, jury, judge, and your client, you must manipulate the press. You didn't leave anyone out your insults. In the next breath, you criticize O.J. for working the press. He was willing, despite your guess that his lawyers weren't in favor of it, to be interviewed publicly about the case. He could easily have stayed out of the limelight and avoided the risk of incriminating himself. You believed he was very savvy and would not make statements that could be used against him. You continue your mantra, *"Simpson was the killer, he knew when he killed Ron and Nicole, he knew how. He knew that he got away...."* [10] Again, not only are you rushing to judgment, but prejudicial to boot. You are convinced that O.J. would commit perjury. *"Lies equal guilt, an innocent man does not lie."* [11] Isn't this a shallow conclusion? Couldn't there be situations that an innocent man may lie, perhaps to protect a loved one? But, again you insist on absolutes. You tell us again *innocent men don't lie.* You insist that people lied to protect him. Remember the stunt Fred pulled on you? He tells the world that you are his attorney before you agreed to take the case. You told him specifically that you were not prepared to represent him until the details of the financing and other matters were worked out. He lied to the press. You were announced as his attorney. You accepted the lie and proceeded to act as though you were his lawyer, when in fact you had no agreement. You misled the public. Is it then true if a person that a person in search of the Truth does not have to lie? Or is there a free pass when there is *a lot of money to move around.*

Notes:

[1] Daniel Petrocelli, *Triumph of Justice*, (Crown, 1998), pg. 66

[2] Ibid, pg. 66

[3] Ibid, pg. 72

[4] Ibid, pg. 72

[5] Ibid, pg. 72

[6] Ibid, pg. 75

[7] Ibid, pg. 79

[8] Ibid, pg. 80

[9] Ibid, pg. 80

[10] Ibid, pg. 81

[11] Ibid, pg. 81

FIVE

You Said You Had Your Quarry,
Why Still Hunting?

The Hunt Begins

You now present us your parade of witnesses, you select Paula Barbieri to be the first; an odd selection because she was reluctant to testify and was O.J.'s girlfriend for the last few years. You hoped Paula, as a jilted lover would give you information that would incriminate O.J. Good premise, but how reliable is the testimony if she was jilted and knew something of value. You've heard about women scorned, I am sure.

"Paula Barbieri was a figure of intrigue to the press. She was an aspiring actress and had appeared nude in Playboy. *She had not spent a single day at the criminal trial, and few in the media had had access to her. She arrived represented by three lawyers."* [1]

You criticize the lawyers for showing up at the *O.J. media circus.* They want a piece of the celebrity and were looking to drum up some business. Why this would surprise you, Mr. Petrocelli surprises me. You already admitted that you coveted the publicity and the business this celebrity would attract. *"...everyone had a lawyer."* [2] Even the lawyers had lawyers. There was a lot of money to move around and why would these lawyers not want to play? You also let us know that none in Simpson's circles were anxious to talk about him. What is surprising about this? You continue to claim that O.J.'s friends are all liars covering up a horrifying double homicide and pandering to a hero.

"Moments before her testimony began, Simpson showed up. As a party to the suit he was allowed to attend all the depositions." [3] You had a real problem with meeting O.J. for the first time. You didn't like how he referred to himself. *"'I'm O.J.'" Not 'I'm O.J. Simpson.' Not, 'I'm Mr. Simpson.' Smiling. I'm O.J.'"* [4] When you shook his hand you claim to have felt terrible, realizing it was the hand that committed the double homicides.

"I felt terrible. This was a double murderer. I shook the hand that held the knife that killed my client's son, the one that cut a huge, gaping hole in Nicole's throat." [5]

There's your mantra again. You have him convicted before the depositions and the trial. You believe that it is a victory for O.J. to have the opportunity to shake your hand. Didn't you think about this beforehand? A good lawyer doesn't lose ground unnecessarily. But, isn't this point so irrelevant as to embarrass your profession?

You conduct the deposition with Paula realizing that she is not going to be a cooperative witness. Since she wasn't an eyewitness and it's not likely that O.J. confessed to her, what did you expect from this witness? Your questions made your strategy clear. You want to establish that there were events that happened the day of the murder that could have contributed to O.J.'s state of mind and perhaps she was part of why he became a raging murderer. You were looking for something in her conversations with him the day before and the phone messages during that day that would reveal O.J.'s reasons to become one of the most vicious murders in recent times. You want to find information that would lead us to believe O.J. would kill with a knife, the ex-wife he loved, with his children in the house in a premeditated act of rage. Paula could help lead you to this conclusion if she provided information about O.J.'s state of mind the night of the murders.

You make several attempts to determine who controlled the relationship between O.J. and Paula and who broke off from whom. All your theories confuse me. Sometimes it was O.J. that broke off, sometimes it was Paula, and sometimes it was by mutual agreement. A key fact that you were trying to get clarified was what happened the morning of June 12th, the day of the murders. Paula testified that she left messages on O.J.'s cell phone in the morning, letting him know that she wanted to stop seeing him. It was important to you to determine who broke off the relationship. Paula wasn't cooperating so you claim to have needed your lawyering techniques to get the answers from her.

While O.J. was in jail, Paula was supportive, so whatever her intention the morning of the murders, it did not lead to a permanent breakup. You confuse us as to where all this is headed. Even if O.J. did get a *"Dear John"* message, what makes you believe he took it as an absolute? You use Paula's rebuff as part of your psychological proof that the stage was set for O.J. to go into an uncontrolled rage and kill two people. Meanwhile, O.J. is checking out another Playboy model to date. It doesn't sound like his self-confidence was totally shattered as to drive him to commit an atrocious murder. You make a powerful statement when you say that O.J. would not have killed Nicole if he didn't love her. It was the rejection of a woman he loved that he couldn't handle that drove him to murder. Pretty good, Doc. O.J. couldn't live with her rejection so he killed her. What type of rejection causes suicide? Suicide, Dan, because being caught could bring the death penalty. I am not a psychologist, either. You state that throughout the criminal trial O.J. sought to confuse us all by suggesting he had a life with Paula and Nicole was out of the picture. Daniel, O.J. didn't testify in the criminal trial, how could you forget? Also, what evidence do you have regarding the nature of O.J.'s feelings for Nicole? Love comes in different packages, different definitions. You are giving us unusable generalities to arrive at your conclusion, again.

You find it incomprehensible that O.J. and Paula would not discuss Nicole's' murder while he was in jail. That is a strong opinion. Why? I wish you had given the reader alternative natural subjects about Nicole's death that would make good conversation. How much did she bleed? Wasn't it cooperative she made such little noise? How she was so helpful as to turn around and allow O.J. to attack her from the behind? How interesting she ended up in the fetal position. Please, Dan, help me out; is there something I am missing? What discussion of Nicole would have made good conversation with Paula? Still you insist that Paula was lying to you and would not be candid. She was remaining loyal to O.J., a man who was clearly a vicious killer on the loose. You don't believe her when you asked: *"Was Nicole ever a topic of controversy or conflict between you and Mr. Simpson?'.... 'No'"* [6] You took her answer to show foolishness, disrespect of the law, and perjury. You were convinced that she was lying to protect a killer,

"*...this woman would lie, to protect a man who killed two people."* [7] "*After a murder, what's a little perjury?"* [8] you ask.

Dan, Paula isn't the suspect here. What are you doing to the readers? You are saying that Paula is belittling perjury because compared to murder it was nothing? That wasn't Paula's problem. She didn't commit murder. Why are you convinced that Paula had to believe that O.J. was the murderer and she would commit perjury—a prosecutable offense?

"*Now, I decided, it was time to zero in on what happened with the breakup the morning of the murders."* [9] Sometime between 7 a.m. and 11 p.m., on June 12th, the day of the murder, O.J. got Paula's message about breaking up and Paula got a message back asking, "*...what was wrong?"* [10] You make a point of guessing that women just don't break up with O.J. Therefore, if two women reject him it's enough to push him over the top and become a killer.

In your opinion, it is absurd that Paula and O.J. didn't discuss Nicole's beating or that Paula never confronted O.J. about the beatings, even though he killed Nicole and was in jail. You are seriously getting ahead of yourself here, making assumptions that fly straight in the face of finding justice. O.J. and Paula sleep together two days after the murder, she must have been rather certain she wasn't with a killer, a thrill seeker or suicidal.

This deposition appears to be meaningless. Continuing to analyze your antics seems purposeless. However, I take you through the process because it is demonstrative of the systematic way this case was handled. You give us a series of fishing expeditions into preposterous areas and conclusions that wouldn't be used in a cheap novel. Let's not forget there is much money to move around and $1.2 million in billable hours to suck up. Yes, there will be some expenses.

"*Paula was the sex object. Paula was an arm piece. She was the person Simpson would summons during interruptions in his relationship with Nicole, or even on the side"* [11]

Paula, how do you like being described by Mr. Petrocelli this way? He says O.J. has no love for you; you were merely his sex object. You are digging a hole here, Dan? On one hand you want us to believe that being dumped by Paula added to O.J.'s rage the night of the murders and you want him not caring about her. According to you Paula is just his *ho*. I would guess that a person of O.J.'s celebrity persona getting sex objects would not be much of a challenge. Besides, he called the recent centerfold of Playboy for a date the day of the murders. Since you painted O.J. so much in love with Nicole that he couldn't handle her rejection, you couldn't have him also in love with Paula. This diminishes your argument. You want us to believe that both rejections on the same day drove O.J. into a killing rage. You want it both ways.

I don't see how your psychological arguments carry much weight. I did check the description of your formal education; psychologist or psychiatrist isn't part of your training, yet you give us no expert testimony to back up your conclusion. Back and forth we go. Paula dumps O.J. O.J. dumps Paula. They mutually dump each other and we are not sure why. Some of these dumping stories are suspect. Let's dump Paula as a witness that was supposed to show us conclusively that O.J. murdered two people. All we are getting are a lot of dumping theories enjoying lots of billable hours. On a contingency fee would you have been down this road? Excuse me; I forgot this was not about the money.

Because Paula had testified before the Grand Jury her concern about O.J. committing suicide, you now move us back to O.J. running around the L.A. freeways considering suicide. *"Suicide was an issue forced on Simpson. The world had seen him running around the freeways with a gun to his head."* [12] Dan is he trying to escape the police or is he trying to commit suicide? Aren't these somewhat mutually exclusive concepts? Why would someone who intends to commit suicide get in his vehicle, with a close friend and drive at a slow speed. Was this to escape or a suicide attempt? These are the reasons you forward to the reader as clear indications of admission of guilt? Which is it? Nothing is clear here; just a pile of suppositions that are contradictory and you are not giving us any solid evidence or some help in connecting the dots. Then you catch yourself. You are undecided and offer that maybe it wasn't suicide or running away. It was something in between. In between, what's that? What is the word for it, suiscape?

Paula testified that she had never seen O.J. in a rage, he had never hit her, never hit a wall, or broke a glass, or thrown a lamp. He didn't have a knife collection or knife training. Unless Paula lied to conceal a mad killer, she portrays O.J. as a guy under reasonable control. Again, you insist that Paula dumped him the day of the murders. Why do you press this so hard? Even though just a sex object, you insist that this so called *dumping* contributed to blowing O.J. out of his normal clever, calculating, and shrewd behavior to become an enraged killer; *"…the sense that Simpson's life was spiraling out of control --…"*.[13] How very dramatic.

O.J. could not produce anyone who could give him a definite alibi as to where he was between 10 p.m. and 11 p.m.

"This was a big problem: Simpson could not identify a single living human being who could vouch for his whereabouts during the time of the killings."[14]

There wasn't one witness to verify where he was for that one hour. Whoa, pretty incriminating. How could O.J. be missing for one whole hour without an alibi? Looks like you got him there, Dan. O.J. has a *big problem,* no alibi for one hour. Actually it was more like 40 minutes, but no need for you to be accurate on such a critical point. To you "It is *entirely unbelievable that Paula Barbieri never once asked him,* 'O.J. where were you?'"[15] Well, not everyone is as confrontational as you, Dan. Is it so impossible for a person one knows well to be a suspect murderer, that a question to their guilt or innocence would be an unspeakable insult? What happened to your sensitivity training, Dan? You can't comprehend this being possible; therefore Paula must be a liar protecting a killer. You dig the hole further when you ask Paula while O.J. is present at the depositions, "And d*id you love him? I said softly. She spoke more softly that I did. 'Yes, sir.' …'And you* still *love him, don't you.'…* 'Yes, sir.'"[16] I guess she didn't realize as you did that she was only O.J.'s sex object, someone to hang on his arm. If Paula read your book, I bet she had a few expletives to launch your way. After more than 11 hours interrogating Paula you conclude you didn't make a dent. You are frustrated. There was more to this story that you couldn't finesse out of her. You admitted you used all your lawyer tricks and they didn't work. You claim she knew more--you were convinced she was lying and couldn't be tricked into answering. You also state that Paula's love for O.J. destroyed her credibility as a witness. What were you thinking, Dan? If you had this case on contingency you would have come to this conclusion without the 11 billable hours?

You clue us in to the fact that you believe all of O.J.'s loyal friends were going to be difficult to crack. *"...there was a circle of people around him who would lie to protect him. I didn't know how wide or deep that circle would be."* [17] Yet, you insist that Paula's phone call to O.J. the morning of the murder was *"...a crucial piece of the puzzle that would help reveal the motive for these murders".*[18] There is that dumping theory again. Dump it, please! Though Paula may not have helped you, she did help us. We got to learn more about Daniel Petrocelli, attorney, his skills in amateur psychology, aggressive grilling techniques, and making inane suppositions. These are the weapons of a litigating attorney, ICBM's of the legal profession, WMD, destruction of the legal system for the benefit of billable hours.

Notes:

[1] Daniel Petrocelli, *Triumph of Justice*, (Crown, 1998), pg. 85

[2] Ibid, pg. 85

[3] Ibid, pg. 85

[4] Ibid, pg. 85

[5] Ibid, pg. 85

[6] Ibid, pg. 86

[7] Ibid, pg. 95

[8] Ibid, pg. 95

[9] Ibid, pg. 95

[10] Ibid, pg. 96

[11] Ibid, pg. 92

[12] Ibid, pg. 99

[13] Ibid, pg. 102

[14] Ibid, pg. 104

[15] Ibid, pg. 104

[16] Ibid, pg. 104

17 Ibid. pg. 105
18 Ibid. pg. 105

SIX

Who's the Liar Mr. P?

Locked In To Lies

Lawyer antics cause it to "...*heat up in the courtroom*"[1]. The court was going to consider if punitive damages would be granted in the event of a guilty verdict. The money thing, again although it isn't the reason for the trial, was producing heat in the courtroom. You were proud that you took the preemptive steps to secure a punitive payoff.

"*We went to court in December to request discovery of Simpson's finances and could start laying the groundwork for punitive damages.*"[2]

Daniel, you're kidding me again. You knew or should have known that no one was going to get any serious money from of O.J. You had to have known that O.J.'s attorneys took all measures to judgment proof his assets. Going after more money is merely an additional way to create more billable time. Not very professional, Dan. This is another instance you are abusing us, your client, and those who donated to the defense fund.

Before the depositions take place you admit, "*I was on overload with all this information.*"[3] Nevertheless, you are determined to question O.J. about everything because "*I didn't really understand why he did it.*"[4] Let's take a pause here. Many, many times you tell us your reasons for taking this case and explanations for why O.J. killed Nicole and Ron. You announce it to the press. It is part of your mantra. It was what you used to justify your aggressive attitude regarding bringing this killer to justice. Although you are not required to establish motive, you feel you need to show why O.J. had sufficient reasons to kill his ex-wife. *This question had not been adequately answered at the criminal trial."* [5] Isn't it late to be raising questions about this important issue now? You knew he abused Nicole and was rejected by her from time to time. Yet, you are uncertain about the motive. So now, I am not sure. Before you were sure, now you are questioning your own logic. This confusion on your part points out another contradiction. Wife abuse and rejection are suddenly not enough. To back up your accusations of O.J. the killer it's important for you to find the motive for the murders. No motive, means not such a good case, eh, lawyer. You promised the reader that you would use commonsense to show why O.J. had a motive to pull a knife on his ex-wife, stab her in the head repeatedly, and finally slash her throat.

In your opinion,

"Simpson had pulled off the biggest fraud on the American public ever seen in a court of law, and now he was trying to perpetuate a fraud to reclaim his position in society." [6]

Did you forget, again, O.J. didn't testify in the criminal trial? Obviously he didn't have to testify. The government didn't prove their case. They weren't showing why O.J. committed the crimes. Attack his lawyers if you must. They are lawyers, after all, defending their client. He was not convicted. Did the government reimburse him the cost of the trial? Why not? Now he is also a victim and you have the gall to criticize him for wanting to repair his image. You are convinced that O.J. would lie about every important fact in the case without even thinking about perjury. *"Having beaten a double-murder rap, perjury was small change for him."* [7] This bias throws additional questions regarding your quest for justice. You have completely made up your mind about his guilt and there is no room for doubt. You even accuse the government of giving O.J. an unfettered license to lie in court. *"On the issue of perjury, Simpson had a 'Get Out of Jail Free' card."* [8] Government, did you catch this one? Mr. P. is accusing you of being a co-conspirator to the crime. Despite all the problems you feel you are facing, you are still optimistic that you can *"...reduce him to dust"* [9]. This is an impressive display of your killer instinct.

There was some speculation that O.J. wouldn't show up in court. Perhaps you were wishfully thinking that he would default to get this terrible chapter of his life done. You could not insist that O.J. testify. A judge would decide the damages, if any. Neither you nor Fred liked this much, but O.J. did decide to go on trial because he didn't want to settle or compromise. He exposed himself to your interrogations and all the terrible facts of these murders. He was fully willing to be deposed and have a jury deal with his fate. Explain how these are the actions of a man who is guilty? He took the risk of being found responsible for the deaths, loss of money, and the specter of a guilty verdict. Still he took that chance when he didn't have to.

You remind us "...*almost everybody even vaguely related to the case was trying to make a buck*"[10]. You had "....*never seen anything like it*".[11] Faye Resnick, Nicole's best friend chose to write a book and not testify in the trial. *"People were selling everything."*[12] Despite this environment you were going to discover the truth and justice would be served. At what price? Your actions are reminding us this case is all about money. Not that we forgot you original noble mission, but Dan, unfortunately you seem to, from time to time. Are you suggesting that you and Fred are the exceptions and not ones who are trying to make a buck or a few millions?

You believe that Simpson's most ardent cronies would break the law to get him off again. You are consistently painting O.J. as a powerful person able to get people to do his bidding. You have many co-conspirators to this crime. These are serious allegations derived from your speculations. Paula's a *ho* and O.J.'s friends are liars. You get very tabloid, Dan.

On the next several pages you give a lecture on lawyer strategies in taking depositions that is oh so boring. I know you feel proud that you know the rules of engagement so well. You state that O.J.'s blood was all over the crime scene. Yet, the reality is since only a few little drops at were found created an important problem in the government's case in such a vicious, bloody dual knife murder. The small amount of blood evidence was highly suspicious in such a horrific crime. There could be a good explanation for the very few drips of blood, but it was not in O.J.'s interest to do your work for you. You constantly present your explanation of events and actions as the only possibility. This is an important reason your story is not reasonable. You are managing the questions very well with clear avoidance of important areas when you are not sure of the answers. A lawyer's credo: *Don't ask any question when you do not know the answer in advance.* This is great strategy for moving money around, but I find suspect when used searching for the truth. You complain that O.J. hired the preeminent experts to prove his case in the criminal trial because they couldn't be used against him. Now you have the best experts as co-conspirators. Dr. Baden, are you listening? Dr. Lee, do you hear? Clearly to you, O.J. was playing unfair by hiring the top experts, shame on him. I guess you will have to settle for less than the best experts to testify on your side to prove you didn't commit the crimes. Mr. P. you can't be telling me this and want me to buy into your conclusions.

At the beginning of the depositions you deliver a question to let O.J. know that you would be challenging his honesty and credibility right from the start and you *"...knew he would be lying about everything."* [13] He had never been questioned under oath about the events surrounding Ron and Nicole's death. When asked about the statement he had given to the LA police on June 13th, O.J. did not believe he was under oath. Step-by-step you take us through all the boring lawyer histrionics of the deposition.

"....O.J. Simpson was contemplating suicide because the media was attacking him. He was forty-six years old, wealthy, celebrated, he had four children, two very young who had just lost their mother, he had women at his fingertips and fans worldwide; he had suffered a horrible tragedy, but he was going to kill himself because he was being falsely accused by the media?" [14]

I don't feel totally comfortable with your assessments, Mr. P. We are again delving into areas that require some professional expertise. How do people act when they are seriously considering killing themselves? In the murky world of suppositions, generally there are no specifically accurate indicators to chart the true intention. Suicide threats are often calls for help and are not the real things, but it's difficult to know for certain. Most importantly, Dan, couldn't there be other plausible reasons for O.J. to consider suicide? Maybe he was afraid of the consequences he must cover up? He may know who the killer was and that was tantamount to ruining his life.

You continually criticize O.J. for being concerned with his public image. *"The reaction revealed how extremely important his public image was to him. It also revealed that Simpson was more concerned about the media attacks than about his wife.*" [15] You hired a public relations firm at the start of this case to protect the images that you wanted to portray. You must have also been concerned about how the public viewed you. The goose and gander theory comes to mind here. O.J.'s public persona was a very important source for his livelihood. Even though declared not guilty, the criminal trial was still an ugly affair.

You discover there was an incident you were not aware of between O.J. and the press. O.J. assumed you knew of this matter. "*I was only beginning to go down that road*" [16] of knowing everything, you admit. Let's take a look at your confession. You start the O.J. depositions only beginning to know all the facts of the case. Despite this, you are certain he is the killer. You have already made your mind up about this. Now you are searching for the story that will lead the listener to agree with you. You will not accept what was just said to you. One of the reasons he was contemplating suicide was that his wife was just murdered. A woman you insist he loved enough to kill. Now just one page later you criticize O.J. by saying, "*The fact that his wife had just been brutally murdered didn't enter into it.*" [17] You further condemn him for claiming that he loved his wife, but didn't want to live with her as though this is a contradiction indicating he lies. You feel his answer was rehearsed to wiggle out of this dilemma.

"*Simpson was smart. He had thought all this out in advance: He would confess to still loving Nicole—any decent man would still have feelings for the mother of his two children, a woman he had known for nearly seventeen years— but would make it clear that he was no longer attached to her.*" [18]

You are not able to accept that a man could love his wife, but not be able to live with her? This is so naïve you leave me speechless, sort of.

O.J. admits to being in a lot of pain during the week following the murders. You believe it is because his media image has been shattered. You try to have us believe that he didn't care a thing about Nicole, though he admits to loving her. "'*Just everything that was going on was my source of pain*'." [19] This is a most telling statement from O.J. When you asked for more clarity, he refused to give it, "'...*I can't be more specific*'." [20] This would have been the perfect time to ask if he knew

47

something that he was reluctant to reveal, possibly regarding Jason. In your eyes, *"I had done my job."* [21] You were not interested in finding out what he meant. Your goal was to cover yourself in case he wanted to introduce additional information regarding his motivations. You didn't want to be surprised. Then you tell us you have pinned down O.J. for the count. You have him on the mat. 1, 2, 3, it's over at this point, according to your score sheet. You now mix the sports metaphors to wrestling. This is the same metaphor that I would use in describing the tactics of lawyers in pursuit of the prize.

O.J. didn't present you with one additional reason for feeling suicidal. Why would he need to? Those were his reasons and they were good enough for him. Why didn't you bring in experts to tell us all that these are not plausible reasons for considering suicide?

"I establish that Simpson saw his children for the first time after the death of their mother on Tuesday, two days after the killings, and they left the next day." [22] You criticize him for this. I am feeling manipulated, again. O.J. was visiting the police and responding to questions to counter the theory that he committed an atrocious double homicide. You never ask him when he did talk to his children. You use this as a characterization that O.J. is an evil man and it's revealed by how insensitive he is to his children. You would have to track all that he did during the 48 hours that spoke to priorities. He was in an incredible spot and probably didn't do many things he would have done under normal circumstances. This type of an attack brings the encounter to a personal level. The seriousness of accusing someone of a double murder should confine your activity to those things that could possibly have to do with the crime to stay on the high road. These post murder observations leave me cold.

Continuing on with your theory that he knew he was guilty and had to run away, *"…he was definitely fleeing"* [23]. Remember, it was a slow chase, more like a crawl. You try to catch him in a lie about the bag with the goatee and mustache found in Al's Bronco. O.J. claims he never opened the bag and thought Vannatter had opened it. *"He… couldn't wait to accuse Vannatter of perjury, when all I had asked him was whether the bag had been opened."* [24] Suggesting that O.J. intended to use the goatee and mustache to elude the police is a comical notion. He was avoiding the police with the slow chase. This point has been made. If this clever, shrewd, and calculating man wanted to run from the police there were far better ways than a moustache and goatee. You press this position of running away and a suicide attempt to back up your assessment on page one that anyone who runs from the police is making a statement of guilt.

You remind us that he had $8,000 to help him escape. How far would $8,000 take O.J.? This is small change in his world, in your world too. Dan, those that move money back and forth between rich people wouldn't believe for a moment that $8,000 would help in a getaway plan. Having only $8,000 is a strong argument he wasn't planning to go very far. According to your theory, he asks Al, his longtime friend to be an accessory in a crime. Poor Al, getting into trouble helping a raging killer escapes by staying below the speed limit. I don't think Al, as his close friend, would have taken a Sunday drive down the freeway if he truly thought O.J. was going to kill himself. Al, if you didn't think you were helping O.J. run or commit suicide, would you please tell Dan? It is hard to believe you are really that cold hearted and naive. Yet, Mr. Petrocelli characterizes this whole episode is *"…an astonishing evidence of guilt. Nobody who is innocent acts that way, Nobody'.* "[25] O.J. didn't run and he didn't commit suicide. Look at the *chase* again. O.J. is still alive. Even if he did run or kill himself, you still don't have a conclusive argument. There might be more compelling reasons that present serious problems for O.J. while he was completely innocent. You insist *"….Simpson had no innocent basis for his pain"*.[26]

Back to what you consider a very important element in your case, the 1989 incident of O.J. admitting physical confrontation with Nicole. Under oath, Nicole testifies that this was a lone incident.

"But Simpson and Nicole both denied, under oath, the existence of any other similar such incidents. In my view, they had chosen to cover up the dark, dirty secret of all their other episodes of his violence in order not to destroy Simpson's earning ability, which would injure not only Simpson, but also Nicole and her children."[27]

Now you are accusing Nicole of perjury. You insist there must have been other beatings. You speak with certainty. You claim Nicole lied to the court when she said there were no other incidents. These are points you present to have us believe that O.J.'s abuse of Nicole should naturally lead us to believe he is the killer. The reason, according to you, Nicole lies is because she wants to preserve O.J.'s ability to make money. According to this notion Nicole lied to not interfere with her access to O.J. making money ability. Yet, Nicole did report this horrific incident to the police. Didn't she think this would hurt O.J.'s image? Now she is not able to answer Mr. Petrocelli's accusation of perjury, but he says it was for the money. If Nicole would perjure herself to the court and to the IRS then it would follow it is possible that when she tells her friends he regularly beat her she might not be telling the truth. After all, lying to her friends would help her get $15,000,000. Lying to the court helped keep her money spigot open. That is consistent, except according to you, Mr. P, only O.J. lies for money.

You go back once more to the suicide matter. *"...why did you want to kill yourself?' 'Because that's why I felt at peace: I thought all my pain was about to end.'"*[28] O.J. hesitates with his answer and you accuse him of doubletalk. You weren't satisfied with his answers. You want to pin him down and you believe you did. This is the suicide world according to Petrocelli. You want us to believe that O.J. considered suicide because he murdered two innocent people and wasn't willing to face the consequences. Again, you forget he didn't commit suicide and faced his accusers, and was acquitted. He could have run and didn't. You finally admit after the first day of depositions, there weren't any great revelations. I fully agree. I saw the Bronco ride, I was told he was considering suicide, and I knew that he beat his wife one time. This all came out in the criminal trial that you didn't have time or interest in watching. Talk about beating a dead horse. You are very good at this and it does eat up many billable hours, but it was painful for the reader who was looking for new information the criminal trial didn't reveal. So far the score is: New Information: Zero, Old Information: Ten. Your strategy was to wear O.J. down so he could possibly make a mistake. Oh, Teacher of billable hours, how faithful Dan is to your lessons.

Notes:

[1] Daniel Petrocelli, *Triumph of Justice*, (Crown, 1998), pg. 106

[2] Ibid, pg. 107

[3] Ibid, pg. 108

[4] Ibid, pg. 109

[5] Ibid, pg. 109

[6] Ibid, pg. 112

[7] Ibid, pg. 112

[8] Ibid, pg. 112

[9] Ibid, pg. 113

[10] Ibid, pg. 115

[11] Ibid, pg. 115

[12] Ibid, pg. 115

[13] Ibid, pg. 117

[14] Ibid, pg. 128

[15] Ibid, pg. 128

[16] Ibid, pg. 128

[17] Ibid, pg. 128

[18] Ibid, pg. 129

[19] Ibid, pg. 130

[20] Ibid, pg. 130

[21] Ibid, pg. 130

[22] Ibid, pg. 129

[23] Ibid, pg. 130

[24] Ibid, pg. 133

[25] Ibid, pg. 133

[26] Ibid, pg. 137

[27] Ibid, pg. 134

[28] Ibid, pg. 136

SEVEN

Beware of the Two Edged Knife

Deep Cuts

The second day of the depositions you ask O.J., *"'Were you a cocaine user in June of 1994?'....."* *"'No,' Simpson said firmly'."* [1] You were very specific and narrow in your questioning. You present Faye Resnick's reference that she observed O.J. using cocaine in 1993, claiming that many people spoke to you about O.J.'s drug use. You ask him about drug use over a long period of time. It would have helped us if you had explained why you needed to know if O.J. had used drugs in the past. I did not understand why. Since O.J. was not on trial for drug use and this is a very sensitive area that could possibly open dangerous doors, the whole subject smells like a trap. Except, Mr. P. you are forgetting a critical piece of information which destroys this line of questioning. O.J. voluntarily went to the police the morning after the murders. They took some of his blood. We heard nothing about him being on drugs. Your questions try to plant the idea that drugs may have caused O.J. to act so irrationally. No drugs were reported the morning after the crime, but you insist on playing the drug card.

When you ask the question of his awareness of Nicole using drugs, contained an inherent dilemma. If O.J. says "yes", that may be considered a trashing of Nicole, which might be bad form since she's not here to refute the accusation. O.J. surprises you by saying that Nicole told him she was using drugs and in trouble. Nicole's lawyer objects. Since he wants to protect his client, you are working at cross-purposes. He let you know that he was concerned this information would hurt Nicole's case. You see his point and agree to cooperate with him leaving this subject alone for now. Sounds like a conspiracy is taking place, Mr. P? We will see if we ever get back to it. You need to walk carefully, Dan, you don't want to tarnish Nicole's image. It is not in your interest to portray Nicole "...*as some perfect angel*",[2] you admit, but you will avoid some truth if it hurts your case. You could manage some of her imperfections as long as O.J. admitted to all of his.

"*I wanted to bring out the warts in her life because I thought it would make her a more real and understandable as a person.*"[3]

A bit of Goldilocks here, not to hot and not too cold, just right, leads to a magnificent manipulation. Let's show just enough of her imperfections to make her real, but not too many to turn the jury against her. You use your lawyering skills to walk a fine line that should be missed by the jury.

Now, you accuse O.J. of asking you to examine other causes of the murders. Faye Resnick's known use of drugs and the fact that she was staying with Nicole does create a possibility that drugs may have been involved with the murders. You treat that as a far-fetched theory. What reasoning lets you says that those who use drugs are immune from getting in trouble with their drug suppliers? This is an option you don't even want to be examined. How do you explain that the LA police failed to use their sources in the drug world to investigate, especially if Faye and Nicole were drug users? At no time in the criminal trial did the L.A. police give us a reason to dismiss the possibility. Did they check for leads and come up dry? No checking out an obvious alternative explanation gives the appearance of a cover-up. You show no interest in examining any other prospect. Let's just dismiss this leap to buy into your sarcasm that considering this possibility is tantamount to "....*Columbia cartel hit men running amok in upper-class Los Angeles?*"[4]

Maybe something less than the cartel had a problem with Faye and Nicole and Ron became an innocent victim. My research revealed that knives rather than guns are favored as weapons in the drug trade. Guns used while conducting drug business brings very long prison sentences. Knives are preferred especially when there are several accomplices. You see there is a high likelihood of noise using a knife.

Yelling and screaming for help creates problems. So a clever, shrewd, and calculating killer who decides to use a knife will probably have an accomplice. A knife is a risky weapon since there is no assurance you will hit the places that will kill the person immediately. This murder needed a fast resolution so the killer could make an appointment to meet his driver in a few minutes. My South American sources say that anyone who uses a knife as weapon alone trying to commit murder is asking for big trouble. Strictly dumb, more than dumb--suicidal, and count on getting caught. Most likely the result would be a wounded victim and a jailed idiot. Anyone who would premeditate murder this way is an absolute fool. It is just too risky, an uncertain result, likely to produce incriminating evidence, and difficult to hide. You know want us to believe that O.J. is an absolute idiot after you tell us he is shrewd and calculating.

You want us to rule out that it is possible for Nicole and Ron to have been victims of a drug deal that went bad. Could it be the drug dealers didn't necessarily mean to murder? Is it possible things got out of hand and they had no choice? Picture Ron turning up on the scene of Nicole talking to a drug dealer and his presence confuses things. Commonsense tells us, there are a number of possibilities that were not considered. In the criminal trial there was a commitment made that O.J. was the killer. The risk was that looking elsewhere would have given the impression the prosecution wasn't 100% sure O.J. was the killer. You are not interested to look elsewhere for the killer(s). Is this because it could prevent you from moving money around easily? You show no interest in any other explanation of what caused these murders. You are going to leave well enough alone. It fits your purpose that O.J. is the killer, period. This writer doesn't automatically dismiss Faye's drug problem accidentally causing these terrible crimes. Faye did the smart thing. She went off to write a book, exempt herself from testifying at the criminal trial, abandon her friend's right to justice, and freely accused O.J. without rebuttal. Clever lady, the drugs didn't burn up all the brain cells. Then you jump to another subject entirely, Dan. Figured you would. This one is dangerous and could cut you down at anytime. Let's take a moment and tally up where we are:

1. Fred Goldman wants to pursue the killer of his son in a civil suit.

2. He finds a commercial litigating attorney who knows nothing about the case to get roped in before the finances have been settled.

3. You take the case because you are certain that O.J. is the killer and justice must be served.

4. Money is not the reason you and Mr. Goldman are passionate about taking the case. The motive is justice.

5. The jury in the criminal trial just didn't get it and the judge favored the defense.

6. Neither you nor your client wants to contribute any money towards the pursuit of justice. You work a plan to get the public to pay for the legal fees and expenses.

7. Paula Barbieri is interviewed and does nothing to help you.

8. Your interview with O.J. begins.

The Score: I'm into your book 191 pages and there has been no new information that helps prove O.J.'s guilt. All you have done so far is work over the old stuff of the criminal trial and produce a mountain of irrelevancies.

The old stuff didn't work in the criminal trial. This reader is getting impatient. Remember the cover of your book advertises the *conclusive proof* of O.J.'s guilt. Maybe you are just teasing your readers since you have 650 more to go. I am still curious and annoyed why it is taking so long. I hope my reader is, too. In the land of lawyers billing by the hour and probably being paid by the word this makes sense. I guess we must be patient. Back to the depositions:

During the O.J. deposition you wanted to establish when O.J. spoke with Faye Resnick last. You ask O.J. *"...is there a buzzer at the front that you could ring the doorbell?"* [5] He answers, *"Yes."* [6] You ask, *"And was that operable?"* [7] He replies, *"As far as I knew, yes."* [8] You remember that Detective Tom Lange indicated the buzzer was not in working order. This raises several serious questions. If O.J. had planned to murder Nicole; he gets dressed in the knit hat, a dark sweat suit, black business socks, Bruno Magli shoes, packing a knife, and thinking how he was going to murder Nicole. If the buzzer were not working, he would have to use a key. He would get in the house, find Nicole, avoid his children, commit the crime in silence, and exit without leaving any evidence, all in about 10 minutes. That sounds like a bad pre-meditated plan, Daniel.

You want us to believe that Nicole angers O.J. again and he decides to drive over in his conspicuous Bronco, go into the house, and kill her. He had to be thinking that he would kill her quietly enough not to wake the kids. Or because it's only 10:00pm they may be up. Bad plan, O.J. if you want to leave the kids out of the murder. This continues to beg the question; would a shrewd, cunning, calculating, wealthy, attractive and often dissed by his ex-wife icon consider pulling off a knife murder under these circumstances? And in trying to answer this question please don't confuse possible with probable. If the buzzer were working then at least he could get Nicole out of the house, somehow get her to turnaround so he can make on perfect stab to the neck, and not have her make any noise to attract attention. With no working buzzer, O.J. must go into the house to commit the murder. It doesn't seem like O.J. is that dumb or cruel despite some of his odd behavior. Nicole was a big problem for O.J., but to kill her in front of the kids? How do you get this to compute, counselor? If you believe Detective Lang, your logic is even more flawed. Either way the whole pre-meditated murder plan doesn't make sense. This is just another attempt to catch O.J. in a lie. All you did here was to prove to me that your theory is implausible.

You take great deal of literary real estate on the cut on O.J.'s hand to account for his blood being found at the scene. This is a critical matter in this case. You make as much as you can about finding O.J. blood at Bundy and his home. I didn't inspect the gloves, but fully expect you and those involved in the criminal trial to have examined them carefully. These should be the most inspected gloves in modern times. In both the criminal trial and your findings, no one produced evidence of a cut on the gloves. If O.J. was cut during the commission of the crimes, it seems logical that the gloves would be cut or at least conspicuously marked in the same place. From a cut in the gloves, then O.J.'s blood could flow. No cut on gloves then how does the blood get on the gate at Bundy? Was there blood inside the glove where O.J. had his cut? If so, why wasn't this brought out in the criminal trial or the civil trial? That would then make a connection of when the cut took place. **Without a cut on the glove and O.J.'s blood inside the glove, the glove might fit, but it still acquits, but for more compelling reasons.**

Wouldn't it take effort to remove these tight fitting gloves? You ask the reader to believe that if O.J. committed these crimes, he took one of these bloody gloves off and dropped it at the crime scene then cuts happened. Then he carries the other bloody glove back to his home and leaves it on his lawn near Kato's quarters to be found later that night. According to you, these gloves are drenched with the victim's blood. You want us to believe he somehow manages to hide the knife and other clothing including the shoes, but he leaves the so-called incriminating evidence for all to easily find. He might have well just put up a sign saying, "I confess." The gloves are left behind along with the Bronco that he didn't have time to clean. Then he leaves on a trip to Chicago, but returns upon hearing of the death of his ex-wife, returning to L.A. to meet with the police and answer their questions without an attorney.

Is this man acting like a guilty murderer in the face of the evidence he supposedly left behind? Everyone knows how effectively police forensics is in identifying suspects. If he had committed the perfect crime and was willing to be interrogated, I might have been taken off guard. Such an imperfect crime would have a guilty suspect hiding behind lawyers; you know the ones, Dan. Your questioning of O.J. regarding how he got the cuts on his hands is meaningless if you don't explain why there are no cuts on the gloves. Forget if they fit or not, I can't convict if the gloves are uncut. You brand him as a liar, because he can't give you a satisfactory answer why he got the cuts. His explanation that he broke a glass while in Chicago doesn't fly with you. Can you give a better explanation? Since the killer with the knife was administering the cuts with great accuracy doesn't let me believe that the cuts no his hand occurred during the crime.

There were other markings on his hands that you attribute to the murders. If O.J. had gloves on, how would he get additional scratches? Any number of ways comes to mind. Perhaps at a different time while retrieving a golf ball or finding a cell phone in his car. Have you ever gotten a cut that you couldn't explain? I have and it is not unusual to have a cut and notice it sometime later. Yet you attribute these marks to scratches made by the victims. It is elementary that L.A. forensics would have checked under the victim's nails for evidence of skin and blood. No DNA testing for material under the nails was admitted as evidence during the criminal trial to my knowledge. Mr. P, if O.J.'s blood or skin would have been found under the victims nails then end of story…guilty, prepare for lethal injections. He would have known that too, leading to his running away or committing suicide, but talking to the police without an attorney under the circumstances that you portray, no, no, no.

O.J. loses his patience with you over the questioning of his cuts. You tell us that breaking down a witness is one of your strengths. By breaking down the witness, getting in his face, asking the same question over and over, and examining tedious details your strategy worked. O.J. stormed out of the room. He had enough of your brow beating. Convinced that O.J. was programmed by his lawyers never to lose his cool because that would confirm he was a wife beater and killer, you were surprised. Controlling his anger, he just left. This doesn't sound incriminating to me. Again you assume that his lawyers orchestrated this, but you don't really know. This is all part of your package of presuming guilt and building arguments to support your theory. You state flat out,

"What was clear that Simpson was lying about it all; he had not, in fact, accidentally broken a glass and cut himself on hearing the news of Nicole's death. He cut himself while killing his ex-wife and Ron Goldman."

Still, you do not show us how the killer got a knife cut on the back of his hand through a glove that has no cut on it. You owe it to the reader to supply answers to elementary questions. Your silence here, as well as in several other areas, prevents me from believing your theories.

Notes:

[1] Daniel Petrocelli, *Triumph of Justice*, (Crown, 1998), pg. 139

[2] Ibid, pg. 142

[3] Ibid, pg. 142

[4] Ibid, pg. 143

[5] Ibid, pg. 143

[6] Ibid, pg. 143

[7] Ibid, pg. 143

[8] Ibid, pg. 143

9 Ibid pg. 157

EIGHT

If the Shoes Fit Someone Else, O.J. Walks

Those Ugly Ass Shoes

We are now told of your strategy for dealing with the press. You believe that O.J.'s team wants to keep a low profile. You feel it is your team's responsibility to deal with the press. Your partner, Mike Brewer, was assigned the job. He enjoys talking and the press likes him. Let's not forget that you criticized the O.J. team in the criminal trial for using the press to help their case. You claim that influencing the press help taint the results. Your team works overtime to persuade the public that O.J. was guilty of these crimes. You doing everything you can to create bias in potential jurors. Good strategy, Dan, when your goal is to move money around, but it makes you a phony if you want the reader to believe you serve a higher cause; like fixing the legal system or fighting for Ronald and Nicole's life.

Alas, the press wants to hear from you, the main man. With some encouragement, you decide to meet with the press after each deposition session. You realize you are *"…smack in the middle of one of the most high profile cases in our history."* [1] The public wants information. *"By giving it to them ourselves, we had a better chance of controlling how it came out."* [2] Why do you have this concern about being able to control the issues? You tell us you need to be in charge so the public will get the truth from you. This is another clear instance of lawyers seizing every opportunity to shape a case in their favor. OK, move those bucks around, but please, don't try to delude us into believing this case is about anything else, but money. You even used a special lectern with your firm's name advertising your business. Proud of the opportunity to hawk new business off your celebrity, you complain if they don't mention your firm's name in newspaper articles.

You show your sensitive side to us, Dan, when you decide it is a better strategy not to anger O.J.'s lawyer. *"I made a conscious effort to pursue a more friendly approach with Baker."* [3] You couldn't stand hearing O.J. referred to as *Juice.* It reminds you that he got away with two murders. *"...Simpson tried to seduce us with his personality."* [4] This is a rather dramatic interpretation that is another rush to judgment. While you fellows are playing your game, how do you apply that to the billings?

When O.J. is interviewed on BET you retaliate by offering the L.A. Times an exclusive copy of the O.J. Simpson deposition transcripts. This is done despite specific instruction from Judge Haber that it would be unethical to take any action that might taint or prejudice the jury pool. Since the other side was appealing to the press you felt it was okay for you to do the same. Did you bother to go to the judge and ask him if it would be stepping over the line? That is part of the big picture thing. Dan, you were just doing what lawyers are supposed to do, right? Win, Win, Win, at all costs, even if ethics get trampled. You were consciously manipulating the system. This information would probably have fetched serious money from the *National Enquirer*, you say, but the *Times* would provide an analysis that would prove most beneficial. *"...I knew their analysis would be good for us."* [5] The fact that you considered the *National Enquirer* speaks of sleaze, and legal whoring. Selling out where to get the most juice?

The *Times* agreed to mention your firm prominently. *"...the Los Angeles Times did not ordinarily engage in what they call 'promotion' of law firms",*[6] but with your great negotiating you get them to lower their standards in repayment for information that could prejudice a jury. What a coup! Lawyers and the press conspiring for economic advantage and your name plastered all over L.A. You proudly report that this entrepreneurial encounter generated a lot of new business for your firm, affectionately called *rain* in your profession. Did this move your name up the list on your firm's stationary?

Yet with all this exposure you provide the public, you are still "… *feared that some people did not get it*".[7] They didn't see O.J.'s body language, you say, so some of the press gave O.J. good marks. You are afraid your strategy is backfiring. *"They didn't understand that his answers could be shown to be provable lies."*[8] I don't understand your premise. The things you call lies may have reasonable explanations. I know that you believe innocent men don't lie, but what you are saying is preposterous. You take much credit for making everything extrapolate an admission of guilt. The reasons people lie are highly complex and not simply a direct line to a murder confession.

You now bring up *the shoes*, the Bruno Magli shoes, bought at Bloomingdale's. We are now in very important territory. You want us to believe that the shoes identify the killer. You accuse O.J. of lying about owning or wearing the shoes. You want to connect the dots. One, a Bruno Magli shoe print at the scene and in the Bronco. Two, O.J. owned the shoes. Three, therefore he was at the crime scene. Four, therefore he was the killer. No, no, Dan, not so easy. It would be good for you if it were that simple. You have two issues in dealing with the shoes and you artfully only deal with one. Your omission of the second casts suspicion on your theory.

Dan, is it possible that someone else could have been wearing the shoes you insist belong to O.J.? Isn't it possible that Jason, O.J.'s older son Jason, could have been wearing his dad's shoes the night of the murder? Did you ever wear your father's shoes? My research found that it is not unusual for a son to wear dad's shoes. For one, I did. Jason looks like a size twelve, just like his famous Dad. It also seems reasonable that O.J. had many pairs of shoes, some bought, and some given to him. You may pay close attention to the brands of shoes you buy, Mr. Petrocelli, but that doesn't mean everyone does. Some of us have shoes that go out of style, ones we particularly don't like, and keep anyway. Your deposition has a mission that O.J.'s unfamiliarity with the Bruno Magli shoes is highly incriminating. Some of us are just shoe dumb, as crazy as that sounds, but if there was a possibility that O.J.'s son, Jason, had access to the shoes, he possibly could be the wearer at the crime scene. Your justice conscience should have demanded that you find out the answer to this question.

We know that Jason was in L.A. after the murder. He could have been in town when the crimes took place. We saw him greet his father after the Bronco ride. He was there. Where else was he? Did he have a motive? Did he have access to the Bronco? Did he have access to Nicole? Was he big and strong enough to commit the murders? Did he know that a knife murder should have more than one killer? Could he have recruited someone to help commit the crime? Since Jason did not have to meet a driver and leave for Chicago that night, he had the time to dispose of the murder weapon and the bloody clothes. Am I missing anything, Dan? How can the L.A. police or you not question such an obvious suspect? I have not read anything that explains away Jason as a suspect. I don't know that Jason had anything to do with these crimes, but it is important that the murderers be apprehended. The silence on Jason leaves us with a suspect that is scrupulously avoided. Silence on this matter raises questions in my mind, not only about the possibility, but the position of refusing to seriously explore any other explanation of how the crimes were committed. The Browns, Goldmans and the public seem entitled to a thorough investigation.

I will develop these theories later on, so back to your interrogation of O.J. and the shoes. You admit that during the criminal trial there was no evidence of O.J. owning or ever purchasing Bruno Magli shoes. Since this was a critical part of the case considering all the publicity about the shoes, if O.J. had actually bought the shoes, wouldn't it be likely someone would have come forward and confirmed that to be the case? It's hard to imagine a salesperson or the cashier not recognizing O.J. and feeling the same excitement as you did. How about any of their friends on hearing that an O.J. sighting had taken place? It is a favorite sport to tell about personal meetings with celebrities; how they acted, what they said, were they cheap, were they nice. No one, but no one remembers O.J. buying these shoes. Don't you find this very strange? Other than the controversial photos at the Buffalo Bills game, no one ever saw O.J. wearing these shoes. Not one person ever has confirmed he ever wore these shoes.

You want us to believe that for the murder, O.J. picked these shoes out of his wardrobe as being the most useful and appropriate. The

Bruno Magli people might be uncomfortable with this notion. Their very expensive sports shoes are the choice of murderers. It must be that unique sole that helps in the commission of a crime. Or maybe it's just the in-thing to get dressed up for knife murders. Aside from my jibbing, the footprints were at the crime scene, but we are still not certain who was wearing the shoes or when the prints were made. Dan, how is it you know for sure? Yet, you want to send O.J. to the financial gallows based on your supposition that shoes convict.

You have difficulty with O.J. referring to the shoes as *"those ugly ass shoes"*[9]. You want an explanation, a fashion critique. O.J. criticizes the shoe you were confident would impeach him. You were set to prove he was lying through his teeth when you got him in court, but he just stepped in it. Dan, I think the do-do is on your soul now. Despite my attempts to blow your specious logic, I know you would be more effective if you were on my side. I can just see you kicking the shoe theory into orbit.

The fact that Geraldo Rivera, a retired lawyer, television personality was delving into the case in great depth had you reveling. *"He also believed Simpson was guilty and said so—repeatedly."* [10] You felt this would help your case. Remember, helping here means influencing the jury, creating bias before the trial, all the unethical things the judge warned you about. What an insensitive judge, wanting to prevent you from trying the case in the media. He must be losing it; he wanted to have a fair trial. Makes you wonder if he was ever a lawyer.

Eleven days of deposing O.J. you state, *"…was the launching pad for our case."* [11] You have fleshed out his explanation for the suicide note, the contents of the black bag, pills, his having a key to Nicole's condo, a green towel with blood on it, his underwear, and the clothing found in the back of the Bronco. According to you, *"None of his explanations was believable."* [12] Aside from these issues, you fail to explain to us how you came to your conclusions. For his explanations to not be believable you must give us better reasons. You don't. Under the promise of giving your ready reasons to believe O.J. the killer, this is very disappointing.

Grilling O.J. on the cuts, he didn't have an explanation acceptable to you. Mr. Petrocelli, since you are portraying him as bleeding murderer leaving evidence all over the place, would you please answer a few band-aid questions? If he received those cuts in the commission of a crime and was leaving drops of blood all over the place, wouldn't it be reasonable for him to return home and put band-aids on to stop the bleeding? If he didn't return home after the crime and put band-aids on, how did he stop the bleeding when he was in the limo? He signed autographs at the airport. Did anyone notice bleeding on his signature? Did anyone see him with band-aids on? Tan band-aids on a black O.J. are not easy to conceal. And there were several cuts, so several band-aids. Still no one reported seeing band-aids on O.J. on the trip to Chicago. If the objective is justice, did you ask anybody about seeing O.J. with band-aids? You asked many of questions regarding the cuts and didn't like any of the answers. According to you, he didn't have one satisfactory one. Maybe it's because you didn't ask good questions. Or like the shoe stuff, people get cuts they can't explain. I find it happens all the time. Check your hands now, Daniel. Do you have any cuts? Can you explain them all? In the future when you get a cut on your hand that you can't explain, remember how absurd this *cuts on the hand* chapter has been.

At best the gloves that O.J. were a snug fit. If these gloves fit so snugly how did they fall off at the crime scene? It is hard to visualize the circumstances that allow removal of bloody gloves during a violent struggle without the cooperation of the killer. You not only have the killer cooperating with the assailant, but also with the police by conveniently leaving one glove at the crime scene and another on the lawn of his residence. This cooperative killer was screaming to get caught; this doesn't fit with O.J.'s intelligence or his persona.

Questioning O.J. extensively about his ownership of guns and knives; "*To no one's surprise, he collected guns, not knives.*" [13] According to your book, you never asked him about any training he had with either weapon. From what I am told, using a knife as a murder weapon presents several serious problems. Since you didn't discover that O.J. had extensive training in the use of a knife as an assault weapon, we have a problem understanding why he would make a knife his first choice. There are many circumstances that a knife, when available during an argument or fight, would be used. Kitchen knives, switchblades, pocket knives, killer weapons all, but, if you hope to get away with a murder you have made a poor selection, unless you are an expert killer and have help. Mr. P, I believe you had a duty to establish if O.J.

had any training to qualify him as an expert with a knife as a murder weapon. Now a gun is an altogether different proposition. A gun, with a silencer, is an effective murder weapon. In a premeditated murder, which you tell us this was, a gun would have been a better choice by far. In addition, with all that was involved you have failed to show that a lone person could have committed this crime.

You acknowledge a key point, that years earlier, after the beating of Nicole, O.J. had a written agreement that would wipe out the prenuptial agreement which at the time of the murder would cost him approximately $15,000,000. (About half of the $30 million reported assets) Nicole could simply go to the cashier's window in the courthouse and collect 5 to 15 million dollars if he ever hit her again. Yet, Nicole never collected on this agreement. If she had proof that he hit her, wouldn't it be reasonable that she would have exercised her rights to the money. You expect us to believe that a woman beaten repeatedly, would not cash in on her due, or do anything to protect herself? Daniel, you plainly state that Nicole felt desperate about her finances. She was willing to cheat the U.S. government and risk getting into serious trouble; yet, unwilling to collect money O.J. owed her, after she was beaten. The response of O.J. that Nicole was trying to build a case to break the prenuptial by advertising to her friends that he beat her rang true. If she had bruises to prove the abuse I believe she would have put them to good use and collect; not just complain to her friends.

O.J. gives you detailed information regarding his activities between 10 p.m. and 11 p.m. the night of the murders; he hit some golf balls, walked his dog, and took clothes out to his Bentley. You found it remarkable he had these details down. Why should that be remarkable? In the morning, when told of the murders while in Chicago, he probably reviewed what he had been doing. It would be natural that he would anticipate being asked every detail of his activities. At this time the events would be fresh in his mind. He might even have gone over them from time to time to make sure he had it right. At least that is what I would expect a person in his situation to do. Your characterization of his memory as remarkable under these circumstances doesn't make sense to me. You contrast his good memory for events about the evening before the murders with the vague recollections regarding the cuts on his hand. To you, this indicated he was lying about one or the other event. I see no connection between the two. As you point out later, your problem is, the entire issue of the cut on his hand doesn't do what you want it to. You never give us an explanation of how the killer, gets a cut with gloves on and yet no cuts are in the gloves. There were no band-aids on the trip to Chicago and his best explanation is he broke a glass in his hotel room. I give this round to O.J.

Convinced that O.J. did not have a good explanation for the missing 90 minutes at the time for the murder; you want us to believe he was up to something sinister, even murder. No one saw him between 9:30 and 11:00 p.m., a whole 90 minutes! I would think you would agree that even O.J., a special celebrity of football, movies, commercials, and guest appearances could be alone for 90 minutes without fault. In this specific incidence, his crime scene time would have been twenty minutes or less, according to you, Daniel. Be precise. Absolutely O.J. had no one to verify what he was doing during the time the murders took place. Absolutely no one can account for him. You keep trying to make us believe that a small window of time unaccounted for has meaning. You state again that he was lying about beating Nicole. I will repeat, in response to your repetition: Nicole should have, could have, and most likely would have reported any beating by O.J. to the authorities. This truth would have been worth millions of dollars to her. If she was silent on this subject then she was lying to the courts. Why would she be silent to the courts with all she stood to gain? You go on to criticize O.J. for not finding the killer. WOW! Now that is a good indicator of his guilt. Hope you are not planning to use your newfound wealth or celebrity to become a Judge or Attorney General. After his depositions you find that O.J. was not the charismatic *Superstar in a Rent-a-Car,* but rather a lying witness and a lying murderer.

You continue to be concerned that a jury would not get it. They wouldn't listen or use their commonsense. Dan, with all the good work you are doing to prejudice the jury ahead of time, what's the problem? This disrespect you show for the jury cuts both ways. If you lose, they didn't listen; if you win, the other side says the jury doesn't listen. I hope that isn't too tough for you to understand, Dan. I know you don't trust juries, you settle cases. You only went to court once, but if in this case the jury rules in your favor, justice will be served. This convoluted thinking is polluting the court system. It is a trillion dollar felony perpetuated on the American people. Lawyer congressmen make the laws they advocate, lawyer judges preside over that law, and lawyers benefit from the enormous economics this system provides. Excellent work, esquire – from the word, squire, nobility, the upper class; respected and feared.

On to the depositions of Fred and Kim Goldman: You admit that the defense was respectful. Ronald was a clean living, healthy man, with black belt karate skills, of 25 that walked into Nicole's condo area and became a victim of murder. This is a tragedy that hits our consciousness hard. It reminds you that we are not as safe as we would like to believe. The visual of such a brutal murder is sickening. But in the specifics I have a problem picturing O.J. subduing a healthy guy so quickly, and preventing any calls for help. The crime took place where there were people around who you would presume would have helped in some way. The short time line that you calculate for O.J. to kill Ron, doesn't allow for much resistance on his part. Didn't they find 58 stab wounds? He put up a heroic, yet silent, fight for his life. Your theory doesn't allow for that much time. You need a lethal blow by the murderer and many follow-up stab wounds as part of his rage. The defense didn't have to ask the Goldman's too much about the murders, since they didn't know much. They were victims, too. You supposed that the defense would attack the Goldman's, but they didn't. Guess they didn't need the billable hours. Not as sinister as you had guessed.

Notes:

[1] Daniel Petrocelli, *Triumph of Justice*, (Crown, 1998), pg. 162

[2] Ibid, pg. 162

[3] Ibid, pg. 163

[4] Ibid, pg. 164

[5] Ibid, pg. 167

[6] Ibid, pg. 167

[7] Ibid, pg. 168

[8] Ibid, pg. 168

[9] Ibid, pg. 171

[10] Ibid, pg. 174

[11] Ibid, pg. 174
[12] Ibid, pg. 174
[13] Ibid, pg. 175

NINE

Faye Ran Away For Pay, With Nothing to Say, To Help A Killer Pay, No Way!

Faye Tells the Truth

Now the long awaited truth according to Faye Resnick. I've been looking forward to this deposition. I've wondered how you were going to turn this pathetic druggie into your star witness. This is the woman who sold out her friend, Nicole.

"Rather than testify, she had written a book for money.... The prosecution, believing the book had destroyed her credibility as a witness, never called her." [1]

That was probably a good decision. You, however, feel differently. You believed Faye would help your case. Dan, let's examine the essence of this woman. Her close friend is brutally murdered and she may have information to bring the killer to justice. She decides that making money from writing a book is more important. Not only did she let her friend down, if what she had to say was important, she let every battered woman down, and hard. She compromised on of the most sacred responsibilities we have to our society and could possibly let a killer go free. If Faye had anything to contribute to the justice of the O.J. Simpson trial, and failed to testify, you committed an inexcusable crime against a friend, women, and society. Since she sold out for money, Mr. P probably empathizes with her. You criticize the O.J. defense team for calling Faye for what she was, a liar. She either had important information that was withheld from the court or her book is full of lies written in a way that would attract a publisher. Either way, what she did was evil.

We are now deep into depositions you tell us you are still not up to speed with the information in the criminal trial. Seems backwards to me, Dan. At this stage of the legal proceedings I'm surprised that there is still important information you have not covered. Why aren't you reserving your conclusion as to O.J.'s guilt until you are finished with your study? Again you tell us that you formed opinions before you began your research of the evidence. You give the appearance that you are searching for a story line that gets you to your predetermined destination – victory and money. Did they teach you this form of logic in law school? This seems to be a consistently used strategy of attorneys, especially prosecutors. More on this later.

Faye tells us in her book that O.J. degraded, beat, stalked, and threatened to kill Nicole. She even purports a lesbian relationship with Nicole. Reading Faye's book, you determine it is "...dynamite" [2] *"The essence of it rang true."* [3] You accept Faye's account and believe that her book *"...confirmed Nicole's side of the story, while entirely eviscerating the spin Simpson was putting on everything."* [4] Mr. P your choice of words says a lot about your use of language to stir up the listener. Eviscerating—meaning disemboweling—something one does with a knife, cutting out the guts. Faye's book attacks O.J. and cuts the guts out of his testimony - good writing and good manipulation. This woman is an obvious low life, selling her friend out for money. You buy her story and want to use it to bury O.J. There is a whole lot of sleazy lawyering going on here, partner of MSK.

Eagles fly with eagles and chickens with chickens, so goes the cliché. You attempt to get confirmation of Resnick's story from Nicole's friends. Nicole lies to the IRS, to the court, has a close friend in Faye, who is lying to everyone and you go to Nicole's friends for confirmation of Faye's book. All I know about Faye and Nicole is what I heard about in the press and your book. These girls are living the party life under their own set of rules. Drug addicts, lesbians, and generally promiscuous people's friends are all saying the same thing. O.J. was a bad guy. Yet, not bad enough for Nicole to go to the court and properly register her concerns, but bad enough to be a raging killer. If all these people were aware of O.J.'s threatening conduct why wasn't someone proactive? They heard Nicole's story, but didn't really believe her or didn't care very much. Dan, would you stand by while a close friend's life is being threatened? A friend that you know was being regularly beaten. Would you just commiserate and do nothing?

You point out that not only did Faye decide to write a book instead of coming forward, she ran away to Vermont, out of reach of a subpoena. When you needed her for her deposition, she was writing a second book on the Simpson saga. You knew that O.J.'s lawyers would remind the world that Faye sold out, but you needed her. She was reluctant, but your selling job assured her she would be safe. That safety came with additional Faye sellout material. She makes a deal with Geraldo Rivera to be on his daytime and nighttime shows in exchange for an all expense paid trip to New York City. So you agree to go to New York to take her deposition. She promises you that she will not compromise her testimony during the television interviews. Faye wrote a book, is writing another, and makes a deal for TV interviews and you expect her to be truthful? Faye explains to you that she was terrified of being in the same room with O.J. If all she was doing was telling the truth and being a responsible citizen you would expect O.J. to be the one afraid. Truth is a powerful thing. You try to defend Fay as being responsible because she had been to many drug treatment centers. Unfortunately, she had a history of relapsing. Still you want to convince us that Faye wasn't the self-serving person her critics accuse her of being. You believe that "…until a month or so before Nicole's murder…"[5] Faye relapsed back into cocaine use. Faye claims it was only a $20.00 a day relapse for only ten days, totaling $200.00 before she readmitted herself to treatment. Dan, either you are completely naïve about cocaine use or you think us readers are fools. In Brentwood, CA, $20.00 worth of cocaine would buy very little *blow*. For the non-savvy folks, it would be like an alcoholic having a 1/3 of a glass of beer a day for ten days and then seeking professional intervention. You go to lengths to minimize the drug use. You would like Faye to be a believable witness and with no chance her drug dealer might have paid a visit to the premises to collect the money or just making a sales call. Sometimes during a collection visit, things happen, like murder. In your attempt to claim this not possible you use two tricks. One, you offer a small amount

73

due would not likely cause a collection visit and second, you send the bill to the Columbian Cartel. Your double theory does sound absurd. Let's consider a more likely case. Faye was using enough drugs to cause a collection visit and the visitor was a local drug dealer and a few of his associates. The visit was not intended to be sinister, just a business call to either get the money Faye owed or saying "hello" to a good customer. You never establish that Faye had an independent source of income. Did she work or was she wealthy? Where did her drug money come from? She was living at a friend's house and she did use the dour events in her life to create income. It sounds like she had a budget problem and sought professional help to rid her of a habit that she just couldn't afford. Silence on her financial situation raises doubt about the role a drug dealer visit might have played in causing this crime. Remember she sold out her friend and justice for money.

How about the following for a possible scenario? The bill collectors arrive and they encounter Nicole. Faye told the drug dealers that Nicole would take care of the bill. Nicole freaks out and someone panics. Ron Goldman arrives on the scene. He tries to help Nicole. The bill collectors are in a predicament. People get killed. Is there anything original about my little story, Mr. P? Are you absolutely sure that this could not have happened? This version takes care of three important problems: the lack of noise at the murder scene, the knife as a murder weapon and the missing clothes and knife. If there were several assailants, two could hold the victims and cover their mouths, while another does the awful killings. This would explain the multiple stab wounds, the use of a knife, and most importantly, the lack of O.J.'s blood on the scene, since this would be removed by the now bloody clothing they were wearing. **The medical examiner reported that the murders probably took place after 11:00 p.m. based on the wet blood found at the scene.** The timeline is no longer an issue because after 11 O.J. is cleared, but you don't want to have any of this, Mr. Lawyer since there would be no money to move around. Others have guessed the same possibility, but it has been dismissed as not possible. The reasons for the dismissals are lame and beg for further investigation.

Faye Resnick's deposition stays consistent with her book. You could have just read it to us aloud. You tell us how much you like reading her book. She testifies that she was *clean* the two years before Nicole's murder. It was only a few weeks prior to the relapse did she resume taking only a small amount of cocaine. Good, Faye, your testimony would therefore be truthful and accurate. Let us not forget the addiction you have not yet conquered, lying. We remember you bailed out when the courts, your friends, and Ron and Nicole needed you most. In the quest for justice, you wouldn't get on the stand to tell the truth to catch a killer. Dan, you thought Faye did a great job during the depositions. Other witnesses, you claim, lied to the police, were vague, indirect and difficult, hedged on their bets, and were otherwise annulling prosecution witnesses. You accuse others of believing O.J. is guilty and yet selling out in order to keep O.J. on their good side. "…*most notably Faye herself. But this time Faye came through.*"[6] Please counselor, she is writing another book. She has a story, tells it well, and is sticking to it. You accept it as gospel and she is successfully capitalizing on the murders.

Faye tells us that she has personally seen O.J. in a rage. She claims that O.J. lost control and screamed at Nicole in public. According to Faye, he was a jealous man, possessed. That is pretty scary. When he was in one of his rages, he obviously didn't resort to killing. So now there are different types of rages; ordinary rages, that scare and apparently another kind of rage that leads to killing two people. Demonstrating one type of rage is a precursor to another type of rage that leads to murder seems to be your theory. It is evident that, while O.J. was in a state of rage, he was fully able to control his emotions and not kill. You describe him as animal like when raging. Yet, this is the same man that Nicole wanted to reconcile her life with, over and over again. I know there are sick relationships that are hard to understand. Couples fight, yet continue to live together, or split up and continue the relationship. There are abusive relationships that shouldn't continue and end up in murder, but counselor, you insist on connecting dots that are based on vague generalities, not conclusive evidence. Paula, in her years with O.J. never experienced these frightening outbursts. O.J. dated other woman with no reports of violence.

Nicole calls the police in 1993 because O.J. frightened her. She tells the police how scared she got when he was crazed. I can't help but wonder if these types of accusations were part of her building the file to prove her right to the prenuptial agreement being rescinded. Nicole admits to the police that she doesn't think O.J. will really do anything because of the 1989 agreement. If it did happen one more time, she knows it would be the last. The last time, because she would go to court and get a restraining order? You want us to automatically assume that this was a forecast or premonition that her life was in danger. It can surely look that way since she was murdered eight months later. Is this your way of connecting the dots to build the story that leads to your preordained conclusion?

Faye reveals that Ron Goldman wasn't just a delivery boy the night of the murders. This was news to me. Faye says Ron and Nicole went dancing with Faye and some of Ron's friends. They also met in front of Starbucks. This is getting a little more complicated. Ron heads over to Nicole's with glasses and Nicole has her bathroom prepared with dozens of candles; a solo bath with candles? Possible, but this is seriously suspicious. I'm not ready to develop any theories yet, but from what Faye is telling us there could be more than a casual connection between Ron and Nicole. Or, is this just Faye's way of writing a more intriguing story? You don't have to answer this one yet, Mr. Petrocelli. We are still in the midst of Faye's *truthful* deposition.

Ms. Resnick now adds Marcus Allen to the mix. The book just gets juicier. She is giving us a reason for O.J. to become a killer. His rival, friend, and younger man is doing it with his ex-wife. That's a perfectly good reason to kill - uncontrolled jealousy. Faye claims that Nicole's relationship with Allen was widely known in 1993 and Nicole admits this to O.J. when they reconciled later that year. How do we know this for sure, Daniel? Faye tells us that the affair was brief and resumed shortly before Nicole died. Faye saw Allen's car parked in front of Nicole's home. I guess the parked car had a sign on it advertising what Allen was doing at Nicole's. Dirty minds can have a field day with this kind of scene. Faye tells us that Nicole was in love with Allen and was no longer seeing O.J. *"I told her...I felt she was setting herself up for murder."* [7] My goodness, if Nicole had listened to Faye she would be alive today. You should have been more emphatic, Faye. You sensed that O.J. could commit murder and the best you could do was throw a one-liner at her? Why didn't you set her down and give a real friendly lecture with a strong message to get a restraining order or some act that sincerely protects a friend in danger?

Faye accuses O.J. of being a drug addict. Mr. P you say it takes one to know one. A good cliché' and when you are looking in the mirror, you should ask yourself how you know so much about deception. Faye is taking cheap shots at O.J. with the perception of fast living and celebrity crowds in L.A. viewing cocaine as a part of life. It is easy to paint with a broad brush here. Your testimony loses credibility when you say,

"'Nicole had said that O.J. was addicted to (?), from when he was a football star, that he became addicted to every pill there was, to uppers, to downers,... She said he had a 'Christmas tree' jar full of every kind of pill...He called it his Christmas tree because it was every color of the light that we would see on a Christmas tree. ...that he was addicted to every kind of pill there was'" [8]

This is the kind of exaggeration that you, Dan, like to use; *every pill there ever was.* Truthful people don't resort to ridiculous statements. After all this double hearsay testimony and you admit it is irrelevant. Still, you make sure that we, the reading jury, hear it all. I'll try to ignore the statement, counselor, especially because you can't prove any of this libelous testimony. You want us to believe that Nicole was a strong gal in the midst of all this heavy drug use and only took *"...took drugs once in a blue moon.'"* [9] Her husband, close friends, and live-in lover were all drug users, while she passed. This may be so, Dan, but you are going overboard trying to keep Nicole angelic and O.J. a raging, jealous drug addict. In the realm of manipulation this is clever on your part counselor. Turn O.J. into a druggie out of control the night of the murders. The problem I have with this theory is that O.J. voluntarily gave the LAPD a sample of his blood with he returned from Chicago. If he was using drugs less than twenty hours later isn't he running a risk that drugs will be detected in the blood samples? He was in a hurry to be cooperative. Is this the way a drug addict who just murdered two people act?

Faye takes us on a trip to Cabo San Lucas, Mexico where Faye, Nicole, O.J. and some friends vacationed in the spring of 1993. Nicole and O.J. were examining the possibility of getting back together at Rockingham. O.J. was doing those things to get the marriage back together. He is quoted, "'*We were like lovers. We were planning to be together. She was planning to move in. You know, we had the best sex,*' *he said* '." [10] Faye says this is untrue. He had to leave to shoot a movie, *Frogman*. Now this must have been planned in advance and shouldn't necessarily be something negative. The money needs had to be fulfilled. You make it a point that O.J. played a Navy SEAL trained at killing with a knife. My, my, aren't you taking the movies too seriously? O.J. is an actor, a bad one, according to you. Now you want us to believe he was really trained in killing people, like a Navy SEAL. Dan, this was a movie. What O.J. might have learned from this experience is how much serious training it takes to kill with a knife. The art of attacking the victim, striking the few and difficult to reach vital arteries, the resistance, the noise attracting help, the possibility of dropping the weapon and becoming the attacked, the certain evidence left behind that had to be cleaned up removing any traces of evidence, a trail of blood that would lead to the killer that had to be cleaned up and so on. These are some of the reasons O.J., a clever and calculating man would not have selected a knife as a weapon for a premeditated murder. This elementary introduction to the risks involved using a knife would likely have warned him of the dangers of either failing to kill or get caught.

Meanwhile, Faye tells us Nicole jumps into the sack with a guy named Bret while O.J. is off working on this killer training movie and hoping to get their lives back together. As soon as he leaves for work, Nicole finds a new guy, and reports to Faye that she and O.J are finished, *for good*. Faye then reveals that Nicole had a long talk with her when she learned in full detail the extent of O.J.'s threats, mistreatment, and beatings. Liars are having a juicy discussion. Whom in this duo do you believe? Or do we believe either of them? Or is Nicole confessing to Faye to ease her conscience? I have trouble with all this gossip and hearsay. Mr. P you are trying to build a case using pathetic sources and compromised positions, pardon the pun. According to Faye, Nicole claims,

"'*[He] had threatened her life many a time, threatened to take her children away from her. He had beaten her too many times to count; he had locked her in a closet and beat her with wine bottles.*'" [11]

Faye continues on and on with more accusations of brutality. O.J must have forgotten the judge's order that he would have pay millions of dollars the next time he hit Nicole. I guess these vicious beatings affected her memory. Faye goes on to testify that O.J. tells her he would kill Nicole if he caught her with another man. O.J. warns you that he intends to kill Nicole and shortly thereafter, she gets killed; yet you won't testify to this information in criminal court? You didn't go directly to the police with this incriminating evidence. No, you went off to write a book and make some money. Dan, you even admit that this whole business of Faye's is questionable, yet you want us to believe it is true. You knew there was no way a judge would let you use this dribble in court, but it did consume some very good billable hours.

When the defense cross-examined Fay you say they could not show her as lying. *"They had nothing on her."*[12] You suspect them of *sandbagging* you. More lawyer strategy and paranoia. I suspect they were. What a great witness to cross-examine, a druggie, lesbian, opportunist book writer who betrays her friend for money and infamy.

Notes:

[1] Daniel Petrocelli, *Triumph of Justice*. (Crown, 1998) pg. 182

[2] Ibid, pg. 183

[3] Ibid, pg. 183

[4] Ibid, pg. 183

[5] Ibid, pg. 185

[6] Ibid, pg. 187

[7] Ibid, pg. 185

[8] Ibid, pg. 189

[9] Ibid, pg. 189

[10] Ibid, pg. 189

[11] Ibid. pg. 190

[12] Ibid. pg 191

TEN

Kato Babbles with Nothing To Say

Katospeak

Kato Kaelin is another celebrity manufactured out of the criminal trial. You want to find out what Kato really knew and whether or not it would help your pursuit of the money. After you read all his testimony and press interviews you were sure he was getting a bad rap. His story was inconsistent and you worried that he might be withholding information from the police and the court. You felt he was lying to cover up O.J., and would perjure himself, permitting a killer go free. O.J. had such a hold on Kato that he would put his freedom on the line to defend him. Dead people didn't count; he was totally immoral. You describe him, *"More like a kid who never grew up."* [1]

Kato meets Nicole in Aspen, shortly after the divorce from O.J. She was having an affair with a friend of Kato's, Grant Cramer. Kato joined them as *"...a kind of a court jester..."* [2] Nicole hires Kato to be a babysitter in exchange for living quarters and a little rent money. Kato becomes good friends with Nicole and her children. The kids love him. Kato claims that Nicole once told him, *"'I think I am falling in love with you.'"* [3] This was just after a double date with Marcus Allen. Whoa, Nicole's eyes do roam. Kato brushes this off, as he was not attracted to Nicole. He claims they did not get involved romantically. Since the new residence at Bundy doesn't have a guesthouse, Nicole had him take a room in the condo. Sounds like they have a good thing going here. This was a time when O.J. was seeking reconciliation with

Nicole. O.J. didn't like the idea of Kato living in the house and so offered him the guesthouse at Rockingham. Kato wants us to believe that this made Nicole unhappy and their friendship came to an end. It is a bit confusing, but it must be a California thing.

"*Courage was not one of his primary virtues.*"[4] This criticism comes from Kato withholding information from the police. He only answered the questions he was asked. He didn't volunteer any information. This is hard for you to understand. You claim the police conducted a superficial interview; softball questions that permitted him to hide crucial evidence. L.A. police, are you listening? A high profile, double murder just took place and you accuse the seasoned L.A. detectives of being incompetent. How could it be possible that they treated Kato casually? He was familiar with all the parties, was with O.J. an hour before the murder and was awakened by loud thuds on his wall. You reviewed his testimony thoroughly and found it was unlikely that you would make any ground proving O.J. was the killer. Yet, you say that he was in a position to destroy O.J.'s alibi. Make up your mind, Danny boy. Can he help or not? The deposition should tell us. Start the legal clock rolling.

You first discover that Kato doesn't speak in complete sentences and is unable to answer you directly. A good start, this witness needs your management skills. He has trouble understanding the questions. You poke fun at him by relating Marcia Clark's frustrations. You tell us that each time she got the answer she was looking for, she threw him a pretzel. What an entertaining witness. Marcia considered him hostile; meaning his testimony would be favoring O.J. This seems hard to understand since he had a decent relationship with Nicole. When Nicole is murdered, O.J. did not have a chummy relationship with Kato. Their drive to get the hamburger was unusual. Kato worked for Nicole and met O.J. through her. Now you have him covering for O.J. This doesn't hang together, Dan. Though, your concerns limit his testimony as much as possible as he is a dangerous witness. You characterize Kato as being "*...deathly afraid of Simpson.*"[5] Nice choice of words, counselor. O.J. is now being seen as capable of another murder. You relate the meeting Kato had with O.J. and his advisors after the murder. Upon seeing O.J. with "*a big, bloody bandage*",[6] he was scared for his life, poor Kato. You conclude that Kato at that moment, believed O.J. was the murderer. Slow down a bit, Dan. This is the first reference to a bandage on O.J.'s finger. It would make sense that if he cut himself in Chicago; he would have a band-aid on. It also makes sense that if he cut himself during the murder, he would have a *big bloody bandage* going to the airport, signing autographs, and checking into the hotel. Again, isn't it reasonable that someone would have had to notice: his chauffeur, the passenger sitting next to him on the airplane, or the man who handled his luggage at the hotel? Too many people missed this important piece of evidence, wouldn't you say?

You uncover that Kato was terrified of O.J. Did he actually tell you this and when? The best you give us is a quote, *"I thought something might happen to me."* [7] You don't develop what that *"something"* could possibly be. Yet this fear alters his testimony in some way. O.J. was able to strike fear into Kato to a degree that he would lie to the police and in court. Your theory has this fear turning him into a perjurer. He decides to let a murder go free rather than testify truthfully and completely. You claim this fear tainted his testimony during the deposition. You tell us how Kato and O.J. hooked up the evening of the murders. O.J. was watching the *World According to Garp.* Two years earlier, O.J. had related the oral sex scene in the movie to catching Nicole giving oral sex in the living room of her Gretna Green apartment. Kato offers to set O.J. up with a Playboy model. Kato shows O.J. the magazine and they call the girl, but she is not in. Let's remember this all takes place the day before O.J. turns into an enraged killer. The day of the murders the Playboy model returns O.J.'s call.

You accuse O.J. of setting up an alibi to cover where he was leading up to and including the time of the murders. Mr. P wants us to believe that during the day O.J. is planning to visit Nicole that evening, confront her, and teach her a serious lesson. He wants to prove who is boss and may have decided to kill her. This is a major thesis, counselor; premeditated murder and setting up an alibi with Kato. Merely hitting Nicole would be very expensive - fifteen million dollars worth. Not a good plan. Nicole continued to do Nicole things. Let's try to imagine how O.J. would think through the murder plan.

In the planning of a murder there are many issues to consider. What is the best weapon to use? There is no room for anything less than the victim dying. Next you need a plan that will avoid being caught. When is the best time and place to commit the crime? What is the backup plan in case something goes wrong? How do you get rid of the evidence? Dan, you expect us to believe that O.J. plans to murder Nicole within an hour of being picked up by his driver and his choice of weapons is a knife? Let's see how these two factors line up with alternative methods of killing someone. O.J. would know that a knife produces blood evidence. Blood evidence is hard to remove. Blood manages to get on your clothing in places you would least expect, on your body, in your hair, and other places you can't even imagine. Deciding to use a knife means you are ready to get real personal. A knife attack brings you up close with the victim. You must gain access to the vital organs. There is a risk there could be a struggle that raises the possibility of noise that could attract unwanted attention. There will be clothes to dispose of and a weapon to hide. There will be endless details to take care of since many things could go wrong, and the victims aren't going to cooperate. O.J. would have to think through each of these elements of killing with a knife and determine how to do it and not get caught. A shrewd and calculating man, as you have described O.J., should have a sensible plan. He knew his two children were in the house with Nicole and could be awake or be awakened. With the very short timeline he had to believe that he could remove all the evidence from the crime scene and his home before meeting with his driver. Add to this the surprise visit from Ron Goldman. O.J. may have been quick earlier in his life, but this game plan is very risky and the consequence of anything going wrong is capital punishment by lethal injection. When you use the theory of a rejected man in a rage, you present a better argument. That man is capable of doing desperate and foolhardy things. Making this murder premeditated completely loses me.

Kato's testimony about O.J.'s demeanor during the day before and the day of the murders doesn't give us any clues to confirm that he was in a rage and planning a murder. Kato tells of O.J.'s account of Nicole giving oral sex, giving O.J. information to make a date with a Playboy model, his relationship with Paula, another model who is incredible in bed, a round of golf in the morning, and watching a movie on T.V. Sounds like a normal day in the life of a Superstar. Kato is not giving us information that O.J. would have been in a state of mind to risk his life and all that he had, to teach Nicole a lesson that night.

At 9:10 the evening of the murders, Kato and O.J. leave Rockingham to go to McDonald's. 95 minutes before he is expected to be ready for his drive to the airport. If he is planning a murder, his mind must be calculating very carefully. Let's get to McDonalds and hope there isn't a long line of any delay in service. Wait in line, place an order, eat the food, and return to Rockingham to change into killer attire. This phase must go smoothly, the clock ticking loudly. You know the problem with fast food restaurants these days. Not always fast. Kato doesn't testify to any unusual behavior by O.J. regarding the time it took to get to and from McD's. He did say that O.J. inhaled the burger. If it took 10 minutes to get there and return, and let's estimate, an additional six minutes to drive through and get the order, that is a total of 26 minutes. Still seems a little tight, but this is Kato's recollection. O.J. would then have to go into his house, up to his room, and change into murder clothes. It is now about 9:40, an hour before Mr. P's theory of when the murders took place. The drive from Rockingham to Bundy is only a few minutes. This means O.J. waited an hour before leaving his house to commit the murders. This time frame raises some questions. Under such a tight time frame, why would O.J. linger at his house for about an hour? Wouldn't a clever murderer get to scene as soon as possible in order to handle any surprises? I cannot imagine what the reasons would be for O.J. to delay carrying out the murder plan. I had hoped you would provide an explanation for this long time gap, Dan. Each second that ticked by shortened the time to commit the murder and dispose of the evidence. Was he debating with himself if this was the right time to kill Nicole? Was he concerned if he got there too early the kids would be awake? This question has a problem because if he is considering the children at all, 10:00 pm is a chancy time, since the kids could still be awake. Was he deliberately setting a tight time frame as an alibi? Was he using this time to evaluate his choice of weapons? All of these reasons are counter productive, counter intuitive, and doesn't make sense. You give us no reasonable explanation why he would wait for almost an hour, increasing his chance of getting caught through things going wrong. This hour is a very important piece of the puzzle. A key element in a premeditated murder is doing everything one can to get away with the crime. All Mr. Petrocelli is giving you is 10 minutes to kill someone with a knife and dispose of the evidence. If O.J. headed right to Nicole's he would give himself an additional hour to commit the crime and get back to his driver at 10:45. Even an hour is a short period of time for a knife murder. Without your explanations I have a problem concluding that this would be the way a clever man would plan to kill his ex-wife under the circumstances of that evening.

Though you are clearly having problems with Kato being a witness who would help you prove O.J. was the murderer, you are not dissuaded. You didn't agree with the public who considered him a flake. You claim that you just couldn't get him to admit that he really thought he saw "...*returning home from the murders...*" [8] You couldn't get him to tell you what you perceive as the truth. Dan, Kato was not at the crime scene, O.J. didn't confess to Kato he committed the murders, and all he could tell you was he recalled O.J. wearing a sharp looking dark sweat suit. What evidence did Kato have that would convince him that O.J. just committed a double homicide?

You did say O.J. acted unusual towards Kato the day of the murders, implying he was setting up an alibi. Kato was just able to get a Playboy model to call O.J. for a possible date. Maybe O.J. was impressed and a bit surprised. Who knows what else this flake is capable of doing? So O.J. invites him to get a burger. Kato fits into *The World According to Daniel Petrocelli*, a useless witness building up some terrific billable hours. I found nothing in the information that Kato provided in his deposition that wasn't already old news, but *"As advocate, you can never give an inch. You can never let the other side get away with anything; you cannot let them pull even the first fast one."* [9]

A little lawyer paranoia is showing here, counselor? Aren't lawyers supposed to be trying to discover justice? The truth, you know, Dan. You accuse Kato of wanting to be agreeable, non-confrontational and easily persuaded. Yet, when you had what you thought to be a vital point in the evidence chain—was the driver inside the gate or outside the gate? Kato stood firm with his testimony, he didn't remember. You criticize Kato for not being clearer, concise, and complete about what he saw while the events were still fresh in his mind. The Petrocelli Curse; when the witness fails to tell the story the way the lawyer wanted it costs the witness the burden of guilt forever. Kato fell apart when O.J.'s lawyer, Mr. Baker, examined him. You say he was overmatched, and instead of backing up his testimony, he backed down. Still, you felt that Kato could be useful at the trial. He would need a lot of managing and you would have to confine his testimony because he was a difficult witness. Score for Round 2: DP=Zero.

When you meet O.J. in the men's room he points a finger at your chest and says, "*I don't care what you say to me, but leave my kids out of it!*"[10] You interpret that to being part of his raging personality when things don't go his way. Why do you have a problem with O.J. being protective of his children? This is just what I would expect of O.J.— to protect his children at all costs. I will bring this up later when we develop the Jason theory. It might be seen as a corny theory to some and a loving father to others. Sounds like you are in the corny theory group. In the description of yourself, early in the book, you go into much detail bout how you became a lawyer and met your wife, but you make no mention that you are a father. O.J.'s admonition to you, regarding the treatment of his children seems perfectly natural. Since you choose to come off as an aggressive, in-your-face, confuse as much as possible and win-at-all-costs lawyer, this is the price you have to pay. You should not be surprised that a father would want to protect his children from your assault.

Notes:

[1] Daniel Petrocelli, *Triumph of Justice* (Crown, 1998) 193

[2] Ibid, pg. 193

[3] Ibid, pg. 193

[4] Ibid, pg. 195

[5] Ibid, pg.198

[6] Ibid, pg. 198

[7] Ibid, pg. 199

[8] Ibid, pg.206

9 Ibid. pg 205

10 Ibid. pg. 209

ELEVEN

Talking, but Nothing New

Everybody's Talking

You tell us "*Nicole's friends knew Simpson did it...*"[1] Let's examine this observation carefully. You use the word, "*knew*", not "believed", "thought", "assumed", or "guessed." No, you choose the word "*knew*". The definition of knew comes from know: to be certain of...beyond doubt. This is a word that I wouldn't expect you to use lightly. You are stating that Nicole's friends "knew" that O.J. was the killer. How did they come to this absolute conclusion? We can assume they weren't at the crime scene. Therefore, they must have heard about it from a reliable witness that did see O.J. commit the crime. Why would this witness share information with Nicole's friends and no one else? How preposterous you are, Dan, how sloppy and manipulative. With this same brush dripping with illogical paint, you indict all of O.J.'s friends, with one exception, as knowing O.J. committed the double homicide. They "*...were prepared to look the other way.*"[2] This is a serious accusation. O.J. has many friends. You are now grouping them all into a pathetic bunch that would prefer a killer go free than be truthful. Mr. P. this is not a harmless crime, like speeding 65 in a 55 mph zone. This is letting a murderer go free and be free to do it again. You are claiming a mass cover-up is taking place because he is the *Juice*, a moral *mulligan*. For you non-golfers, this is a friendly free shot you get in a round of golf. A do-over if you will. O.J. was such a terrific guy; his friends gave him a pass on a double homicide. Dan, you are way out of bounds on this one, a major bogey.

You criticize the prosecution of the criminal case for handling this portion of the case poorly because they were rushed and didn't have time to prepare properly. The criminal defense team claimed the prosecution "....*rushed the case...*"[3], you are agreeing. There should have been no scrambling by the prosecution. They should not have indicted him until they had their case worked out, but alas, are they lawyers trained to come to conclusions before all the facts are in? Isn't the better criticism that the prosecution should have had done their homework so they wouldn't have an excuse for rushing to present their case? No, were they were as anxious as you to get in front of the TV cameras? You know the feeling, Dan. Pretty powerful stuff that makes careers, win or lose on the lawyers part. The prosecution fell short of establishing O.J.'s motive for committing the crimes. With all the information laid out before you in the criminal case and over $1 million to work with, you promise us that you will do a better job of convincing the public and the jury that O.J. had sufficient motive. This is what you advertise on the cover of your book to get the public to part with their $29.95. Your first claim is that the prosecution made a mistake by asking the powerful, status conscious wealthy to demean themselves by going to the grungy courthouse to answer questions. This crowd had to be treated differently to get to the truth. They needed the proper atmosphere. You accuse Clark and Darden of being insensitive to their needs. It should have immediately occurred to them that to get to the truth in this case the surroundings had to be more suitable. Possibly they could have imposed on one of their defense attorney friends to loan out their offices. This would be the friendly surrounding they needed, but darn it, they blew another chance to bring out the truth. A bit tackier here though they are not just moving money around, they are moving lives. They shouldn't have been in such a hurry. They might have gotten it right, but you Dan are not going to make those same mistakes, are you?

First you are going to bring them to your fancy offices, the kind designed to impress clients and their adversaries. All the furniture victory can buy. All the intimidation wood paneling can muster. The witnesses told you that they didn't like the atmosphere of the prosecutor's office. You empathized with them. Wow, Dan. Great lawyer strategy, fine furniture makes better witnesses.

You give us a look at the District Attorney's office and the police detectives. They are skeptical, with limited tolerance, and show it.

"They tend to demand rather than request-usually have the power to back it up-and not above strong- arming people when they need to move things along…they don't like to lose. They have their own set of rules, which they insist others follow."[4]

You are confusing me, Dan. This is the same description you gave earlier of how lawyers work. The in–your-face, break down the witness, confuse, and other aggressive tactics you are so proud of possessing. I don't see any differences here. By the way, aren't you an officer of the same court, sworn to uphold justice as the law enforcement folks are? It seems like you have similar training and pride in your tactics.

Letting the witnesses know that they would not be treated like they would in a D.A.'s office, you pay for parking, serve lunch, and interview them in a fine office building in the right section of town. You make it as comfortable and un-intimidating as possible. Then you tell them,

"'Look, you have to tell me now *what you know or it's going to the grave with you. Nicole's already in her grave and she is entitled to have the truth known. This is her last chance for justice.'"*[5]

Good speech, Mr. P. Dine them, make them comfortable, and then make it clear they should not hold anything back or lie to you, a definite insult to any person not intent on shielding a murderer. I wonder if the L.A. detective's offices are paying close attention to your tactics at getting the truth. They should definitely clean up their act and to get at the truth make sure when interviewing the upper set in California; they are as comfortable as possible.

Now you bring us to David *Pinky* LeBon who may get you some results. Pinky lived with Nicole when she dropped out of high school and became a nightclub waitress. One night she came home with her pants ripped open. Her explanation to him was that O.J. had picked her up and "*…tried to be forceful in his Rolls Royce*".[6] "Tried" usually means he was unsuccessful. If Nicole's story was truthful O.J. tore her pants, but didn't go any further. Since Nicole was living with Pinky, wouldn't she tell her story in a way that put her in the best light? She didn't say O.J. tried to rape her. Whatever happened couldn't have been so out of place since she takes up with O.J. in the future. Do you want us to add Pinky's testimony to confirming that O.J. is a person capable of rage at the murder level? Not yet, counselor. Pinky says that he and Nicole remained friends and he was protective of her. He often reported on O.J.'s cheating on her, but O.J. bought her off with a Ferrari. Pinky, what are you telling us here? As long as O.J. would compensate Nicole with a gift, it was okay for him to play around? Nicole, I guess, could handle infidelity as long as she was being lavished with gifts. Pinky also tells of Nicole confiding in his wife, after the 1992 divorce, Nicole *"confided that Simpson was going to cut her up in pieces and throw them over the freeway"*.[7] How coincidental. Someone hears from Nicole that she had a premonition of being murdered with a knife by O.J., but it didn't stop there. O.J. would do a _Friday the 13th_ thing, cutting up the corpse and distributing it along the freeway; tabloid stuff here—directly on the grocery store newspaper rack. If Nicole were truly feeling this way in 1992, she didn't act accordingly. No restraining orders; instead attempts at reconciliation, I guess to keep those Ferrari's coming. You felt this testimony, which had no place in court was helping you understand the complex relationship between Nicole and O.J. You didn't quite know what you were going to do with this stuff, but if there were enough you would surmise, *"...that much of it* was *true. It all fit."*[8] So far all I am hearing is Nicole telling many people she was in fear of her life. The problem is she is not telling the right people. All this looks like Nicole building a case to get the prenuptial rescinded. There were lots of millions of dollars there.

Robin Greer, a Nicole confidant, and a woman you say O.J. despised, introduces a letter from O.J. to Nicole regarding her illegal use of Rockingham as her address. It was causing a problem with the IRS and had to do with the prenuptial agreement. In 1985, O.J. gave Nicole a condo at the signing of the prenuptial. When Nicole divorced she got $400,000 and moved into an expensive condo in Brentwood. She sells the condo given to her in San Francisco and takes the money to buy the new condo. This left her with $90,000 in the bank. There was a significant profit on the San Francisco condo that was subject to capital gains tax. It was Nicole's plan to avoid that tax by claiming that she was living in O.J.'s house at Rockingham, whereby the Bundy address would become a rental to avoid paying the tax. Since it was possible that Nicole would return to O.J. he didn't have a problem with the arrangement, as long as she put the money away for the taxes. The tax was estimated to be from $90,000 to $100,000. The letter to Nicole put her on notice regarding the taxes and was written with an attorney's assistance. O.J. was taking this matter seriously. The prosecution wanted the jury to believe that the letter was part of the murder motive and added to the rage that drove him to planning her murder.

Mr. Petrocelli wants us to believe that this was part of a strategy by O.J. to put Nicole out on the streets to become a homeless person. Let's slow down a little here, counselor. Nicole puts herself in this predicament by buying into a luxurious condo leaving her no money to pay the taxes that she owes. Hey, Nicole, how about selling the Bundy place that should have never been bought in the first place and living in a residence that cost less than a million dollars? Nicole had a choice. What about the concept of living in a place she could afford, pay the taxes, and not be dependant on O.J? As Mr. P points out, Nicole had no way to earn money. She had failed as an interior designer and had no other skills. She put herself in a totally dependent situation. Her family, friends, or O.J. would have to help her out. It seems he was fed up with her needy money situation. Remember, you let us into Nicole's very promiscuous life. You want us to believe that this letter was retaliation for Nicole not wanting to return to Rockingham. It sounds more like a $100,000 scam O.J doesn't want to accept responsibility. You try to turn Nicole's poor judgment into an O.J. being dissed. That is a far reach from where I read.

When O.J.'s letter was delivered to Nicole, she went wild. This is one of those hyperbole words that require a better explanation. What was Nicole like when she went wild? Was she in a rage? Would she attack someone with a knife? Would that knife then be used against her? Maybe the drug money collection guy turned around an attack and whoops, a dead lady. Robin reports that Nicole told her Simpson was going to have her arrested for tax evasion and take the kids. This made Nicole freak out. Robin and Nicole, it doesn't work that way. Yes, Nicole was supposed to report the gain on the sale of property, but there are timing issues. There is not enough information here to tell us that Nicole would have been arrested for tax evasion. The *kinder, more gentle IRS* would probably have given Nicole a chance to fix the problem before sending her to the slammer. Your attempt to quote Nicole from beyond the grave is very imaginative, counselor.

You want us to believe that O.J.'s letter to Nicole put her on notice he wasn't going along with her tax scam drove her to finally cutting off from him forever. This theory is filled with contradictions. You want us to believe that O.J. couldn't live without Nicole, yet you have him driving her off over financial matters. You have O.J. strategizing to put Nicole and their children on the streets and at the same time despondent over Nicole having affairs with younger men. You have him jealous and at the same time rejecting her. A whole lot of guessing is going on here. What you want to believe as fact, is O.J. being emotionally attacked enough to commit murder. Robin Greer says that O.J. keeps repeating, "*'...I'm sorry'.*"[9] At the funeral, Robin believes this to be a confession. "*She says that it was understood by everyone that he had killed her*"[10] Here we are again, in the deep valley of suppositions. "*Everyone*" knew O.J. committed the murders? This guess was based on what evidence, counselor? Please, at best some may have guessed O.J. would commit these crimes. At the time of the funeral none of the flimsy evidence was known. Robin and you share the same nonsense of conjecture by trying to claim that O.J.'s guilt is obvious. Again, the only thing that is obvious at this point is your willingness to accept any piece of trashy testimony.

Now you turn us to a conversation between Al Cowlings' and Robin Greer. Al wants to know if Nicole and Faye were dealing with *cartel drug lords*. Greer answered sarcastically to imply that was crazy. Dan, why didn't you ask the more reasonable question? How much drugs was Faye using drugs before the murder? How would Greer know unless Faye or Nicole told her or she saw them using. If she were there, which would be the best testimony; she might be opening a door to a space that you may regret. Then Robin answers the big question from Al,

"*Who could have done these murders?*" Greer's answer: "*It was either O.J. or you.*" Your reaction is that, "*This woman who took no shit.*" [11]

Why Dan, when you said earlier that "*Everyone understood O.J. killed Nicole*"[12], is Robin now wavering? She says it is either Al or O.J.

or someone who might have framed him. So, Robin is not that sure that O.J. committed the murders. It could be Al or someone framing O.J. What happened to knowing, along with everyone else, O.J. is definitively, conclusively, absolutely the murderer? Cowlings' realized that the conversation with Robin was going nowhere. You are right on that one, Al. Robin is full of shit, (not my choice of words) just as Dan pointed out. Well not precisely, but one full of shit doesn't need to take on anymore. You conclude that Robin is not a good witness. She exaggerates and has details wrong. She is also into exaggeration. Not a witness, but certainly birds of a feather and more good billable hours, counselor.

Let's take a look at the score. You deposed O.J., nothing new here. Faye's no help. Kato brings nothing really new and now Robin Greer. It looks like the score is Dan Petrocelli – zero new evidence, zero convincing proof; O.J. – four. The real winner so far is billable hours and your exposure to the press in behalf of your firm.

It should be pointed out that the real losers here are O.J.'s kids. You are dragging their father and mother through this slimy process once again, so the kids are victims. You want their Dad to be a killer and reveal some of the seamy side of their mother. According to the testimony, their Mom's a *ho*, a tax cheat, and a druggie. You and Fred have put the kids through this ordeal and have come up with nothing convincing. We still have over 500 pages to go so maybe something redeeming is as yet to be revealed; hopefully some truth, for all of our sakes.

You now interview Cynthia Shahian, another friend of Nicole's. She was proud that she turned down an offer to write yet another book about Nicole. Cici is another friend that Nicole told O.J. hit her. You make a teasing reference to O.J. having an incident with Tawny Kitaen and to the police coming after Nicole. What did the police report actually show? You never say. Cici says she heard that O.J. kicked Nicole in the stomach and punched her in the face. Nicole told Cici that she went to the hospital and told the doctor she fell off her bike. Why would Nicole lie to a doctor? And wouldn't a doctor know the difference between a beating and a fall? Why would Nicole protect O.J.? Unless it was to keep the money coming, but there was bigger money to be made in telling all. Cici tells us that Nicole wanted to reunite with O.J. in 1992 because she needed him and wants to get her family back together. O.J. accepts the idea as long as she dropped Robin Greer as a friend and would be monogamous. He wants her to take up golf so they can spend more time together. His plan was to give the reconciliation try a year. Cici encourages Nicole to go back to O.J., yet later regrets giving her that advice. When does the person who is getting dumped make the rules? The main reason Nicole's interest in returning to O.J. is to restore all the nice things O.J. did for her friends and family. It really hurt when they split and O.J. cut off the spigot. Here's that money thing again. Now, Cici's testimony gets juicy. Nicole mentions to Cici that her extra set of condo keys are missing. Cici says sarcastically, "*I wonder who could have taken them?*" *They both knew it was Simpson.*[13] Is this another message from the beyond? Nicole complains to Cici, "*He does not love me, he is obsessed with me. He is going to kill me and my friends are going to sell me out.*"[14] The next night she lay in a pool of blood. According to Cici, Nicole has this premonition of impending death. I don't know exactly what this means in the context of O.J.'s violence. Cici speculates that O.J. and Nicole fought on the phone the night of June 12th, about 9:00 p.m. She and you are convinced that this call triggered O.J.'s rage. I see too many problems with this theory, Dan. In your deposition with Kato, you theorize that O.J. was setting up an alibi for a murder he had planned. If he were planning the murder, then the conversation with Nicole wouldn't make sense. He admitted that he called at nine to talk to his daughter. If he is talking with Nicole and expecting to speak to his daughter at nine, it seems unlikely that he would be planning to come over in 45 minutes to commit murder. Then in the midst of this murder plan, he calls Kato to go out for a burger. Does this sound like the MO of a raging killer planning to commit murder, a murder plan that runs the risk of having his own children as witnesses or victims? Come on Mr. P how can you feel good about this killing theory? Yet, at this point you maintain that O.J. was lying about being interested in talking to his daughter, but was having a nasty argument with Nicole that triggered her death.

You are looking for a witness that would say, "Nicole broke up with O.J." You desperately need O.J. to be the rejected one, abandoned, cast aside, and divorced. This rejection led him to murder. You wanted a witness that would line up with your research regarding people who kill their spouses. Your research showed that recently estranged spouses kill! WOW, any of you recently divorced spouses, better get restraining orders. In O.J. and Nicole's case recently estranged happened over and over in their on again off again relationship. There would have been several incidents that would have driven O.J. to become a raging murderer in this theory. Well, it's a Mr. P theory so on with the search. Who would tell you that O.J. says Nicole dumped him? With that testimony, you could then tell the jury, "See, O.J. admitted he was rejected by Nicole, therefore we have a clear motive for murder." Maybe one of O.J.'s friends could help you in your quest.

Let's try Kris Jenner, Bob Kardashian's ex-wife. Nicole also told her that she thought O.J. would kill her and get away with it. A rumor from Faye revealed Nicole saying on May 2nd that O.J. threatened to kill her if he saw her with another man. Kris recommended that Nicole get someone to stay with her. She was quite surprised that Nicole would have told her she was threatened by O.J. She viewed Nicole as a very private person who did not discuss personal problems.

Kris, what Nicole was doing was equivalent to committing conversational adultery. She talked to many people, but effectively gave the impression that she was sharing a deep dark secret. Bob Kardashian is one of O.J.'s friends and Kris is his ex-wife. I see a conflict of interest here. I would like to know more about this before I have to listen to hearsay, tabloid type testimony.

Kris leads you to Allen Austin, a long time golfing buddy of O.J.'s. Allen tells you that he thinks O.J. committed the murders, though he didn't think so during the criminal trial. Austin is concerned that O.J. didn't have any explanation for the blood evidence or testify in his own behalf at the trial. He was offended that O.J. went to black churches to speak, after the trial. He thought that was hypocritical. *"O.J. didn't give a shit about the black community!"*[15] Austin, don't you need better reasons to be convinced O.J. committed these murders. Austin adds on that it was out of character for O.J. to come home for his daughter's dance recital. Again, how do these observations help us understand why O.J. would want to slash Nicole's throat.

O.J. was constantly away from home and would regularly miss important events. So why did he come home for this recital? Austin thinks it was because he was planning the murder of Nicole. We are back to the premeditated theory. This doesn't line up with the rage theory. Which is it, fella, planned or spontaneous? You make it seem like both. Austin says that O.J. told him instead of moving to Rockingham in May of 1994 Nicole pulled the plug. Simpson said Nicole had broken up with him. Here is your admissible evidence. Bingo, O.J. admits he was dumped, but guys, that was in May, Nicole didn't get murdered until June. A month is a long time in the lives of these people. There could have been several reconciliations and partings in the meantime. Even Allen admits this was not unusual. They were always breaking up and getting back together. Nicole constantly changed her mind. Allen is getting weak as a witness. He really doesn't know the status of the situation on the day of the murders. Sorry, Dan, this one just came unglued. The blood evidence haunts Austin. I don't know how much Mr. Austin studied the suspect evidence, but the best forensic guys in the business convinced a jury that the blood evidence was not conclusive. The blood evidence created more confusion than explanations. He is convinced that Marcus Allen had something to do with the reason O.J. murdered Nicole. Another regretful reach since Marcus denies such a relationship. When any of these witnesses put out a theory of O.J.'s possible motives for killing Nicole they are pure speculation. In an accusation as serious as murder, these guesses are totally out of bounds. You need a whole lot more to get to murder than the possible rejected lover story. Pulp fiction is filled with jealous husband theories that hold together much better than this.

Austin goes on and on with preposterous assumptions for filling up your billable hours. He comments on O.J.'s behavior the morning of the murders on the golf course. The criminal prosecutors said that O.J. blowing up on the golf course that day was an indicator of his state of mind, but Austin said these outbursts were "*...nothing. That happens all the time.*"[16] Yet, Dan, you want to interview all his golf partners that day. Austin volunteers to arrange for you to meet all but one of them. He warns you it would be a waste of time, but that was fine with you, since your motive is billable hours. Then Austin really drops a bomb. He tells us that O.J. cheats at the game of golf and this makes it easier to accept as true that O.J. killed Nicole. We have now entered the land of the totally preposterous and unbelievable. We are now given testimony that those who cheat at golf are especially likely to kill ex-wives. This guy tops Kato in being an airhead. Allen leads you to a witness to an O.J./Paula incident in Palm Springs. She's a woman who was speaking to O.J. at a birthday party. Who knows, maybe she can shed some light to help convince us that O.J. is the killer. I can't help thinking of the good intentioned, innocent people that invested in Fred Goldman's legal fees. If they knew their money was being burned in these useless fishing expeditions wouldn't they want a refund?

Allen and Pam Schwartz are the next to be subpoenaed. They are social friends of Nicole and O.J. Allen was convinced that O.J. was the killer. Pam couldn't believe that O.J. would commit such a crime. They both admit they are confused. They are upset that O.J. wouldn't testify at the trial and that the race card was used. You show them a letter from Nicole to O.J. before their divorce that brings them to tears. Allen speculates, ""'I'm telling you. In my opinion, this involves Marcus. For him to do what he did, I think this involves Marcus.'"[17]

Allen offers additional evidence that would suggest O.J. could be the killer. There was an annual softball game between Jewish businessmen and black professional athletes that included Allen and Simpson. Simpson's teams won routinely. One year, Schwartz loads the Jewish team with good athletes and by some miracle they won. The next year, O.J. brings on his "A" team and humiliates the Jewish team. O.J. let his competitiveness show and got in Schwartz's face over the victory. The fun of the yearly contest was now gone. You admit, Dan, that there is no significance to this incident. You defend yourself by claiming it gave you insight into understanding O.J., the icon. Good investigative work, Dan. We now have clear authority that O.J. cheats at golf and is aggressive in softball games. Is this part of the convincing evidence of O.J.'s guilt you promised? The way your case is developing is intellectually insulting. It becomes clearer each chapter that you are burning up lots of billable hours and achieving giving us no substance.

Pam Schwartz now contributes her evidence. At the recital rehearsal, the Saturday of the murders, Pam reports that Nicole was finished with O.J. She guessed it was because of the IRS matter. Nicole discloses to Pam that she loves O.J., would always love O.J., but he would never change. Since O.J. wouldn't change, Nicole decides to look for another direction in her life. Let's take a moment to look at Nicole's options. She didn't finish high school, which seems a bit unusual for an attractive girl from a middle class family. When she met O.J. she was a waitress. She had a short-lived career as an interior designer. She's a mother to two children and she has no disposable income. Her only money is tied up in her expensive condo. What could be her dreams and prospects? For a high maintenance, thirty-something, attractive blond, it would seem that her best prospect would be to find another man to support her lifestyle. What she needed was a single man with a handsome income or a sugar daddy. Though she has been divorced for two years, this hasn't happened. What would make this prospect even greater? O.J. gave this woman a taste of the expensive life. He supported her family and friends. He was a celebrity and came with the full package. Isn't this the Beverly Hills standard we have learned so well? In the land of many, many beautiful women, Nicole didn't seem to have much else to bring to the table. It is tough enough to be a single mom, but when you are a very high maintenance lady it narrows the field considerably. And let's not forget her choice of a drug-addicted roommate. This is not the best thing to expose the children to, Nicole, let alone a mate. This testimony of Pam's contradicts the statement by Nicole herself that she had lost her love for O.J. after the 1989 beatings. Pam believed all of Nicole's stories were true, *"She didn't lie..."*[18] Pam, explain that to the IRS, Pam.

From this dribble you extract that

"Little by little, I was not only piecing together what really happened, but also developing evidence to impeach Simpson's many lies."[19]

I don't understand what you mean by *"..what really happened."* After hundreds of pages, I haven't found anything that could be considered reliable evidence proving O.J.'s guilt. You didn't get it from O.J. Kato gave you nothing. Paula couldn't help and these acquaintances of O.J. and Nicole's admitted they were guessing. Sum total of good information: still Zero, Dan. At least you feel you are getting somewhere in piecing together convincing proof. I don't see it, but read on we will.

You now spend some time with Jackie Cooper, the tennis pro at La Quinta Country Club in Palm Springs, another lead from Allen

Schwartz. Cooper and Simpson have known each other for several years. He has information from a visit with O.J. over Memorial Day, 1994, two weeks before the murders. During this weekend spent with Paula, O.J. expressed to Cooper his devastation over the current break up with Nicole. Simpson told Cooper he thought that his was the final split.

What does this mean to the reader? O.J. and Nicole had been divorced for two years. Though they talked about getting back together, it didn't look like it was happening. One of the theories being put forth was that Nicole was furious O.J. wouldn't let her use the Rockingham address as her own. She was misleading the IRS and he didn't want to be part of this ruse. This sequence of events makes no sense to me, counselor.

If O.J. wanted Nicole back at Rockingham, why is he complaining about her using his address? If O.J. wanted Nicole back how would a $90,000 IRS debt interfere? It would be simple for Nicole to sell her condo, pay the IRS, and still have cash from the proceeds of the sale. In living with O.J. she wouldn't need the condo. If Nicole went back with O.J. her IRS problem could easily be resolved, if he wanted her back. We know that logic doesn't always prevail in these situations, still Dan; you want the reader to believe that Nicole dumped O.J., which led to his rage to perpetrate murder.

The IRS letter can't logically serve two opposite purposes. It can't cause Nicole to want to dump O.J. because he wants her back. It is a letter telling Nicole in no uncertain terms that she wasn't coming back to Rockingham. You think that O.J. is devastated because she is seeing Marcus Allen. You feel the combination of jealousy and rejection is something new with O.J. and yet the facts speak differently. Nicole took up with many young, attractive men. What makes this combination so special?

The witness testified to the fact that Nicole and O.J. were regularly getting together and breaking up. Every time they stopped seeing each other they knew it could be the final time. They may hope for a different outcome, but definitely run the risk that this is the last time. The history of these two lovers shows many inconsistencies. They are both very attractive people, used to a lot of attention, and live in the upper echelons of society; spoiled in many ways. It is no big surprise that many superstar relationships have these qualities, but don't necessarily lead to a knife murder. You didn't give an example of other knife murders in similar situations.

Much of the tension between O.J. and Nicole including spousal abuse, on both sides it seems, could lead us to imagine murder among us usual folks. Even then, this is a dangerous generality and less likely the higher up the economic ladder you go. Those with more to lose are less likely to risk the chance of being caught and loosing all that they have gained. Not always, I have to give you that, Dan. If you need a motive based on the marital and post-marital relationship O.J. and Nicole had, it is hard to conclude with conviction that O.J. would premeditate to kill with knife. It seems less likely especially because the kids were in the house and the high risk of being caught. All this speculation leading to a disappointed, devastated O.J., even if true, still does not add up to him having enough motive to be a killer, but I am still reading on in hopes that you may provide the dripping knife that cuts to the truth before you run out of $1.2 million.

You congratulate Cooper for being a real hero for testifying about his conversation with O.J. leading us to evidence that O.J. was dumped by Nicole. Aren't heroes supposed to do a bit more than that, Dan? First, he has an obligation to tell the truth. Secondly, if he did have important information that would bring a case to justice, he has a duty to testify. One does not become a hero by merely testifying in court. You say that Cooper has nothing to gain by talking to you. On the contrary, counselor, haven't many made millions telling their side of the story? You know the publicity was priceless, Dan. All those cameras, the press, the attention could have incited the same publicity seeking virus that was infecting you.

Now you return us to the Schwartz's. They asked you,

"Dan, why did he do it? Did he go there with a knife and gloves? Did he plan it? Could he have done it alone? Do you think somebody helped him clean up? What about the fact that they found his sock on the rug? Why is it there?"[20]

You had to convince them that O.J. was guilty because they knew in their hearts he did it, but didn't want to acknowledge his guilt. Whoa!

What did you tell them, Dan? Why did he do it? You are groping around to find out what the motive might have been. You even asked these questions yourself pages earlier. The only answer you have come up with so far is that O.J. couldn't handle being rejected by Nicole and Paula on the same day so he decided to kill Nicole. I submit that with all that has been put forward so far, this is not nearly motive enough to murder or many, many people out there better get restraining orders.

Did he go there with a knife and gloves? You haven't established that yet. The knife is still missing. Wouldn't a knife be hard to hide given the time frame outlined by O.J.'s activities of the evening? If he went with the knife, it would have to have been premeditated. Did he plan it? The premeditated theory doesn't hold up against the activities before the murder. Could he have done it alone? A great question; reminiscent of the Kennedy assassination accused murder, Lee Harvey Oswald. Yes, it's possible, but commonsense is uncomfortable with the facts supporting a single killer. In O.J.'s case it seems even more likely there was more than one killer. Oswald could have launched shots that happen to hit the target. Unlikely to have happened, but possible. The circumstances create enough doubt to demand a thorough examination. In O.J.'s case the thorough examination didn't take place. I'm not a professional detective and I see serious questions and reasonable suspects. The absence of investigation is the single most troubling aspect of this double homicide.

The crime doesn't look like one person could have done all that damage alone. The absence of noise, the short time frame, getting rid of the bloody evidence all point to having more than one person involved. Another great question: Did he have help cleaning up? What did you say? That the sock in his room certainly looked planted, the strange way the blood drops, all two of them, were bleeding from inside the sock. Criminals make many mistakes, O.J. gets rid of the major pieces of evidence: knife, clothes worn during the crime but he leaves a pair of blood spotted socks in the middle of his bedroom. Doesn't make sense. A spectator naturally asks, "Who put that there?" What was your answer?

You had only to convince them of what was in their hearts. That O.J. was the killer. You have introduced a novel way to convict someone of murder, just trust what is in your hearts. The evidence is apparently not important. The convincing evidence you promised us, Dan, where is it?

Schwartz gives you another person with information. He suggests you contact one of O.J.'s friends, Joe Kolkowitz. He tells you that O.J. was a complete mess after the divorce in 1992. He had lost 25 lbs, and was a pathetic, sniveling, crying person according to Joe. You feel this establishes his emotional attachment to Nicole. Joe, who stood by O.J. during the trial, believed that O.J.'s unwillingness to testify convinced him that O.J. was the killer. Simpson told him repeatedly that he would testify. His failure to clear his name brought him a judgment of guilty, again. Joe felt he was misled by O.J. regarding the awareness of Nicole's relationship with Marcus Allen. This too became one of the themes to pronounce a guilty verdict among his friends.

The decision to have the accused testify is largely the attorney's decision. There are good reasons for an innocent person not to testify in their own behalf, especially in a murder case. The burden of proof is on the prosecution to establish evidence that the accused is the murderer. A failure on their part provides no reason to take the stand. Witnesses under pressure innocently may portray an incorrect impression on the jury. Forceful prosecutors can make witnesses look like they are lying, turning small inconsistencies into large issues.

Lawyers' tactics, when the rules are focused on winning, sometimes succeed whether the accused is innocent or guilty. Come on, Dan, you must remember Intimidation 101 in Law School. O.J.'s lawyers probably insisted he not take the stand. If these friends would put themselves in his shoes, they would understand. If you were winning the case 12 to 0, would you jeopardize victory to testify? Think about it, the only thing you can do absolutely is to provide an airtight alibi. Short of that, you are asking the jurors to guess.

O.J. said consistently, "I didn't commit the murders. I wasn't there. I was at my home getting ready for a trip to Chicago."

The prosecution would challenge and ask him to account for some of the so-called evidence. They would ask O.J., "how do you account for your blood being found at the scene? It is on your hat, etc, etc."

He would deny every allegation and it would be up to whether the jury believed him or not. If the prosecution had not proven their case, there was no need for him to testify.

He made the correct decision. If you were a friend, would you say, Well, O.J. must be guilty because he didn't testify." That would be ridiculous. Mr. P wants us to believe that friends that believed he was guilty drew these conclusions. Couldn't he come up with something better than that? How about some sensible evidence, a witness, something new? It's not enough to build a case on rumors and gross speculation to convince this reader.

This reminds me of a story about a young man I know deciding not to go into law after graduating from law school. He said that in law school he would be challenged to argue both sides of a case to a mock jury. He was good enough to win on both sides. He was concerned the process wasn't a process of justice, but more aligned with how much justice money could buy. How good was your lawyer compared to the other lawyer? He chose to go on to medical school and become a doctor instead. No justice here, so far, just extensive lawyering.

Dan, you continue to burn up more billable hours interviewing people who knew O.J. and Nicole. You search for information as to how O.J. was handling the on-again, off-again relationships with both Nicole and Paula. You find that O.J. was upset as to how he was being treated. All of the principles involved have a common problem. They don't really know what they want. All three had many relationships under their belt and seem to be seeking more. All were very attractive people, the Hollywood image, rarely satisfied, selfish, money driven, image crazed, and unpredictable. Surely these on/again, off/again relationships cause feelings to be hurt leading to angry responses. There is abuse, but you want us to believe, Dan, that this is certain recipe for murder.

Exposing the lifestyles of the rich and famous we do find too much spousal abuse (any is too much), broken hearts, transient relationships, but when do you hear about knife murders? Gun murders, paid killers, drug administered killings, and drowning, but when are there knife murders? Knife murders take a special brand of courage. The in-your-face, skillful performance required is the opposite of the cowardice of a scorned lover in a rage.

Even though a movie actor may play an expert Navy Seal, we must remember this is not real. The actor would not be trained to handle the real deal. The tabloids liked to make hay over O.J. playing this part in preparation for this double homicide. This is not reality T.V., Dan. It's the movies. Make-believe, remember? Your lengthy excursion into developing motive and capability has proven to be more about burning billable hours, providing no substance into proving in a convincing way that O.J. is the only possible killer.

Another acquaintance, Mr. Hughes, is now given, to relate another incident in the early '80's regarding O.J. hitting Nicole. In his account, Nicole first attacks O.J. because he gave jewelry to someone else. O.J. said the bruise came from his trying to restrain Nicole, who was upset that O.J. could get away with this bad behavior, leaving her the victim. All Hughes could do is to remind Nicole that if she left O.J. she would be losing all the financial benefits. He regretted giving her that advice.

What is this supposed to be telling us, Dan that we didn't already know? O.J. had a pretty, but untamable wife; Nicole had a superstar, but untamable husband. They both abused their marriage and each other, they got divorced, and they kept in contact and tried to rekindle their relationship. It didn't work and you want us to believe it led to knife murder. Not a probable conclusion with the information at hand. True it is possible, but not likely. Still you may find a new witness to shed a more convincing light. We are only a third of the way through your story with lots of creative billable hours ahead.

Notes:

[1] Daniel Petrocelli, *Triumph of Justice* (Crown, 1998) p.210

[2] Ibid, pg. 210

[3] Ibid, pg. 210

[4] Ibid, pg. 211

[5] Ibid, pg. 211

[6] Ibid, pg. 211

[7] Ibid, pg. 212

[8] Ibid, pg. 212

[9] Ibid, pg. 214

[10] Ibid, pg. 214

[11] Ibid, pg. 215

[12] Ibid, pg. 214

[13] Ibid, pg. 218

[14] Ibid, pg.218

[15] Ibid, pg. 225

[16] Ibid, pg. 225

[17] Ibid, pg. 228

[18] Ibid. pg. 230

[19] Ibid. pg. 230

[20] Ibid. pg. 231

TWELVE

A Killer Lawyer in Training

Lethal Paralegal

Our next adventure is tracking down uncooperative witnesses for you to depose. Apparently, this is not an easy job. Not everyone wanted to make a buck or share the O.J. spotlight. Luckily for you, within the law firm there was a pit bull of a young man that would go out there and get these witnesses subpoenaed. Steve Foster was a very resourceful guy. He will go far in the legal industry using these tricks to get his quarry. In a civil case there are several reasons for people not wanting to be deposed. One is that they have nothing to contribute and don't want to be inconvenienced. Depositions are not fun, and people don't want to be used just to burn up billable hours. There are improper perceptions associated with being called to testify. Merely avoiding being served does not proclaim that someone has something to hide. The many tactics used to serve many of O.J.'s associates were fascinating and cunning.

One of the things you felt needed clarifying was a "*...screaming argument*"[1] O.J. had the morning of the murders with one of his golfing buddies. You wanted to establish his mood that day. Baumgarten notes that though O.J. was unusually pissed off at him, it wasn't really that serious; two competitive guys facing off on a golf course.

He gives us a different picture of O.J. and Nicole's relationship. He tells us that Nicole was interested in getting O.J. back. She was taking golfing lessons and bringing the kids to the golf course. She would go unannounced to the Rockingham estate. He also reveals to you that O.J. told him he and Paula had a big fight the night before the dance recital because he didn't want her to attend. Paula was pissed off. You believe, Dan, that this treasure hunt has produced a valuable nugget in this "...*big slip-up*".[2]

He had just badly impeached Barbieri and Simpson. O.J. felt that Paula's presence at the dance recital would make everyone uncomfortable. Paula was upset about this rejection. Contemplating this, the reader has to guess what would have made Paula so upset. Did she want O.J. to display her to his ex-wife, family, and friends as a statement of his love for her? Was he insinuating that she was not that important to him by not letting her come? Was Paula actually interested in the dance recital and supporting Sidney? Did she feel that if she missed this recital, her relationship with the child would be undermined? Did being left alone, while O.J. was with his family and friends make her feel bad? Poor Paula. Baumgarten offered, "*I'm so sure that when I heard about Nicole's murder, I thought Paula did it*".[3] Craig, this is not the time for joking around. Don't you realize that everyone is listening to each word and making interpretations? Lawyers will seize any kind of juice that will give their cause a good perception. Paula was annoyed at not being with O.J. at the recital. From her testimony, we have seen she is not a dumb person. Paula had experienced many instances where O.J. had to make politically correct moves that annoyed her. Do you really want us to believe that this is the straw that broke the camels back? There is not enough here and Mr. Baumgarten is too flippant to be taken seriously. Your nugget is fool's gold, Dan.

Enter, Cora Fischman, one of Nicole's closest friends. Quite a lady, Nicole, with all these close friends in which to confide. Cora says they ran together, shared stories about their affairs with younger men and confided in each other about their husbands. Barbara Walters came to her for some of Nicole's stories; lots of juicy stuff here. During the criminal trial, Cora tried to get on the money bandwagon and spoke with National Inquirer reporters and also with the publishers of Faye Resnick's book about developing a project of her own. Dan gets a copy of the taped interview. They were looking for exploitive sex secrets involving lesbianism and threesomes. Cora must have had some or she wouldn't have been talking to the National Inquirer. Pretty tawdry stuff, eh? Cora didn't like playing second fiddle to Faye Resnick so decided to become an O.J. supporter. Can this woman actually help you establish O.J. had a motive to kill Nicole, uncovering this sick stuff?

Cora and Nicole had a falling out because Nicole, who was supposed to cover an affair from Cora's husband, failed to do so. Cora tells us that Nicole participated in a threesome with Faye Resnick and a man. Cora wasn't present, but as with the rest of this motley crew of witnesses, she has a lot of trash to spread around. The big problem is who to believe. Which, if any, of these storytellers is telling the truth? What you consistently do, Dan is selective acceptance of testimony. If a statement makes your case better, you claim it is believable. If it hurts your case, the witness is a liar. This convenient creation of truth to suit your desired conclusion is nasty lawyering with no apparent interest in establishing justice.

You are not happy when Cora won't confirm that O.J. has a violent temper. You never ask whether she witnessed any displays of violent temper. All you are seeking is second-hand knowledge, rumor, if you will; that O.J. was a violent man. Then, you get your needle stuck on finding out if O.J. was obsessed with Nicole or was Nicole obsessed with O.J. or was it mutual. This is just like the dumper/dumpee exercise. We never do find out. We are now lost in who was obsessed with whom and what it means.

Cora is not cooperating with you. She tells that O.J. would come to her for reports about Nicole's love life. Cora would snitch on Nicole, excusing her because she was afraid of aging and having younger men made her feel good. According to Cora, Nicole bragged about seeing both Marcus Allen and her Cabo lover on the same day. Nicole complained to Cora about O.J. stealing her friends. He was buying them things and abandoning her. Friends going to the highest bidder aren't friends at all. The bottom line for Mr. P was that Cora "...*soft-pedal O.J.'s behavior and inject unflattering sexual innuendos into Nicole's portrait*".[4] Another round of billable hours for Dan and no more information for us; you win and nobody else.

Now, we come to Christian Reichardt, a chiropractor in his forties, Faye Resnick's fiancé, and "...*a male equivalent of Cora Fischman*".[5] Reichardt and O.J. have conversation 90 minutes before the murders and before O.J. went for a burger at McDonalds. You interpret this as part of O.J.'s strategy to set up an alibi. Let's go back to the premeditated theory, Dan. The more you cook on this burner, the more we see how desperate you are. Remember premeditation would have us believe that O.J. wanted the perfect knife murder, no evidence, no chance the victim could survive, and, of course, no witnesses. Do you forget the children were at home? You have O.J. scheming the perfect murder by calling Reichardt. He tells you that O.J. sounded relaxed and happy to be seeing Paula, didn't say anything about Sydney or the recital, and told him he was packing to go out of town. This all seems to you, Dan, as a transparent attempt to establish an alibi and paint it impossible that he would be capable of committing a murder an hour later, but, you are not all that sure about this wild scheme, are you, counselor? You ask yourself if O.J. is really that clever. This phone call between Reichardt and O.J. does nothing more than portray O.J. as a man under control. It doesn't place O.J. at a different location at the time of the murders, which is the most important part of an alibi. If this were a set up for an alibi, the conversation would seem O.J. would try to place him far away from the murder site.

The most important information we receive from Reichardt is regarding Faye's cocaine habit. This turns out to be problematic for you, Dan. If Faye was addicted again, spending a lot of money on cocaine, she may have charged up a bill large enough for her dealer to come over to the house to collect. You need to dismiss this possibility. Earlier you accept Faye's version of spending only $20.00 a day on her habit. Of all the ridiculous theories you set forth in this book, this one is particularly special. If you believe that Faye was spending only $20 daily on a cocaine habit you will believe any piece of garbage that fits into your case. This really impeaches your lack of integrity, commonsense, and interest at unveiling the truth, Dan. There is no such thing as only a $20.00 cocaine habit. Ask anyone who has dealt the drug and they will laugh at you. This is either a case of either being naïve and unwilling to do basic research or you think your readers are dumb.

This is not a small point; being in debt over drugs could bring a nasty collection call from her pusher. A collection call could get messy when Ron Goldman enters the scene. You have to press hard that Faye could not be in debt. There can be no other option, other than O.J. being the killer or it seriously messes up your easy pursuit of moving money around. This possibility should have been dealt with seriously, but you make a sham of the whole process with your Columbian cartel gambit. Lady Justice is squinting here, Dan. It would be understandable in your zeal to succeed in this case, if this was the exception instead of the rule. Time and again, you abandon logic, reason, good judgment, and the obvious truth at the same time promising us clear evidence that O.J. was *indeed* the killer.

Your method of legal combat ranks with the athlete that cheats, the prosecutor who lies, the cop that plants evidence, the businessman that deceives, and the politician who steals. They are all your colleagues in the crime against our value system. You must win irrespective of the cost and the methods. You don't seem to get the impact of the damage you cause. You are a very, very bright guy, resourceful and clever, yet you use these special abilities in such a convoluted way. You are proud of your ability to win because it brings you bigger and bigger clients, a more powerful position at your firm and in the field of battle. People cower at the thought of facing you. When you look at yourself in the mirror, Dan, imagine all the good that intelligence could be doing, instead of adding up billable hours and letting blood with the craftiness of your ax.

Here we are with you confronting a witness that knew of Faye's condition at the time of the murder. For Reichardt to lie about what he knew in order to help O.J. would make him someone that would be protecting a killer. That is a serious accusation, Dan. Let's see how you handle this.

It causes you concern that Reichardt's testimony would suggest Faye's observations and perceptions were tainted by drug use. You need to blunt this damage, but Dan, why, if it was true? Since you are on a hunt for justice why not just accept it? You carefully select your questioning so as to convey a correct perception. The first word you carefully select is "*'...entourage'*".[6] You felt this as an appropriate dig on the "*...shameless faithful in Simpson's wake*".[7] Again you attack any witness that sheds favorable light on O.J. Simpson. You believe them all to be sinister liars. Continuing with your psychological assault, when Mr. R. refers to a "Dan", you ask "*And by 'Dan', you* *are not referring to me....*"[8] You purposely did this to unnerve him. After sizing him up you concluded he didn't like to be made fun of. Proudly, you tell us, "*I was just playing with him*".[9] You lean heavily on this technique. When one of his answers didn't go the direction you charted, you accuse him of being condescending, in fact, "*The condescension was dripping.*"[10] You accuse him of injecting Faye's drug use unnecessarily. You are offended by his answer because "*First of all, Resnick was taking relatively small amounts of drugs and went into rehab because her friends intervened...*"[11] You feel Reichardt is obstinate and used every opportunity to throw the drugs into the situation. You move to have his testimony stricken from the record. You and Mr. R's attorney get into a verbal wrestling match. You accuse Reichardt of refusing to act reasonably. "*This was unmitigated bullshit, and I wasn't going to let him get away with it.*"[12] Pretty strong vocabulary. Dan you are getting upset. Your *Faye was a good witness theory* is biting the dust. Note my sarcasm here, counselor. Under no circumstances was Faye a good witness. Having another nail driven into her testimonial coffin is not what you expected. You must know that there is some possibility that this murder could have happened because of a bad debt. You can't allow that to be true. You can't afford to have any other possible reason for the murders; so you are sticking to your *little drug use* theory while you slide down the slopes of legal sleaze. Continuing to jockey with Mr. R. you believe you have him rattled. What was this all about? You give us the answer, Dan, "That was an issue of control."[13] You didn't really need the answers you were seeking, but you went out of your way to "...crush him".[14] Impressive, Mr. Tough guy!

This was a reoccurring pattern with the Simpson's witnesses.

"*Rather than be fair and neutral, come in and tell the truth, they chose to be advocates for him and I wasn't going to put up with it. I sat there and wore them out until they had been disciplined. Some fought me more than others, but ultimately it wasn't a fight they were going to win.*"[15]

You continue to characterize O.J.'s witnesses. These are not just any one's witnesses. You deposed these people. Some give you useful information and others do not. You imply that O.J. has some spell or special influence that causes people to lie under oath. There is a conspiracy to get this killer off. They are working for a murderer. This is quite an accusation, Dan. According to you these are really evil people; letting killers go free, especially spousal abusers who kill. Something is very sick here, Dan, and it looks more and more like your zeal to win. This Justice thing you talked about, where did it go? What happened to fixing the mess in L.A.? What's up with your contribution to the legal profession? Dan, you are coming off like the obsessed one. Mr. Fiancé was simply telling his story about Faye at the time of the murders. You didn't like the implication. Faye was a drug addict seeking money and her account of what went on couldn't be relied upon. Somehow you can't accept this reality.

You ask the question, *"Why did no one hold Simpson accountable? Why did they let him get away with it?"*[16] The answer may be, Mr. P., they did not know for certain that O.J. was the killer. Just like you, Dan. They just told the truth, as they knew it. Not just like you, Dan. You are accusing people of shielding a murder. Very nasty business. You even accuse the lawyers of these witnesses of having too good a time playing with "...'the Juice'."[17] Now the lawyers are in on the conspiracy to free O.J. I don't know how to follow-up on this accusation. The thread going through my analysis of your work is that you don't stand alone abusing the law, now you bring your colleagues into the criticism. I wonder how they are viewing your antics, especially if their clients are insisting to them they are telling the truth.

You are disgusted with the witnesses that are not producing the testimony that will help you. *"These people are weak."*[18] They didn't want to admit O.J. was a killer. You claim they are covering up their own bad feelings about consorting with a killer. *"So many of them lied to themselves, to each other, and to me."*[19] Let me spell p-a-r-a-n-o-i-a for you, Dan. It means *extreme irrational distrust*. Seems to fit here.

You also criticize O.J. for not taking the stand in the criminal trial. You have joined in this specious logic. By not testifying, you conclude, O.J. must be guilty. Was this another lesson you learned in law school? You only had one case that went to a jury, so you are not very experienced in these matters, but if you check with one of your 60 partners, maybe someone will explain to you that if the prosecution fails to make their case, it would be foolish for the accused to get on the stand, despite the fact he promised his friends he would do so. This is so elementary, Mr. P. it astounds me that you would try to add this to your proofs of conclusive evidence of his guilt. Did he lie to his friends, or did he say if it were necessary to clear his name he would be happy to take the stand? The prosecution did not prove that he committed the crimes. You haven't added to their case and yet you are coming in with a verdict of guilty.

You want us to believe that the witnesses that didn't contribute to your case were "*...willing to write Nicole off* ".[20] She's dead, but the Juice is still here; I'm going to be his buddy. You call these people, "*...despicable*".[21] You deposed Cora and Christian for five days, and you claim that you needed a shower. After all that billable time did you check into the Beverly Hills Hotel and use the Presidential Suite? A little Dom Perignon, a few candles around the room, caviar and a big fat $35 cigar? Sorry, Dan, just a little jab. I can't afford to have an investigator check out your way of celebrating. Just using the same form of logic you have been using throughout this book. However, you celebrate your financial victories and take us on this narcissistic journey.

Notes:

[1] Daniel Petrocelli, *Triumph of Justice* (Crown, 1998) p. 241

[2] Ibid, pg.242

[3] Ibid, pg.242

[4] Ibid, pg. 246

[5] Ibid, pg.247

[6] Ibid, pg. 248

[7] Ibid, pg. 248

[8] Ibid, pg.248

[9] Ibid, pg.248

[10] Ibid, pg.249

[11] Ibid, pg.249

[12] Ibid, pg. 250

[13] Ibid, pg. 250

[14] Ibid, pg.250

[15] Ibid, pg.250

[16] Ibid, pg.252

[17] Ibid, pg.252

18 Ibid, pg. 253
19 Ibid. pg. 253
20 Ibid. pg 253
21 ibid pg. 253

THIRTEEN
Liar, Liar, Liar

Fuhrman, Fuhrman, Fuhrman

You now bring us to a name we have all learned to dislike, Fuhrman. Your chapter heading gives us his name three times. Three gags from this reader. Don't tell me Dan; he's really a great guy, thoroughly professional, impeccably honest and just a terrific fella that's been misunderstood. Pardon the pre-emptive sarcasm again, but I just feel it coming. Tell me it's not true. Or is he really the low life cop we got to know too well during the trial?

You recognize that during the criminal trial Fuhrman lied under oath, because

"If we could keep Fuhrman's presence minimal and focus the case on the evidence of Simpson's guilt, we stood a much better chance of winning." [1]

This is taking a page out of a magician's book; distract the observer, so you can pull off your tricks. You tell us that Assistant District Attorney, Bill Hodgman told you that Fuhrman did the best detective work at the crime scene. He found a spot of blood on a car at the crime scene and treated Kato as a suspect. He found the bloody glove near Kato's room and summoned his colleagues. He took handwritten notes documenting various pieces of evidence at the Bundy crime scene. Good police work according to you, but pedestrian so far, to this observer. Wish you would give us more, Mr. P.

You point out that when no one at Rockingham answered the telephone the detectives decide to go on the property and they find

119

Kato asleep. Hold here a moment, counselor. Did they have a search warrant? What was probable cause? Who was the suspect? Who was in danger? I recall this was an issue in the criminal trial. Why would a good policeman run the risk of losing evidence found by not having the proper authority to enter? Why leave a possible margin for error? What is good about this police work? Sounds like the police are putting themselves in a predicament. They need to establish probable cause and assuming O.J. was the killer covers their tracks. Otherwise, they are rushing to a judgment, which could blow the case.

As a white person, your next paragraph embarrasses me. You give your version of how Fuhrman should have handled the question regarding using the term *nigger*. You let us on to a little secret. The prosecution tried to prepare Fuhrman and he refused to cooperate. You didn't like the question posed to him in the first place. You thought it had no place in this trial.

Dan, as a resident of planet Earth, you must be aware that in the land of Los Angeles, in the land of the U.S., in too many places, law enforcement has abused the rights of black people. This record is a scar on our history. L.A. has had more than it's fair share of police brutality and race problems. If a policeman is a confessed bigot you are telling us this would have no bearing on a case where a black man is a possible suspect, a black man married to a white woman. In this case Fuhrman, a bigot, and tried to hide the fact. He wanted the world, the TV audience, and the jury to believe he was just a good cop doing his duty. He wanted to deceive us all. Did he lie because he knew that if the truth were known it would shed concern about his role in being a detective in this case?

This was not an accidental lie. This was carefully thought out because he felt he could get away with it. He did not expect that someone was going to come forward with proof that he was lying on this subject. Is this inescapable proof, Dan? Something you have yet to present us with for supporting your premise that O.J. was definitely the killer. You believe that Fuhrman's lie sealed the fate of the two innocent victims. Wrong again, Dan. If the prosecution had other good evidence, something, wouldn't the jury consider it? Saying that no matter what else was presented in the case, the jury would not believe because Fuhrman lied. You level another insult at the jury.

You then give us your version of what Fuhrman should have said. You would have liked him to say,

"*I use the word all the time, I'm sorry to say. It is unpleasant language of the street and the language of where I work. I use all kinds of racial epithets for all kinds of people. That language is directed at me and we direct it at other people. We use it among ourselves, even among police officers. I'm not proud of it, but of course I've used that word. Are you trying to embarrass me, Mr. Bailey?'*"[2]

I have problems with what you consider the better answer than the lie. What I think you're giving us is a bigger lie, Mr. P. You are trying to minimize the use of the word *nigger*. You do this in several ways. First, you assume that no one who uses the word is a bigot. The problem was not that Mr. Fuhrman used the word, but the context in which he was discovered using it; on a tape-recorded message that was part of a book describing police work. The message on that tape screamed bigotry. It was not just the "*N-word*"[3] word. You wanted him to say he was sorry for using the word so often. Now, Dan what makes you believe for a moment that each time he used the "N" word he was sorry? He just couldn't help himself; like a bad habit. Kind of like a $20 a day cocaine habit. No harm, no foul. Balderdash, again!

You try to excuse Mark by minimizing the bigoted language as merely the language of the streets. Everyone else does it so why can't I? It really doesn't mean anything when I call someone a nigger. It is just an expression. My black friends have a problem with that attitude. Just like my Italian friends when they hear the expression, guinea or whap. You know, *just one of those guinea lawyers, acting like a kike lawyer.* Harmless enough, just street talk. Everyone does it. No bigotry here, definitely not. Everyone does it, even the bigots.

"*...the language of where I work.*"[4] How nice Dan. You now have the LA police department regularly using racial epithets as kind of a work environment requirement. Otherwise, you are out of step with police culture. All 30,000 of LA's finest are you smiling at this? He wants to get the bigot off the hook because all the boys and girls in the office are doing it. They are even doing it to each other. That's the clincher. He can't be a racist if everyone is using the "N" word, just another nice guy fitting in with the crowd. Not only have the blacks gotten this treatment from Mark, but everyone. He is nondiscriminatory. He uses slurs on everyone, and they back to him. What terrific example law enforcement is making.

Now, Dan, you must be putting these words in his mouth. They don't have the ring of truth. It is a cop-out. You are either coaching Mark into a bigger lie or not willing to ask the real question. "Do you have a problem with black people?" He does, Dan, and you are not willing to face up to this. Mr. F. felt it important enough to lie about it in one of the most sensational murder cases of the century. He probably knew that if the truth came out about his real feelings, the suspicious nature of how some evidence was discovered would be questioned. Especially with the sorry record of the LA police department at the time. Remember those scandals, Dan? He was blatantly covering up and got caught. You are trying to minimize a critical part of this case. You are coaching the *bigger lie*. You claim that you "...*all*" knew that race had nothing to do with the case. Who are these *all*? You say Fuhrman was not especially assigned to the case. Okay. Why is that important? He was sleeping when critical evidence was found, you say. That theory cuts two ways. What critical evidence are you talking about? He was involved in finding the glove at Rockingham. That discovery begs many questions. In what other way was he helpful in proving O.J.'s role in these murders? You didn't want to lose his honest and important information. What information? Uncertain whether or not you can use him after all, but you keep your options open. This is rather sneaky here, Dan, wanting the reader to use information that would not be used in a trial. This looks like a clever prejudicial trick to me.

One of your legal partners deposes Fuhrman in Idaho. An interesting choice for him to relocate; where several neo-Nazi militia outposts are known to be located. Signs are actually posted by business people there, "*'We don't hate people.' 'We are not racists'*"[6]. Apparently his arrival didn't help the Sand Point Chamber of Commerce promote tourism. At the time of his deposition, the California Attorney General's office was looking into pressing charges against him for perjuring testimony in the criminal trial. Sounds like serious stuff.

Your deposition caused a traffic jam in Sand Point, Idaho. It appears you notified someone as to why you were in town. Just couldn't resist stirring up more publicity. Your colleague was relieved that, "*He did not have the horns he was portrayed with,'*" [7] In fact, he liked Mr. Fuhrman. Hmmm. What made him come to that conclusion? Maybe it says something odd about your friend. Mark took the fifth to most of your questions. Particularly notable was his failure to answer the question regarding his planting of the glove. Mark had a problem answering self-incriminating questions for you or for O.J.'s attorneys. He had a problem telling the truth. The bottom line, "*Fuhrman's deposition ended. He had said nothing.*" [8] Again, lots of billable hours, travel expenses, preparation hours, and the result, nothing. Not even from a guy that you claimed would be "*...a star witness*". [9]

Time now becomes a problem. You are not going to be ready for the April trial. Things are obviously not going well and you need more time. No new evidence, just a rehash of the same old stuff. O.J. hit Nicole back in 1989. Some of her acquaintances claim she complained that he hit her again. Paula=0, Kato=0, Faye=0, an assortment of friends=0, Fuhrman=0. Nothing, nothing, nothing except using up the $1.2 million and lots of publicity for you. Give us something, something, something, pretty please.

You are relieved that the judge grants you an additional six months for more depositions. Fred is not happy; he's looking for his bucks. You try to calm him down by telling him the delay will help the case. "*...'We will benefit from this delay, I promise you.*'" [10] What is it you are promising? This is a major contradiction to your original premise that this is an obvious case, correcting a great miscarriage of justice; everyone knew that O.J. was guilty and the prosecution blew the case. The evidence was so convincing that any reasonable jury would get it. O.J.'s guilt was obvious. Yet you need more time to fully develop the facts and prepare the case. You have a running head start from the criminal trial since you could avoid all the *mistakes* made by the prosecution. Yet you need more billable time. Nothing convincing came from all the witnesses you thought could help.

Now you turn to the heart of his close friends hoping to find information that would shed some light on O.J.'s guilt. You take two months to depose Al Cowlings, Robert Kardashian, Jason Simpson, Cathy Randa, Skip Taft, and Arnelle Simpson. You admit that none of these people are likely to say anything to help your case, but the show must go on.

Al Cowlings, a long-time close friend of O.J.'s refused to testify about his role in the Bronco chase. Your use the word *chase* again, please. You ask Al about the type of player O.J. was on the football field trying to create a metaphor of his brutality. What a pathetic reach here, counselor; the tougher the football player, the more likely the murderer? Is this where you want us to go with this line of questioning? NFL beware, you are all murder suspects, especially Madden's *Toughest Guys* squad. Cowlings would not confirm that he knew of any beatings O.J. administered to Nicole, other than the 1989 one. You point out, Dan, between 1980 and 1985 before O.J. and Nicole were married they broke up regularly.

You offer that it was because of O.J.'s womanizing. This supposition has two edges. I assume you don't have specific evidence regarding this accusation. One possibility regarding the relationship is that Nicole was aware of O.J.'s conduct before she married him and it was acceptable enough to become his wife. Or, this just an example of a couple that were in a perpetual on again, off again relationship. Did each on and off seem like the real deal? We don't know, but in this case the cycle persisted.

In a sad way, these two people seemed to need this roller coaster existence. A need that you want us to believe would be ended with a knife murder. What evidence do you give us that there was anything special going on that night attributing a murder motive to O.J. You need it to be special because you are searching for a motive. The beatings and breaking ups don't automatically lead us to a violent knife murder. Please give us more logical circumstantial evidence if you want us to be convinced.

Cowlings relates an old story from many years back that you describe as "...*comical*".[11] He tells us that O.J. claimed he thought the police were coming after him. They split and lost the police pursuit. Simpson went to his friend, Schwartz, in his Bentley and hid in his garage to avoid detection. O.J. then took Nicole's jewelry, puts it in a black bag, and hides it in a neighbor's garbage can. He looses Schwartz's car keys, climbs over the neighbor's wall, and returns to the Schwartz's on foot. He asks Cowlings to retrieve the keys and the bag. Cowlings says he never looked in the black bag. From this odd story, you conclude that O.J. was hiding dope in the bag. After all,

"Why else would anyone go back into a house to which the police were coming from which Simpson had been expelled, take a bag of something, and then place it in a garbage can?"[12]

Why would O.J. take Nicole's jewelry? You can't explain the reason for O.J.'s actions so you attribute a crime to it, hiding drugs. It was obvious to you since O.J. acted nervously when he got the keys and the bag back. Good police work here, Mr. Lawyer. What do all these presumptions and innuendos have to do with this case? Are you telling us that O.J. was a drug addict? You want us to believe that he is a murdering drug addict? The long arm of a far-reaching attorney does not a case make. Remember that when O.J. returned from Chicago he willingly went to the police submitted to an interview without the aid of an attorney and gave a sample of his blood. The police had an opportunity to examine this blood sample and determine if there were any illegal substances in his system. Nothing was reported. Introducing the possibility of drug use on O.J.'s part in the past is another example of misdirection, manipulation and unnecessary aggressive lawyering in the pursuit of money.

During a discussion with Nicole, after she accuses O.J. of hitting her, Cowlings advises her to "'...go all the way'"[13] and press charges. Sounds like Al is calling Nicole's bluff or giving her some good advice. Either way he is acting decently. Nicole doesn't press charges. Her alibi was that her family would side with O.J. What did they know that would work against her, their abused daughter? Very strange logic here; parents that would cover-up for O.J. even though they were convinced he was beating their daughter. What does that say for what Nicole thought about her family?

At the hospital, Nicole says she sustained her bruise by being hit. During the deposition Cowlings tells us about this incident. He was not there during the incident so all we have is Nicole's word. It is too hard to determine what Nicole might say. Lawyer, you want us to believe that this incriminates O.J. because he denies hitting Nicole. You are still working over old unsubstantiated ground. When you examined Cowlings aggressively, he did not appreciate your tactics and became surly and obstinate. You got him so angry that you were afraid he was going to squash you.

You accuse Cowlings of being coy about the Marcus Allen subject. Dan, you are sure that Nicole used him to enrage O.J. The theory is Nicole knew that it would bother him more than anything else she could do. Was Nicole looking for trouble? According to your logic, if Nicole knew O.J. was violent, her having an affair with Allen would drive him crazy, so what did she have in mind? It all sounds very sick to me, Dan, and highly speculative on your part. You are groping for a motive by saying that Nicole is purposely angering O.J., someone she supposedly fears. Since many of Simpson's friends believed this, you feel better about this theory. You feel they are correct. This is just another instance where you are comfortable believing the speculation of some witnesses and are unwilling to accept the *I don't know for sure* from others who will not support your theories. Al Cowlings becomes upset with your tactics of interrogation and gave odd answers. Yes, he had an obligation to answer truthfully, but by aggressively badgering him aren't you inviting his sarcasm? You are now through with deposing Al and still have nothing new. He did confirm that there was an incident when O.J. appeared to have hit Nicole, but that is as far as it went. You continue to fail to show progress on finding conclusive evidence that O.J. is the killer.

You turn now to Robert Kardashian, another long-time friend of O.J.'s. Cathy Randa was his secretary before serving O.J. You throw out a blockbuster theory. Robert K. is the one who hid the bloody clothes and murder weapon. You remind us that Kardashian had been a lawyer. You guess that there may have been crucial evidence in O.J.'s Louis Vitton bag that he took from O.J. Tragically, we will probably never know what was in that bag; bloody clothing, the murder weapon. You don't know, but you will throw out the nasty assumption that Mr. K is accessory to a double homicide. You want us to believe, without any proof he knowingly conspired to hide evidence to conceal the identity of a murderer. There will be big trouble for Mr. K if he gets caught helping a murderer. Big prison time for covering up a murder. Pretty evil person this Mr. Kardashian and a jerk according to your theory. He allows himself to be photographed taking the bag from O.J. The police and all their fine detectives are desperately looking for the bloody clothes and the murder weapon. In broad daylight, Robert is willing to incriminate himself in aiding and abetting a murderer?

That must be quite a friendship; except this whole theory is very weak. You want us to believe that a successful businessman lawyer is going to risk his freedom to cover up a double homicide. This would be too risky, too dumb, and too unreasonable. Why did it take months before the bag is brought to the courthouse? Were forensics tests done to see if there was any blood in the bag or any chemicals use to remove blood? Who would have cleaned out this bag of any trace of evidence linking O.J. to the murders? The bag was presented to the courts, not burned or lost. You are concerned that there was no guarantee that the bag didn't at one time contain the knife and clothes. You are right, but it is your burden to prove that it did contain the critical evidence that you are alluding to. You cannot guarantee this information, just speculate, and poorly at that.

I see how important it is to you to find an answer to what happened to the murder weapon and the bloody clothes. This is the major problem the prosecution had in the criminal trial and you will have in your civil case. The short time frame between the murders and O.J. getting into the limo strongly suggests that he would not have an opportunity to hide the bloody clothes and the murder weapon; no place to drop them off and no chance to turn them over to someone else. Your theory has him carrying the clothes and knife through the airport, onto the plane, through another airport, checking into the hotel, then leaving them unattended in the room, checking out with the bag of bloody clothes and knife in tow, getting back onto the plane, arriving in LA, bringing it back to his house, and *then* making arrangements with Mr. Kardashian to dispose of the incriminating evidence.

You think we will believe that after a double murder, O.J. as the killer keeps the bag of bloody clothes and knife with him through this elaborate trip, through all the public checkpoints, within a timeframe when the police are frantically looking for the evidence. At any point along the way, O.J. could be stopped, made to have his luggage inspected, and caught red-handed dripping with murder evidence. Most likely double murder would mean the death penalty. You have O.J. carrying the evidence that will have him executed while keeping his cool. No way, Dan, can I believe that O.J. does this. I don't think that Mr. K would put himself in harms way, even for his dear friend. Do you really think he would say, "What a great plan!"? We will all get away with the perfect murder. After all, you are the *Juice*! There is nothing we won't do for you including going to jail for a long, long time. Dan, how can you put out such an absurd theory? The murderer knowing he was the most logical suspect, carrying around a bag of evidence for days, in public places, that would have him executed if discovered; then having a friend willingly participate in covering all this up. Mr. K would most likely have explained to O.J. how smart it would be to plea bargain with the law and throw himself on their mercy. This bag shows up and you want to fill it up with unsubstantiated murder evidence. This is not beyond a reasonable doubt, counselor! Not from this vantage point.

You decide to call Mr. K "'…Skunkhead…'"[14] because of the startling shock of white hair streaked back from his widow's peak. You don't like the way this man looks, so you proudly show-off using childish slang to ridicule people. This is part of the fun of this case, I suppose. You are very critical of the way Mr. K responded when O.J.'s verdict was announced. He had an awkwardly pained smile, not one that you would expect to appear when someone got away with murder. That's just the point; Mr. K's reaction was appropriately relieved; yet you call it unadulterated astonishment. Some people expect the worst, and when it doesn't happen they are relieved. Earlier in the book, you make quite a point about how unpredictable juries can be. Yet, now you say that Mr. K may have even known the night before that O.J. would be declared not guilty. That would make him prepared and his reaction insignificant. Anyway you want us to interpret this small event; I don't see where it gives us any evidence about O.J. being the killer. You take us on this speculative psychological excursion, make a guess that is helpful to your pursuit of O.J.'s money, and want us to come with you to your conclusions. Not so easy with this observer. You also tell us that Mr. K is a pariah in some LA circles. This seems standard for the course, especially if you are an attorney. Sorry for the dig here, counselor. You must know by now that lawyers are not loved everywhere, particularly those who make a living moving money around.

You have a problem with Mr. K invoking the client/attorney privilege in this case. You want an exception because O.J. was proclaiming his innocence on the airways and his lawyers confirmed that O.J. was innocent to the media. You insist that O.J.'s refusal to take the stand was an admission of his guilt. Again, you are ignoring a basic principle of the American legal system. It is not the burden of the accused to prove innocence; it is the burden of the prosecution. If they fail, as they did in this case, you believe that O.J. should be the exception and insist that he testify to confirm what the jury already discovered. He is innocent. It is not a matter of hiding anything. O.J. says he was not at the crime scene at the time of the murders, simply that. You have to prove he was there and committed the crimes. Even though we all know how your case eventually turns out with your jury ruling in favor of your clients, this does not mean O.J. was the killer. There have been many men convicted by juries, who at a later date were found to be innocent. The system is not perfect, even with DNA testing, eyewitnesses and incontrovertible evidence. Too regularly, people are released from jail after subsequent information proving that they were a victim of injustice. It is an embarrassment that there are too many aggressive prosecutors, cooperative judges, dirty policemen, and unreliable witnesses that proclaim innocent people guilty. Despite your success in this case, it is not an absolute that you found justice. To the contrary, your lawyering fits more of the profile of those who have perpetrated the awful miscarriages of justice in this country.

You are utterly confusing me. You criticize Mr. K for going on national TV and telling the audiences that he asked O.J. directly, "'Did you commit these crimes?' He said, 'I did not. I am innocent. I did not commit these crimes'"[15] He tells us that O.J. said he did not commit the murders. You say that Mr. K was wrong in sharing this personal conversation with the world. First of all you tell us that most lawyers would not ask this question, afraid that the answer would be in the affirmative. Earlier, you criticize O.J.'s lawyer, Mr. Baker, for covering up for O.J. because he allegedly knew that O.J. was the murderer. Did Baker ask the same question and break a fundamental rule of lawyers? According to you, Dan, lawyers don't want to know the truth from their clients. I don't see how you can have a Triumph of Justice without the Truth. Since you want us to believe that Mr. Kardashian was part of the cover-up, he wouldn't need to be asking that question, since he would already know the answer. You are not making sense here, Mr. P.

On June 14th, O.J. and Mr. K were driving around the San Diego freeway to relieve tension when O.J. decides to go to the airport and retrieve his golf clubs from American Airlines. This surprises you and you take offense. You tell us,

"There is no good reason why a man whose ex-wife has just been murdered, who hasn't yet seen his grieving young children, is going to drive to Los Angles International Airport to get his golf clubs."[16]

You consider this an obvious lie. You believe that O.J. wanted to get the golf clubs before the police did. Your assumption is that he is hiding something in the golf club bag. Bloody some things, perhaps? Again, there would be blood inside that would not be easy to get rid of. You want us to believe that a murderer would be going after a bag that contains incriminating evidence, though at anytime the police could stop him and catch him with the goods. Under normal circumstances, you presume that O.J. would not go for the bags himself, but would have someone else get them for him, but because they contained special contents, he needed to get them himself. By the way, where was all the LA police or detectives during all of this? Why aren't they rounding up his entire luggage? That would seem like fairly obvious investigating. You are intent on making us believe that O.J. carried the knife on the plane with him, running the risk of being stopped at anytime by metal detectors or the police to show what he has in his bags. You are trying so hard here, Mr. P. Now you have to give us another co-conspirator willing to go to jail for protecting a killer, who would have cleaned up the bags thoroughly to rid them of any blood evidence. Unless you think that O.J. and Mr. K removed the blood from the bags with Comet or some other reliable blood remover. Blood as we all know is an insidious fluid, really tough to get rid of. This would be especially true of luggage and a golf club bag. I am having trouble picturing the two of them scrubbing the blood off Louis Vitton luggage and a golf bag. What do you think they were talking about during this cleaning up episode? We are now through with Mr. Kardashian and still in the same place regarding accumulating conclusive evidence that O.J. committed the murders. Counselor, you have given us a whole lot of nonsensical theories and suppositions; nothing compelling; nothing convincing. I'm still waiting for you to put something on the scoreboard, Dan. All I see so far are a lot of K's and they don't stand for killer. For you non-baseball fans, K is the symbol for a strikeout.

On to your next witness, Ron Fischman. Ron was a longtime friend of O.J.'s along with Fishman's wife, Cora. We met her earlier. Fishman tells you that O.J. and Nicole have a volatile relationship - the whole time - not just towards the end. You hoped, again, that Fishman would help you confirm that it was Nicole that dumped O.J. This was important in your creation of motive. Fishman tells you that O.J. told him that "*He was confused and frustrated.*"[17] by Nicole. Simpson insisted that he finally rejected Nicole. O.J. and Fishman traded stories about their unfaithful ladies. Terrific gossip, but again what does this have to do with finding a killer? You get nothing significant from Ron. Merely another interpretation of who might have been the dumpee or the dumper at the time of the murders. No closer to convincing us of O.J.'s likelihood of killing two people that fateful night.

Over three hundred pages into your book and we finally get to Jason Simpson. Oh, how I have been waiting for this deposition. This could be the core of the honesty in this case, both in how you handle Jason and how the LAPD and the prosecution didn't. You now have the chance to show us what you are really made of Dan. The pursuit of justice, the truth, the noble reasons you took this case is going to now be critically tested. Give me your best shot.

We find out you "*love* Godfather *movies*"[18] Godfather movies. A curious beginning. A curious confession from a lawyer, to love a movie that glorifies gangsters, killers and lawyers that got paid off by the mob and a cast of other unsavory characters. You draw a similarity between Jason and Fredo who was someone that didn't live up to his father's expectations. He had a troubled relationship with his father. Jason did not testify at the criminal trial. You heard that Simpson beat Jason. Now we have added parental abuse to the character assassination. Jason admitted that his dad did spank him with a belt on his butt when he was a kid.

You tell us there was a rumor that Jason may have committed the crimes or helped his father clean up some of the mess. It's very important that you were aware of this possibility. Yes, it was out there during the criminal trial. One of your partners was enamored with the theory, but you decide, absolutely, that Jason's blood was not found at the crime scene and there wasn't a shred of evidence to indicate that he was involved. Why was it necessary for Jason's blood to be at the scene for him to be a suspect? Can't a murderer commit the crime without leaving blood evidence behind? Of course, Dan, yet you give us this as the important indicator that Jason definitely couldn't be involved. You say that there wasn't any other evidence. Is there a requirement that a murderer leave evidence behind? I feel foolish asking you such silly questions, but your presumptions beg the absurd. You considered the suggestion of Jason being involved a "...*running joke*"[19] I'm not laughing just yet, other than at your insistence to cover-up an obvious exploration.

I do not know if Jason was involved. I am going to present compelling reasons that he could be a serious suspect. I must apologize, in advance, to Jason, O.J.'s family, and friends for adding his name to the possible suspect list. This is necessary, however, if justice is really the objective in all this legalism. For you, the LAPD, and the prosecution to not carefully establish that Jason was definitely not involved, incriminates for not going after any other suspects and focusing on the big prize, taking down a celebrity. O.J. was entitled to have all other possible causes of the murders examined and dismissed before he became the only target of the case. I took an informal survey of people interested in this case and we discussed the possibility of Jason being involved. There are several reasons why he is a serious suspect. With that offered, including one of your partners in love with the idea, I must ask you, what should have been the most important questions to ask Jason in your deposition? Readers, can you help me out? Ask yourself, what are the most obvious, demanding questions that Jason should have to answer to?

JASON, WHERE WERE YOU THE NIGHT OF THE MURDERS?

CAN YOU PRODUCE ANY ALIBI'S TO YOUR WHEREABOUTS?

JASON, DID YOU MURDER NICOLE SIMPSON AND RONALD GOLDMAN?

Daniel Petrocelli, Fuhrman, Vanatter, Marcia Clark, Darden, LAPD detectives, why did none of you ask these questions? Or if you did, why weren't we told so Jason could be completely exonerated? If Jason had a reasonable alibi and it held together all this speculation would go away. It appears all of you decided that O.J. was the killer so did not want to ask this question for fear he didn't have an alibi. If he didn't, then all of you are in a mess. The slightest suggestion that there was another explanation of how the murders took place would make it appear that you might not be so certain O.J. was the killer. You have so much invested in O.J.'s guilt you couldn't run the risk.

The other facet of a murder is motive. Did Jason have a motive to kill Nicole? Dan, you put the words in my mouth. Of course he could have a motive. Like in the Godfather movie, Fredo, the failure son, Jason had an opportunity to do something good for his dad. He knew that Nicole was tormenting his father. He knew that Nicole accused his dad of beating her. Jason could remove this woman that brought so much pain to his father. She was a lady who was sleeping around, hanging out with known drug addicts in front of her children, out for O.J.'s money and generally embarrassing him over and over again by flaunting, if you will, a promiscuous life. Jason would put an end to this emotional torture his father had been put through for years; no more pain.

In five minutes of deposing Jason, you got the sense of him; a 26-year-old that would never live up to his father and had given up trying, probably for the better. Jason played some football at USC, but was not a gifted athlete, not a star. You felt sorry for him immediately. Your questioning centered on whether his dad had a violent temper and whether he had seen him hit anyone. You felt badly asking Jason these questions. He seemed like a sad person. He didn't need anyone else giving him a hard time. Did you think asking him about the incident where he lost a job as a dishwasher by attacking his boss with a knife? Why wouldn't you bring up that story, which was out there, to give him a chance to deny the possibility he had a violent streak? Why didn't you give Jason the chance to clear himself, Dan? You ask Jason if he loved his father. A great question there, ol' Dan. A few other inane questions and you let Jason go. This avoidance of Jason speaks volumes about you, the LAPD, and the entire O.J. tragedy.

Jason had access to his father's house, shoes, clothes, Bronco, and Nicole. I wore my father's shoes as a kid. Did you, Dan? Jason and O.J. are about the same size. Do they share similar blood types also? You didn't rule this out, did you? How do you know that it wasn't Jason wearing the Bruno Magli's, the gloves, and the hat? He would not have had the time constraints that his father had on the night of the murder. He would have had time to dispose of the clothes and the murder weapon. We know he was in town because he met his father after the *Bronco Slow Speed Tour of the LA Freeways*. He was on camera and shooed away by people at Rockingham. Jason as a suspect is not just a joke? No, the sad thing is this reader and the world have been denied the airtight alibi that Jason was not involved in this crime.

The theory of Jason could also explain much of O.J.'s behavior after the murders. A devastated father put into the worst parental predicament. What would you do if you found out your son has committed a murder? Most people I have asked say that as a parent they would try to protect their child. In this case, O.J. could go to trial not fearing the verdict because he knows he is innocent. He would naturally remain silent. Even during your case, to continue protecting his son. You are a father, Dan. Did you ask yourself what yourself would do if you were in a similar circumstance? If you haven't, it is about time you did. The absence of making absolutely sure that it was impossible for Jason to have been involved in these crimes brings up the awful reality that you do not really want to know the truth. You did the same thing when you tried to dismiss the theory that a drug bill collection went down badly. You want us to believe this is impossible. Any amateur sleuth would at least investigate this possibility carefully before completely ruling it out.

There are other ways these murders could have taken place, Mr. P. There is no sign of any interest by you or others involved to ask questions that end the suspicion of additional totally natural possibilities. You know it, Fred Goldman knows it, and all of his friends know it, but none of you would dare to ask the obvious questions that suggest you had any doubts. The silence is deafening. It screams out that you all have an agenda and would not allow any possibility of contradiction. O.J. deserved better, the legal system deserves better; the public is being cheated by another legal rip-off if you will.

Jason, I certainly hope it wasn't you, but I would like to know for sure. Maybe drug dealers, a random crime; another Nicole rejected lover, or confusion by one of Faye's friends, any number of possibilities caused the murders. What I'm witnessing is attorneys developing a conclusion and then systematically building a story to justify the theory. Prosecutors, police, and lawyers looking to move the money around are doing it all the time. Shame, shame, and shame again, counselor, lawyer, esquire, barrister, member of the human race.

Mr. P, you now depose Arnelle, O.J.'s oldest daughter. Since you are accusing even the most causal friends of perjury to protect O.J. what did you expect to learn from Arnelle? She testified that she was not in the house during the time surrounding the murders. When awakened at 5:30 a.m. by the police she told them *"…he was out of town"*.[20] On this basis the police were able to secure a search warrant. When the police wanted to enter the house Arnelle selected to meet them at the front door so that she could deactivate the alarm system. You question her motive for doing this; after all it was the police. There are people, who out of habit, ritualistically, like to deactivate their alarm systems once someone enters their house. You attempt to make something sinister about this. The police and Kato remember entering the house from the back door.

You attempt to make this important because Kato was called by Simpson from LAX a little before midnight on June 12th, just before boarding the plane to Chicago and asked him to set the alarm. This is the first time that Kato was entrusted with the alarm code. Kato followed the instructions and set the alarm. When Kato and the police entered the rear door they do not remember an alarm going off or being deactivated. You conclude that after O.J. left to go to Chicago someone else must have been in the house and disarmed the alarm. This may have been possible. Could it have been Jason? Did you ask him, when he was being deposed, if he was in the house? It would be reasonable to assume he had the security code. Dan, the answer to your suspicions that there might have been someone else in the house makes me see failure in not confronting Jason as to his whereabouts that evening. You never checked to see who else might have had access to the house. This blows big holes in your unexplored theories.

You come up with another preposterous speculation by asking if O.J. washed up after committing the murders. To begin with, we have an impossible timeline that makes it foolish to even suggest that O.J. could have single-handedly done the perfect cover-up. Only Arnelle's wet underwear were in the laundry room. You are right in saying that this must have been a very bloody murder; blood all over clothes, themselves, and anything they touched. We all know blood is extremely difficult to get rid of. You ask us to believe that O.J. marshaled a cleanup team to take care of this incredible mess while he was on his way to Chicago. Each member of this cleanup crew would have to know they were becoming accessories to a double homicide. This includes the risk of big jail time with many ways things could go wrong. The possibility that forensics would produce unassailable evidence of the identity of the killer. Preposterously, you have this person or team of people working in the dark so that no one would notice they were in the house. This is how you account for the few drops of blood that were not removed. You must need this because the few drops could also suggest that they were planted. Do you really think this so called clean-up crew is willing to risk their freedom by working in the dark surely running the risk of a less than perfect job? Anything less than perfect is a guaranteed ticket to prison. This is a highly improbable explanation for the suspiciously small amount of blood found at O.J.'s home, Mr. P.

So in the haste to leave the house, the cleanup crew forgets to reset the alarm system? You ask the reader because you don't really have the answer. You ask us many questions. You want us to guess what went on at Rockingham after O.J. left for Chicago. We don't know and you don't know. Merely creating a possible scenario doesn't make it real. If your investigation had come up with something compelling I suppose you would have provided a better theory. You can't answer your own important questions. "Who routinely cleans up after Simpson?"[21] You ask and leave it to us to answer. That is an odd use of the word. *Routinely*, as though this is a routine in the life of O.J. Simpson. Murder two people, make a bloody mess, enlist help to clean up and create elaborate diversions to elude the police. Just routine in the life of a superstar!

Notes:

[1] Daniel Petrocelli, *Triumph of Justice*, (Crown1998), pg.254

[2] Ibid, pg.255

[3] Ibid, pg.255

[4] Ibid, pg.257

[5] Ibid, pg.256

[6] Ibid, pg.256

[7] Ibid, pg.256

[8] Ibid, pg.258

[9] Ibid, pg.254

[10] Ibid, pg.258

[11] Ibid, pg.276

12 Ibid, pg 262

13 Ibid. pg 263

14 Ibid. pg 265

15 Ibid. pg 268

16 Ibid. pg. 269

17 Ibid. pg 271

18 Ibid. pg. 273

19 Ibid. pg. 274

20 Ibid. pg. 276

21 Ibid. pg. 279

FOURTEEN
Randa, No Help.

Help, Help Me Randa

Now the depositions turn to Cathy Randa, O.J.'s secretary. You assume that Cathy would not say anything to clear O.J. If O.J. goes down, so does Cathy. If O.J.'s guilt were discovered, Cathy would be destroyed. Maybe, Mr. P, but if she gets caught lying how would major jail time look on her resume? You ask us to believe that Cathy knew O.J. was guilty and would do anything to protect him. I don't automatically assume that the best of friendships bring cover-up and perjury as a price. You know, there are moral people that will not lie to protect someone committing a double homicide. You use a wide brush to paint all witnesses who do not support your theories as being immoral people. You have Cathy enlisting O.J.'s friends to lie for him. Asking people to go to jail for a murderer? Friends, yes, jail fodder, not so sure. Though you knew that you would not get anything incriminating from Cathy, you depose her nevertheless. You are the billing monster chewing up mucho time here makes good work as a partner at MKS, your prominent law firm with lots of high overhead.

You insist on calling Cathy by her last name, Randa and expect her to be untruthful. You believe you are not mistaken when you talk of an incident where Cathy is asked by O.J. to go to his safe deposit box and remove contents that pertained to his children. She corrects herself to make it clear that it was Skip Taft, O.J.'s lawyer, who removed the contents. A guard claims that he saw a lot of cash being removed.

Cathy denies this. What is the point of all this unnecessary speculation? Even if a lot of cash was removed, what does that tell us? Since O.J. had become a target in a murder investigation he supposedly takes cash from his safe deposit box. What is absolutely incriminating about this? What does this point to that makes us believe he is the murderer? I recognize you are trying to accumulate facts to help point to his guilt. How does stringing together many irrelevant possibilities help us come to this conclusion? Your foundation is weak, your construction is flawed, and the result is worse than a house of cards.

Ms. Randa will not give you anything to help your case. You become exasperated and find her answers unbelievable. I can't see what the problem is here, counselor. If you find her answers unbelievable, then wouldn't a jury? It seems that would help out a lot. Someone so close to O.J. clearly lies. Wouldn't that really hurt O.J.? However you decide that you won't call her as a witness. Something is clearly contradictory here, counselor.

O.J. had Cathy keep notes regarding the physical abuse episodes. O.J.'s version has Nicole initiating the contact. Nicole's diaries say that O.J. started the fights. Here are two people covering themselves for a future legal battle. Since O.J. never accused Nicole of fraud, to Cathy, you feel this will help you in your case. It is possible that O.J. did feel he was being set up by Nicole, but never shared this with Cathy? Maybe he felt it was inappropriate to do so. You lead us to believe that O.J.'s failing to state his feelings about Nicole's motives incriminates him. Maybe sometime later you will show us how this works. It seems far-fetched to me. More far reaching there, Danny Boy, Oh! Excuse me, Mr. Petrocelli.

You accuse Cathy of purposefully destroying information that might have been harmful to O.J. Again, putting her in harm's way with the law. You surmise from the information you get from Cathy, that Paula was heartbroken when she was not invited to the dance recital. Paula let herself get sucked in again; she was feeling dumped by O.J. Then you have Paula retaliating by dumping O.J. Remember the earlier theory you had for the murder motive, O.J. feeling very rejected. Again you confuse us as to who was dumped. Maybe ol' Richman was right, Paula is the murderer. Sorry, Dan, some of my sarcasm leaking out. You are reminding us once again that both Nicole and Paula's actions on that fateful day made O.J. a man in intense personal turmoil. He had struck out miserably with both of them. This is your profile of a murderer? Yet, Kato has him calling yet a new playboy model for a date. There is nothing slowing down this superstar, icon, very attractive bachelor, full of self-confidence, and the object of much adulation. You portray his friends as willing to participate in a co-conspiracy to double homicide and go to jail for him. He is worth 30 million dollars, has a fabulous home, and is sought after for endorsements. He stars in movies, commercials and speaks all over the U.S. He is endowed with the many perks that go along with all this stardom; free clothes, shoes, trips, and meals. He is stopped wherever he goes and receives star quality treatment. Maybe O.J. could have been a tormented man, but most likely he was quite pleased with himself despite having difficulty with two very high maintenance women. This does not sound like a recipe for murder, especially for a guy who played some very rough football ten years earlier.

You acknowledge that you didn't depose Paula very well. You wanted to do it again, but time is running out. This is just another one of your excuses for poor lawyering. Facts existed, but you weren't able to get to them because witnesses were lying and time was running out. You want to leave us with the impression that there was important information that would have proven O.J. guilty, if you could have gotten to it. You give us deposition information that you know is not useable in court to add to the reasons O.J. is guilty. This is mostly all prejudicial and little fact. Well, you have used lots of money and lots of ink, but come up short of the convincing evidence you promised. I am still being patient, but losing confidence, as the book is almost half finished. There is still more to learn before the last nails get put in this coffin.

Skip Taft, O.J.'s business manager and lawyer is the next witness on your list. Skip is in his 60's and has worked to promote O.J. for most of his career. He should know O.J. very well. Since he is really close to O.J. you accuse him of being "...*a loyalist to the end*". *If O.J. was indeed guilty, then Taft had staked his whole life on a double-murderer.*"[1] Mr. Daniel Petrocelli, you have changed your take on this whole excursion in these two sentences. You now question O.J.'s guilt. Join the club. If you were being consistent, you would have said, "Skip knew O.J. was guilty." or "Since O.J. was guilty, Skip was willing to go to jail by lying in O.J.'s behalf." If O.J. was indeed guilty is not the same conviction you have had up to now. Is the truth wearing on you, Dan? Because Taft was with O.J. the day after the murders, you want to know what he knew about the cuts on O.J.'s hands. He said, "It was the middle finger. I think on one hand he had a cut.[2] This was part of the Simpson story. No news so far. You accuse the LAPD of poor police work because they didn't take better pictures. They only caught the two cuts and you accuse O.J. of "...*cleverly keeping his fingers pressed together in an attempt to hide all others."*[3]

Shrewd on your part, O.J., you fooled those detectives. Vannatter and Lange testified they got a good look at his hands and noticed only cuts on the middle finger. I'm a bit troubled here as to where you are going, Dan. Did the detectives lie? Were they covering up poor detective work? You putting words in their mouths, *"'We're stupid, he had all these cuts and we didn't notice them.'"*[4] Dan, if they didn't notice them, how could they say he had the cuts? You concede that this is a problem for you. Two detectives examine a suspect, take the time to photograph O.J.'s hands declare that there were only two cuts, and you want it to be otherwise. You offer that two days later a Dr. Huizenga reports that Simpson had ten cuts or scratches on his left hand and one on his right. You want to know where did he get them? Because years later O.J. can't explain the doctor's observation, you conclude that they were obviously caused during the commission of the murders. Yet you have no witnesses to say, "'I saw all of the cuts on Monday.'"[5] Wouldn't that have been helpful? Again you are going into major wishful thinking, Dan. You really think you need these cuts to win your case. Not only don't the cuts matter, but this is yet another display of constructing theoretical activity in the absolute and misdirecting the reader leading them to come to your orchestrated conclusion.

Since days elapsed between the police photographs and the doctor's exam isn't it possible that O.J. received cuts from other causes? You insist on forgetting that the gloves did not have any cuts through them clearly indicating either O.J. did not get cut during the commission of the crime or that blood could not have come through the gloves to incriminate him. The presence of cuts also suggests a fight. Your timeline doesn't leave room for much of a fight. You are trying to get us to believe that the killer, very quickly administered two lethal cuts, one to Ron and one to Nicole causing almost instantaneous death. You need this theory to explain why there was no noise from the victims. The expected noise that would have been likely during a struggle is being explained away by the killer instantly cutting off the victim's ability to scream. Many cuts on the killer's hand require a struggle and time for the fight. The gloves would need some evidence of penetration to suggest cuts occurring at the crime scene. The victim's would most likely have forensic evidence of O.J.'s skin under their fingernails, if there were a battle. No evidence I have heard of puts O.J.'s DNA on the victims. This entire *cuts on the hands* exploration would strongly suggest that the victims would have had some evidence that they were in contact with O.J.'s skin and blood. Not one hair, drop, or morsel of skin. This is a big problem, Mr. P. You grope for signs of a struggle by having O.J. cut many times, but everything else in your theories contradict the possibility. You get Taft to say he may have seen other cuts on O.J. You consider this a devastating admission coming from a lawyer. Taft says he remembers seeing two cuts on O.J.'s hand and possibly a third within eighteen hours of the murders. Now you really take us out there, Dan. Out to the land of lawyer despicableness, the jungle of misdirection, deception sewer, and into the river of lies by leading us to the conclusion that if he had these cuts on his hand "... *then he murdered those people. Plain and simple.*"[6] Plain and simple to you maybe, but to this reader, three cuts on the back of the hand does not a murderer convict. You qualify your assumption by saying, "*--putting aside the one he claims to have gotten when the 'glass broke' in Chicago – then he murdered those people. Plain and Simple*"[7] You are building your absolute conclusion on one cut on the back of O.J.'s hand as empirical proof he is definitely the killer. *Plain and simple.* You want this reader to be simple-minded to buy into this conclusion. This is the type of reaching is necessary when you have nothing else to go by. Shame, shame, and shame again, counselor. Please pardon my redundancies but you must admit they are following your redundancies. You go on further to tell us,

"*Taft had just buried Simpson on one of the most damning pieces of evidence in the case. The guy didn't know it, but Baker sure as hell did.*"[8]

If this were so obvious to you, why wouldn't Taft have understood? Is he a jerk? Why would he be blind to what is so clear to you, and you guess, to Mr. Baker? You make a very, very big deal of this, Mr. P and I believe the sewerage is backing up on you and you should take a deep breath and realize how badly this reflects on your mission to find justice.

Notes:

[1] Daniel Petrocelli, *Triumph of Justice*, (Crown 1998), pg. 285

[2] Ibid, pg.286

[3] Ibid, pg.286

[4] Ibid, pg.288

[5] Ibid, pg. 287

6 Ibid. pg 288

7 Ibid. pg 288

8 Ibid. pg 288

FIFTEEN

Lots of Talking, Nothing Said

Breaking Ranks

The next chapter you seduce us with a luring title, *Breaking Ranks*. This contains several innuendos on the assumptions you have about O.J.'s friends sticking together to help him cover up this heinous crime. You get another call from Geraldo Rivera's people. They have another lead for you. You seem to have acquired the skill of working with the press. Geraldo, of Al Capone fame, do you remember the sensational build-up he had to the discovery of Al Capone's fortune. It all turned out to be a bust. Geraldo was certainly missing all the attention he got during the O.J. trial. His life was now slow in comparison. He and his staff would be looking to revisit the O.J. magic as soon as possible by looking to find what they could stir up. Just like you, Dan, wanting to interview Faye Resnick again. Geraldo presents you with a doozy.

I especially enjoyed the way you describe her during your questioning. This is someone who would be giving you important information that would otherwise have been concealed because she was part of the O.J. conspiracy. Like the chapter title suggests, breaking ranks. As it turns out, this person Jennifer Ameli claims that she treated Ron and Nicole. Dr. Ameli is a psychotherapist. She did not treat O.J. She was not even acquainted with O.J. so was not in his ranks. Do misleading chapter headings lead to a deceitful author? Maybe not, but why all this hokey stuff, Dan?

Dr. Ameli claims that she treated Ron beginning in October 1993 into 1994. You are concerned that she may be a fraud and questioned her carefully. You felt that *"She had her facts and nuances reasonably straight:.."*[1] According to the doctor, Ron introduced Nicole to her. This could bring to light that Ron and Nicole had a relationship for some time. He was not merely a waiter returning her mother's glasses. I recall that the police found about sixty lit candles around Nicole's bathtub, apparently waiting for someone to enjoy their atmosphere. Nowhere do you explore the full nature of Nicole and Ron's relationship. He is young, attractive, healthy, and fits the description of the kind of person Nicole was sleeping with. You open a door here, counselor that adds confusion to what might have happened that night. The more confusion, the less likely we are to be convinced when you tell us, O.J. is the killer.

Dr. Ameli presents extensive notes and bills regarding Nicole. With Ron, she has less to present, which you call "...*amorphous*".[2] She gives you notes that speak of abuse by O.J. She made an entry three days before the murders that Nicole thought O.J. would kill her. Dan, you are sincerely concerned. "Is this some wacko, or is Jennifer Ameli for real?"[3] If she is legitimate you believe her information is extraordinary. I can't buy into it, even if what she offers is true, it is damning. It still bothers me to know that Nicole who is so outspoken about O.J.'s abuse never took reasonable precautions to protect herself. People get restraining orders all the time when they feel endangered, especially when there could be $15 million at stake. What makes Nicole's circumstances especially difficult to understand is her constant need for money and the possible consequences to O.J. if he hit her? This is too obvious a possible set-up and gives me cause to pause before I reach the absolute conclusions you do without allowing a new insight. We know that Nicole was capable of lying. You are asking us to believe that she wouldn't go as far as building a case to get O.J.'s money. The prenuptial agreement would be broken if O.J. hit Nicole just one more time. $15 million for just one blow. For someone worried that the IRS was going to put her in jail for trying to cheat them out of $90,000, those millions had to look tempting.

You find out that the LAPD had a file on Dr. Ameli. The first problem was that the good doctor didn't come forward until months after the murders. Not until the money feeding frenzy was in full swing. Many of those with information about this case were cashing in with publicity and financially. The LAPD check out Dr. Ameli "...*long and hard and concluded that there just wasn't enough for them to feel comfortable with.*"[4] They wrote her off. Your associate had a big problem with Dr. Ameli since there was no proof of payment from either Ron or Nicole. This is a strange coincidence, no proof of payment from either party. Her explanation was that Ron paid her in cash and Nicole never paid her. She was waiting for payment through her medical insurance. You admit the "*whole story was wild*".[5] Is this the person that is "Breaking Ranks" with O.J.? Important objective, personal, vital information is expected, not a wild story. Both of her explanations could have been checked out. Did she report the fees over two years received from Ron on her tax return? Could she show paperwork to the insurance company requesting payment? You and the LAPD could have corroborated her story if you felt there was some truth in it, but you didn't. Doesn't sound like either of you were convinced about the credibility of this witness. The Goldman's and Nicole's family were not aware Ron and Nicole were going for treatment. This is a bad sign, especially in Nicole's case. You would think that among all her close friends she would have mentioned that she was going for therapy. After all, she shared her intimate sexual encounters, why not a little therapy chatter? You have a problem with the way in which Dr. Ameli would slowly leak the story to you. Her dramatic presentations didn't ring true. She finally gives you a story you cannot accept. She tells you she had a conversation with Nicole on the night of the murders from a pay phone during which Nicole tells her she is frightened about what O.J. might do to her. This is just too much. You send the doctor to a lawyer friend of yours and his investigation gets eight people to verify her story. Worried that she is a fraud, you examine her motives. Because she never sold her story makes her more believable. You tell us, "*People don't make things up out of whole cloth, en masse, especially in a case of such intense scrutiny.*"[6] Dan, please, you accuse all of the witnesses that help O.J.'s case of being liars. You want us to believe that only witnesses in your behalf don't lie. I'm choking on this one, Danny Boy. You decide not to use her in the trial. Here we go again, more billable deposition hours, innuendo, weird stories, but no new evidence to go into trial. I have to beware of your chapter headings. They suggest something good is going to happen that will help your case, but all we get is a *weirdo*. You proudly tell us that you lied to the courts and the defense team about using her. Good deceptive work here, Dan. Make the other side spend money to get prepared. The score is still in horrific shape, Mr. Petrocelli. New information=0, old information=293 pages. Useless, misleading contrived, preposterous theories on most of those pages and no convincing evidence as advertised, NONE!

Now we come to a titillating part of your story, Nicole's relationship with Hall of Fame football player, Marcus Allen, a friend of O.J.'s. You start out by calling Marcus a "...*wild card*".[7] This colloquial expression means different things to different people. To me it means, unpredictable. Let's see what Marcus does for your case. He is certainly good press for the book. Our imaginations are roaring over this new candy. The first thing that comes to mind is O.J.'s feelings about Nicole having sex with his friend.

O.J. gives you a story about Nicole telling him that she was having an affair with Marcus. He calls him and tells him that it is "'...*screwing her up. She is like, going bonkers.*'"[8] To O.J.'s knowledge the relationship is over. O.J. and Nicole offer to have Marcus' wedding at Rockingham. O.J. sounds cool with what is happening. Marcus denies that they were having a relationship; they were just friends, no sex. "'*Nothing happened.*'"[9] What is going on here? Is Marcus just trying to keep his name clean? It doesn't look to good to be doing it with your friend's ex-wife - so deny everything.

You depose Marcus. He's not happy about all of this negative publicity. You find it incredible that Marcus wouldn't interrupt a holiday to attend Nicole's funeral. Dan, the man just got married. There are accusations that he had an affair with Nicole. His name is being dragged into this. He decides it is not a good idea to attend the funeral. Perhaps he was concerned that it would give misleading signals. Not so *incredible* that he would pass on this funeral. Your literary style pushes the old envelope.

You state flatly, "...*it seems clear that they* did *have an affair.*"[10] You have Marcus lying. You can't accept that they might have just been friends. Those visits had to be more than platonic. I don't know where to go with this Dan. Just as it is easy to accuse someone of murder before you have all the facts, it is easy to assume if two people are meeting they must be having sex. You want to apply only one definition as to how someone would react when finding out their ex-wife was having an affair with their friend. You want us to conclude that this would bring murderous rage. How does this connect with the night of the murder? Gathering from some of your other presumptions, you either lead a very sheltered life or you expect your readers to be quite dumb. Don't tell me you have never heard of swinging? Some husbands and ex-husbands get off on the idea of their friends making it with their wives or ex-wives. Some even arrange the deal. The *one reaction fits all* approach that you use is insulting. Let's not forget where all of this is taking place. You have taken us on a trip in the fast lane on a superstar planet. Infidelity with an ex is not the big shocker. What would be more insulting is Nicole getting it on with some sleazy, out-of-shape, money grubbing lawyer. I can see that offending O.J., but another superstar, not necessarily. Your one take is that Marcus was a threat to O.J.'s persona. All those other guys, that was okay. Oral sex in broad daylight, no problem, but another younger football star, that's a formula for raging murder. You are giving us another example of terrible logic and another embarrassment for the legal profession.

You admit that all this speculation wouldn't stand up in court. It does give you more billings and printed pages, but useless information to convince a jury that O.J. is the *killer*. The maraschino cherry on top of this legal seven-layer cake is your analysis of how useless Marcus' testimony is to you. In fact it is dangerous to your objective. If the jury wouldn't believe that the killing was motivated by O.J.'s raging jealousy, your whole case *could topple*. You confess there is not enough evidence to prove that a relationship between Nicole and Marcus would be a motive for the murders. You believe if people were truthful you would get the whole story and the jury would know O.J. was guilty, but people were lying, Simpson was lying, Marcus was lying. You didn't trust a jury to see through the lies. Scratch Marcus, just another liar.

Then you deposed James Merrill, the Hertz employee that took O.J. to his hotel in Chicago. Did you ask him if O.J. had bandages on his hands? Was he bleeding? Did he give autographs? It would have been helpful if someone had seen O.J.'s bloody hands on the way to Chicago or to the hotel, anyone. You give us no one. We really need a person that saw O.J. in Chicago that could confirm if his hand was cut or if he was wearing bandages. You want us to believe there were many cuts. The more cuts the more bandages. We have a problem here; Mr. P and you don't even tell us if you asked the obvious questions.

Allen Schwartz gives you the names of some other people to talk to. This is the same Allen Schwartz that drew the conclusion if O.J. would aggressively stack a softball team with black athletes against Jewish guys, he could be Nicole's killer. The theory went along with O.J.'s cheating in golf adding to the circumstantial evidence that he was the killer. Allen refers you to Louis Marx and Frank Olson. Marx was the principle stockholder in the Forschener Company, maker of Swiss Army watches and knives. Frank was the chairman of the Hertz Corporation. Simpson was a spokesman for both companies.

Let's see what these two fine businessmen know about who killed Nicole and Ron. I get it, Swiss Army knives=murder weapons. Schwartz encouraged you to *"Don't let them off the hook. You've got to shame them"*.[11] He surmised they didn't want to be associated with O.J. You thought this was a good idea. After all, O.J. was looking for financial support for his legal fees and that was inappropriate since he was worth millions of dollars. If you could sabotage his efforts in raising money you could call it a victory for your side. So, that's how lawyers play the money game. Solicit the public for your fees and go on the offense to try to stop your opponent from raising money in his own behalf. Tough thinking here, Dan, did you learn this at Southwestern University of Law?

Yes, you like Allen's idea of speaking to O.J.'s wealthy friends to see who would support him financially. You would then also know who would lie in his behalf. Another good conclusion, Mr. P. Did the folks that contributed to Fred's fees also lie for him in his behalf? Contributors and liars, right?

A few days before the murders, O.J. visited Forschner Company to attend a board meeting. Simpson left with a bag full of watches and cutlery. You tell us a limo driver overheard Simpson saying, *"You can really hurt somebody with this. You could even kill somebody with this."*[12] Wow, Dan, a confession in advance. I suppose when O.J. was planning this murder, he forgot that he told someone about knives being lethal. This is just more legal gibberish. If O.J. was truly planning to murder

Nicole with a knife, do you think he would be so dumb to use one that would so easily associate him with the source? That would be like going to a gun store, telling the clerk, "Gee, I bet you could kill someone with this. Make sure it is registered in my name." No, no, no! If it must be a knife, you find one that cannot be traced back to you easily. Too, too dumb an argument that O.J. gets some free samples, tells a driver he knows they can kill, and then goes out and commits a murder. It is just plain scary that you would take us down such a sophomoric path. You ask Louis Marx if he knew if O.J. got any of his knives. As you suspected, he didn't know. When Skip Taft asks Marx for a contribution to O.J.'s legal fund, he declines. Way to go, Allen and Daniel, high five! Weaken the opposition.

Mr. Olson of Hertz had very nice things to say about O.J., witty, charming, and persuasive. You interpret this to mean O.J. has "...-all the attributes of a functioning con man—and was a very effective salesman."[13] You imagined this might tell a jury not to buy what O.J. is saying, he is just a salesman or a liar, I guess. Let's look at the broad brush you paint with, Mr. Lawyer. If one is witty, charming, and persuasive, they must be...you guessed it, a con man. All you WPC's watch out the law is checking you out. Is this also a sexist remark? Do women get painted the same way? It seems like Nicole was witty, charming, and persuasive. Does that make her a con lady? Are you witty, charming, and persuasive, Danny? I hope not because you know what that makes you! Are any of your partners at MSK, WCP's or effective salesmen? Perhaps they are a group of con men.

Olson tells you that O.J. lied to him about the Nicole beating in 1989. He was embarrassed. After the fact, this is an easy position to take. O.J. was making money for his company. Once the sensational trial took place, innocent or guilty, high profile companies naturally distance themselves from controversy. Too many hired guns out there to be using an accused murderer. It was easy to let O.J. go, throw him under the bus.

Hertz gives you a letter from Simpson in which he quotes Nicole, "'I have given you the best years of my life and all you want to do is control me. Okay, it's all right. I'll just have to raise the stakes in our gin game so I can recoup some of my losses.'"[14]

151

You expect us to take this letter as incriminating evidence against O.J. I don't see it that way, counselor. First, O.J. provided the letter so why would he incriminate himself? Next, it's Nicole accusing O.J. of trying to control her. O.J. does not admit that this is what he was trying to do. She then threatens O.J., by using a gin game as a metaphor. Is she going to retaliate by raising the stakes? Prenuptial stakes, maybe; a $15 million axe over his head and she is threatening to start swinging.

You take this letter and twist it to mean, *"When he could no longer control her, he killed her – the ultimate act of control."*[5] I take exception with your dramatic conclusion. It can be argued that when you kill someone, you lose control over them. Nicole admits to being controlled. O.J. is getting his way according to Nicole and she doesn't like it. He controls the money, buys off her friends and whatever. Is there anything unusual here, Mr. P? Each time Nicole says she is through with O.J. she comes back; just a matter of time and money. What made June 12th any different except at worst, a temporary loss of control? Nicole comes off as a high maintenance, swinging, and self-indulgent LA beauty. Not controllable in the way we more normal folks view relationships. You could give us motives much less suspect. The control spin doesn't fly here as the motive for murder. Realizing that in a knife murder there is a higher likelihood of being caught considering all those forensics problems; O.J. would be trading his inability to control Nicole for being controlled by the California Prison System for life or more likely death for a premeditated multiple homicide. This bad stuff is not usually seen from the types like O.J. Simpson to give it all up because you lost control of your ex-wife. You are skating on razor thin ice here, counselor.

Notes:

[1] Daniel Petrocelli, *Triumph of Justice*, (Crown 1998), pg. 289

[2] Ibid, pg. 290

[3] Ibid, pg. 290

[4] Ibid, pg. 290

[5] Ibid, pg. 291

[6] Ibid, pg. 292

[7] Ibid, pg. 294

[8] Ibid, pg. 295
[9] Ibid, pg. 295
[10] Ibid, pg.296
[11] Ibid, pg. 298
[12] Ibid, pg. 299
13 Ibid. pg. 300
14 Ibid. pg. 303

SIXTEEN

The Brutal Bruno's

The Bruno's

We finally get to a piece of information that may shed some light on who murdered Nicole and Ron. Someone brings you the *National Enquirer.* They are all excited! It contains a grainy picture of O.J. wearing shoes that look like they could be Bruno Maglis'. These are the same style shoes that left the bloody shoe prints near the bodies. You assume the killer wore them. You assume that O.J. was wearing these shoes. There are several problems here, counselor; the authenticity of the photos, was O.J. actually wearing the shoes, and was the killer wearing these shoes? This was new evidence, the only new evidence you have brought us so far. It is not surprising that you were excited about the possibility that this was the *dripping knife* you so desperately needed since you haven't come up with anything that the first jury hadn't seen and they acquitted. Oh! If only these shoes could help your effort to move the money around. How great that would be for you and Fred Goldman and the rest of the public that would like closure on this case.

Right from the beginning you have an insurmountable problem. Hate to put it to you this way, Dan, but the conspicuous avoidance of considering if anyone else could possibly be wearing Bruno Magli shoes, O.J.'s or otherwise, is a serious omission. It is one thing to establish that someone at the crime scene at sometime on June 12th or 13th was wearing these shoes; it's another to say it was definitely O.J.

Earlier we discussed Jason and the possibility that he either borrowed daddy's shoes, or was given the shoes, because they were *ugly assed shoes*. Jason was certainly big enough to fill the shoes. Did you check to see if he was pigeon-toed also? He could have been at the crime scene and not be the murderer. Now I have a nasty for you to consider, Dan. You say in your book that it is absurd to believe that the police would plant any evidence. In my opinion it is surprising that you would say something so absurd. The police detectives were in O.J.'s house. Could someone have put on O.J.'s shoes then go back to the crime scene? Is this too devious, too clever? Not more than dropping a weapon at the scene to implicate a person. Not more than planting drugs or DNA at a scene. I know you think this only happens in the movies or trashy crime novels. I suggest you do some research in the greater community or the police files for evidence that proves differently. You dismiss another scorned Nicole lover owning these kinds of shoes.

None of us really know the importance of the Bruno Magli footprints. Since there is more than one possibility, it is offensive that you bring us to a conclusion that it could only have been O.J. that made those footprints. You claim that

" Perhaps only hole in the prosecution's case was their inability to show through a photograph, witness, or other clear proof that Simpson owned and wore the Bruno Magli murder shoes."

Was this is the only hole in their case, Dan? You are implying that if you could fill this hole, you would have an airtight case. No doubt then about O.J. being the killer. You set the standard for the reader; only one missing piece of evidence and if that is found you win. Sounds like the trick of a sleazy salesman, reduce the choice to one objection, then sell it. Really though, there are many missing pieces. Even if you could fill this one, which you don't, your case isn't any better than was presented to the jury in the criminal case. The lawyer tricks to set up the argument in their favor and then prove their point is a serious problem in the pursuit of justice: backfilling to a contrived conclusion, making the story fit, leaving out reasonable alternatives, driving conclusions out of whole cloth and stacking juries who you think will buy your version of the story.

I'm still surprised how you phrase the importance of a photograph of O.J. wearing a pair of Bruno Magli shoes. You state flat out that if the defense lawyers saw conclusive proof that O.J. did wear a pair of these sporty shoes,

"I wonder how they all felt when they saw Scull's photograph, an image that single-handedly exposed their complicity in perpetrating the most reprehensible miscarriage of justice seen in an American court of law."[2]

Mr. Daniel Petrocelli, Esquire, partner in the prestigious law firm of MSK, graduate of Southwestern School of Law, you just uttered a mouthful. I'm wondering how you feel when you construct ridiculous arguments and preposterous assumptions and get exposed? You are now accusing all of O.J.'s attorneys of conspiring to let a killer go free. According to you, the whole case is based on this one presumption, O.J. could be the only person wearing the Bruno Magli's and they were worn during the commission of the crime. If you had spent a moment examining any other possibilities and presenting cogent explanations that it was impossible for anyone else to have worn these shoes, then I would respect your claim. Your silence is deafening on this one, and you are resting your case primarily on this assumption. The Petrocelli Magic Show, but in this case it is not sleight of hand it is slight of foot, too slight, barrister.

In this chapter you take us through the elaborate steps of establishing that there are pictures showing O.J. wearing Bruno Magli's at a football game in Buffalo. This is in September 1993. The photographers involved make no bones about wanting to make money for this photo. The big problem was, in your estimation, proving the photos weren't doctored. With digital technology, this was not an easy task, especially verifying shoes. You do a decent job at getting a credible expert to say the photos were authentic. Again, allowing that O.J. wore these shoes at a football game some nine months before the murder does not make an airtight case. Would O.J. forget that he had a pair of these shoes? I'm not sure at this point. I don't know the size of O.J.'s shoe wardrobe. Did he have a lot of shoes? Was he given shoes through his promotional activities? Did he pay close attention to who manufactured his shoes? O.J. lived in a special world where it is quite possible that different items of clothing could enter and leave without much notice. You don't give us any supporting information that would let us believe that he paid any special attention to this particular pair of shoes. Is he forgetful? It could be. Dan, O.J. did not testify in the criminal trial. He did not say these were not his shoes. You have him in the civil trial three years later and you want him to answer all your questions about these shoes. You need O.J. back in the deposition chair for one more hour. That's all you want, to nail him on this shoe business. There you spend your time trying to establish that O.J. was at the Miami-Buffalo football game on September 26, 1993. O.J. is not cooperating. He doesn't deny that he was there; he just says he doesn't specifically remember the details of that day. He tells you he covered many Buffalo-Miami games and that he doesn't remember this one. You show him pictures of him doing an interview during the game, to help his recollection. He still gives you a soft answer. He neither admits nor denies that he was at that game. He just isn't sure. You take this as a bold lie. You and O.J.'s lawyer go at it over the questions you ask. You are proud to be acting inappropriately. Baker is fed up with your tactics and tells you his client is finished answering your questions.

After storming out of the room, Baker's son returns and together you come to an agreement regarding how the depositions will continue. O.J. is back answering your questions. You ask questions about each part of his wardrobe that day and he gives you a similar answer to all the questions. He has no specific recollections of any of the items. Nothing was special to him. You want O.J. to tell you if the pictures appeared to be doctored. His lawyer objects to the questions. O.J. is not an expert in photography. O.J. replies that everything in the picture looked big to him and he doesn't recognize the shoes. The deposition is over. O.J. does not admit he was wearing Bruno Magli's at the football game. He doesn't admit owning those "*'ugly ass' shoes*"[3]. If he knew it could be a possibility or a fact that Jason or someone else was wearing the shoes the night of the murder, wouldn't it be natural for him to be denying any connection to these shoes? This is one of the many logical explanations surrounding the mystery of these shoes. You ask us only to consider one: O.J. owned these suede sport shoes and he used them in the commission of homicide. Though it is odd he would wear them with a dark sweat suit, a sneaker would seem the more likely probability. This is ugly ass logic, Mr. P, but beautiful lawyering. How sad it is, that your profession has stooped so low as to resort to these kinds of tricks to move money around.

Notes:

[1] Daniel Petrocelli, *Triumph of Justice* (Crown 1998) pg. 305

2 Ibid. pg 307

3 Ibid. pg 308

SEVENTEEN

Squeezing the Juice – Do We or Don't We?

How Do We Deal with O.J.?

Do you put O.J. on the stand or not? This is the troubling question at the moment. At first it appears obvious, but now you seriously question whether it is a good idea. I'm disturbed that this would even enter your mind. You have insisted O.J. is the killer, it's as plain as can be, he's a liar, and it's as plain as it can be, the evidence is conclusive and everyone knows he is guilty. Then, you are concerned that O.J. will charm the jury, take the ball and run from you. Or maybe he will be called by his lawyer and enter in a better position, leaving you at a disadvantage. From your vantage the only defense O.J. has is his charm, you have all the evidence against him, and you are worried. If his lawyers call him first O.J. would get two chances to testify, rather than one. You can't allow him that edge. He may be convincing. Your stuff may not make sense to the jury. In the quest of justice, why should any of this matter? If he is guilty or innocent why be concerned about how many times he testifies in his own behalf? Why be concerned if he goes on first or second? After all, Dan, you are only seeking justice, not money. Give the man a chance to speak in his own behalf. Let him be charming, whatever that is in a double murder case. Let him lie. Prove him wrong. Let the jury be reminded that many a charming man has committed murder. Bundy was charming.

Ask all his victims if you could. He fried. Charming murderers do get convicted, Dan. The evidence did the job, but you must be very worried about your evidence if you think it can all be scuttled by a football player's charisma.

How was he going to charm his way out of the pictures of Nicole's beaten face? You have that evidence and so did Clark and Darden. The few smatterings of blood, you have that and so did Clark and Darden. The same story with the bloody gloves. What else is there to charm himself out of, Dan? What you don't have and Clark and Darden didn't either, is enough time for these murders to take place considering all the blood and the natural issues surrounding a knife murder. What you, Clark, and Darden aren't doing is allowing any other possibilities that bring about a murder and produce evidence. This creates doubt in some people's minds. To be afraid that O.J.'s charm will defeat your case speaks volumes as to where your mind and heart really are about this whole affair. You are talking the talk, but really afraid to walk the walk. It is simple to accuse. It is a whole other thing to back it up and more importantly to avoid the trickery to cover-up that which you can't prove. For all the suspicious elements of this case, you couldn't resist manufacturing your spin and conclude out of context, driving the readers to follow your story. That is subjecting justice to a neutron bomb. Kill all the living to get to their assets.

You make a confession during this chapter that speaks to your unethical attitude towards the money in this case. You say that unlike a lawyer that takes a case on contingency, you expanded your witness list to even those that did not want to talk to you. You weren't constrained by costs. You are saying several things here. If you take a case on contingency, you make a decision regarding the work done as it eats into your time and capital, if the client is paying then you have an open checkbook and you will depose as many people as you can. In this case Fred was not paying, but you were using the money donated by people who were solicited by you and Fred. You didn't show us a copy of the solicitation letter. I would have liked to see what claim you made to the people that ponied up the money for your fees. You now have clear conflict of interest, spending innocent, well-meaning people's money for your legal fees, whether prudent or not. I would have much preferred to hear you were very respectful of their charity and protected every dime, not wasting it on wild goose chases. Dan, considering the score so far, all you have been doing is chasing wild geese and feeding well while doing it. The benefactor's of this endeavor have yet to get their money's worth. This brings up the question, did you measure the amount of work you were willing to do based on the $1.2 million collected? If you were to have collected $1.5 million, would you have added an extra $300,000 in billable hours? We assume you would have, we know you are very good at this, Mr. P.

Finally you get to business. At a trial you will only call those that will help your case. You question whether O.J. is essential in winning this case. You are not sure. Your gut says yes, but you are interested primarily in winning and question whether you are a good match for O.J. After the eleven days of depositions you are not clear. This seems strange to me. After all that time dealing with him and your attitude about him, it seems that there wouldn't be a scintilla of doubt in your mind. The case deserves to have O.J. heard and for you to reveal all of his *lies*. This would seem to be the moment you have worked for; the confrontation the public and justice deserve, but no, you are worried. If you put him on the stand and can't do much with him he may hurt your chance of winning.

So you seek advice from you associates at MSK. You get differing opinions. Finally, just like on T.V. you go to the *man*, Arthur Groman, your mentor at MSK. He argues that you don't have a choice. You must put O.J. on the stand. You like his arguments, but reserve the decision to a later time. Leaving still more room for debate about the subject. Here you leave us hanging, but make it clear you are afraid of O.J. John Douglas, a renowned former FBI criminal personality profiler is brought in to give you an opinion of the murderer. He tells you this is a classic case of a rage killing. There are several problems with this, Dan. You have already set a stage for a premeditated plan by O.J.; planned it, set up alibis, and carried it out. The motive you give is the combination of being rejected by Nicole and Paula simultaneously, driving him into a rage, thereby killing Nicole. I have a problem with the term rage and how it is used in this context. I can understand that rage drives some to murder, but all rage does not lead to murder. Therefore there are different levels of rage. Some rage brings about beatings, screaming episodes, silent treatments; you can have your own list. You seem to be enraged about O.J. getting off with these killings, yet it doesn't drive you to murder. The application of rage and premeditation has inherent contradictions. Rage implies spontaneous emotional explosion and premeditated implies thought out emotional responses. Profiling has its statistical problems, especially when dealing with the cast of characters in this case. You seek an expert that will describe motive and analyze this crime in an attempt to convince the jury and the public that O.J.'s the killer.

Douglas' theory of how the crime took place doesn't make sense. Maybe he is a little long in the tooth. He pictures Ron getting to Bundy, ringing Nicole's' buzzer. O.J. is sitting outside in his Bronco, contemplating what to do next, kill or go back home and get ready for the trip to Chicago? O.J. sees Ron pull up and recognizes him as the man he saw talking to Nicole and her friends in front of Starbuck's. When he saw Ron headed toward Nicole's it was the last straw. Nicole was flaunting Ron in front of him driving him over the edge. He now had no choice. He got out of his car and began walking. He saw Ron at the front gate, Nicole coming down to greet him. Simpson approached the two of them from behind. He quickly and violently shoves Ron. This is when Ron probably said "Hey, hey, hey."[1] which was heard by the neighbors at 10:40 p.m. This is 20 minutes before his limo driver saw him at Rockingham. In that 20 minutes, according to the scene laid out by you, Mr. P, O.J. kills two people, returns home, does some laundry, changes clothes, and meets his driver to be taken to the airport. We all remember that corny commercial where O.J., late for departure, runs through the airport to meet his plane. Though he was very quick in the commercial, you have him doing this crime at warp speed with an almost perfect cover-up. He should be doing commercials for Star Trek.

Let's go back to the crime scene now and Mr. Douglas' theory of how things happened. Ron gets pushed aside, O.J. punches Nicole, knocks her down, maybe unconscious. He goes back to a stunned Ron and with furious rapid thrusts of a knife, overpowers him. Ron was trapped and defenseless. He collapses. O.J. returns to Nicole, stabs her in the head, then the neck, finally delivering the last gaping wound that nearly severs her head. O.J. unable to contain his rage drops a glove, his hat comes off, and he cuts his finger. He walks out the back of the condo in order not to be seen. Five minutes later he was back at home. Let's rewind this tape and look at it more closely. What are Mr. Douglas and Mr. Petrocelli asking us to believe?

1. O.J. Simpson is sitting in his Bronco looking at Nicole's condo thinking about killing her. If you want to believe he was in a rage, then the idea that he is sitting, contemplating a knife murder doesn't go together. Rage, thinking, rage, thinking, not sure whether or not to be in a rage or let my reasonable side win, go home and get ready for the Chicago trip. This sounds like a confused state, not a raging one.

2. The sight of Ron going into Nicole's condo was too much for O.J. so he leaves his Bronco and approaches the two of them. You want us to believe that O.J. is ready to attack both of these healthy people with a knife, taking on the two of them single-handedly. Kill them both without noise, leave no evidence, and be back to the house in 20 minutes. This is preposterous.

3. In his enraged state, he charges them from behind, knocks down Nicole, perhaps stunning her. Perhaps? If he hasn't knocked her out, he has two victims to deal with simultaneously. You don't back this up with forensic evidence that Nicole received this kind of knockout blow. One that would eliminate any possibility of noise, any cry of help, or scream of pain. In one knockout punch, Nicole is on the ground. O.J. immediately turns to Ron, who is just watching at this point, saying, "Hey, hey, hey." O.J. shoves Ron before hitting Nicole so he is stunned and defenseless. He is overpowered by O.J., trapped against a tree with nowhere to run. O.J. comes at him with a knife and administers 58 knife wounds. Ron is silent while being attacked. Ron inflicts no wounds on O.J. He falls down dead. O.J. turns to unconscious Nicole and stabs her in the head. Then gets behind her, lifts her head, and slits her throat. He can't contain his rage, he is frantic, disoriented, and so drops one glove.

4. Wait just a minute, Mr. Douglas. This glove at best is tight fitting. How does he take it off? It is bloody. He would have

to take a good hold and pull it off. Then he drops it at the scene. This doesn't sound very likely. He has another glove on the other hand. When does he peel this one off? Before he gets into the Bronco or he will leave blood all over the steering wheel, door handles, and seat belt. Where does he put this glove, in his pocket? Later we find this glove on his property. How does it get on his lawn? A man who premeditated a murder is handling a devastatingly incriminating piece of evidence very poorly. A calculating and clever man you called him. He would surely have had a plan for getting rid of his clothes. The foremost thing that he would have been thinking is not to leave anything behind that might cause him to be caught.

5. His hat comes off. Again, no explanation as to how this would happen. Is it being suggested that it came off during the struggle? If so, the victim would have to get very close to O.J.'s head. Doesn't seem like a person being stabbed with a knife would reach up, leaving their body exposed, to pull off a killer's hat. This type of knit hat doesn't just fall off; it must be pulled off. For O.J. to pull off his hat and drop it on the crime scene doesn't compute. Why would he do that? We must consider this because after the commission of a murder, the killer would naturally be reviewing all the aspects of the crime to determine how to get away with it. If he found that he left incontrovertible evidence at the scene wouldn't it be reasonable to assume that he would be preparing an alibi. Maybe this is suggesting something less than premeditated murder. Huddling with his lawyers, scheming the best story to minimize the damage. Several ideas come to mind. I will expound on that later. At this point, Mr. Douglas and Mr. P, we are presented with a version of this double murder that screams with incriminating evidence.

6. You have his finger cut at the crime scene. This is problematic. You have not presented any cut through the glove. Cut on hand, yet none on glove; how could that happen? You give us no plausible explanation as to how this cut could have happened during the commission of this crime. O.J. has the knife, what sharp object would have caused the cuts? Where is that object?

If it were found at the crime scene it would have O.J.'s blood on it. Where is it? We are left guessing. Could it have been during the struggle with Ron? That would suggest bruises on O.J., yet none were reported. Without a cut on the glove corresponding to the cuts on his hand, how does the blood get out of the glove and onto the crime scene? Since you give us nothing, we must guess. These matters are too important to be left for conjecture. With too little of O.J.'s blood at the crime scene we must have answers to these questions if we are to be convinced that O.J. is the killer. You give us a scenario by a top former FBI guy that could, but doesn't, give us any explanations of how a glove can give us blood drops without any openings. *Also and very importantly, we have not heard from anyone that O.J.'s blood was inside the glove.*

I cringe at the thought that you paid for this awful rendition of how O.J. might have committed the crimes. Did you ask if there might be a more plausible way the murders could have taken place? Wasn't it more likely that more than one person committed these crimes? How do you account for the fact that there was no noise? Isn't there a shortage of O.J. blood evidence? How much of a fight would he expect Ron and Nicole to put up? How likely would it be for the knife murderer to incur wounds? Why were there not more Bruno Magli shoeprints in the Bronco? How many steps would a pair of shoes drenched in blood leave? How much blood would have been on the killer? How difficult would it be to dispose of the evidence? There are so many unanswered questions, but, most surprising, so many unasked by you, Daniel. You are adept at keeping this case in your preconceived context. I am not surprised since this is the proud skill of lawyering these days.

You tell us that Douglas is not available for the trial and probably would not be permitted by the judge to testify. Oh, come on now, Dan, more useless testimony and wasted time. However, you say for the most part you buy into the Douglas scenario; maybe a few details could vary. Then to your big conclusion, "But there is one thing that can never vary: the only living person who can tell us is O.J. Simpson."[2] There you go again, insulting our intelligence. You make a declarative statement, "the only living person". You cannot really be sure of that.

You can't dismiss that someone else might know. Even if we bought into your foolish argument, how about the person who would have helped O.J. dispose of all the bloody evidence? When you make these dramatic statements of your belief of the facts you are unabashedly trying to manipulate the reader. This is intellectually repulsive.

Notes:

[1] Daniel Petrocelli, *Triumph of Justice* (Crown 1998) pg. 324
[2] Ibid, pg. 324

EIGHTEEN

No Question Who the Racist Is

Mock Trial: The Question of Race

We are now only four weeks from the trial and you are frantically preparing. You feel it is necessary to have a mock trial. You want to see how your story would play to people similar to the jurists you will find in Santa Monica. You hire a renowned firm to help you stage this. You are effectively spending more money and building more billable hours. These folks are experts in jury selection. You want jurors that are the most receptive to your case. This is now an important science. The more it is used, Dan, the more you can manipulate the results to effectively move money around. That's okay in the world of economic lawyering, but you are forgetting your desire to find justice in this case. Instead, you strive to find the most biased jurors. You show us you are not interested in the fair trial concept. You must load the deck as high as you can on your side. We remember how you did everything to get out in the public eye and tell your story; now you are looking for people who bought into your side. This is the serious edge you want over your opponent. Polling the jury on whether each of them thought Simpson had killed Ron and Nicole, you were stunned when their pretrial verdict came in only 55% thought O.J. was guilty. A full fifteen people out of thirty-three thought he was innocent. *"How could that be?"*[1] Simple, Mr. P, your original presumption that everyone knows O.J. killed these two poor people was wrong. You were not carrying the banner for the citizens of L.A.; they were divided on the subject. The information reported over the past year had confused us. Much of it didn't make any sense making it hard to convict. At this point in your investigation, you have nothing new that the prosecution didn't have with the minor exception of the Bruno Magli shoes. And we know, Dan, though the shoes fit, you can't prove who was walking in them and why.

Your various criticisms of the criminal jury's verdict is revealing of how hypocritical you can be:

1. They were under tremendous pressure. Pressure to do what, Dan? What different pressure than what your jury will be subject to? Are you suggesting that people under pressure make mistakes? You don't explain.

2. They weren't in possession of all the facts. What *fact* are you going to give this new jury that the criminal jury didn't get? I am waiting.

3. They were sequestered. This would seem to be to help make the decision less biased since they wouldn't be subject to the media spin.

4. They had been racially inflamed. What does that mean, Dan? Are you accusing that jury of making a racial statement? Saying there were racists on the jury is a nasty accusation. Twelve people or some of the twelve, thought it more important to make a racial protest than convict a murderer? Nope, Mr. P.

5. Dazzling defense team. You are going to try to dazzle them, aren't you?

6. Dizzying display of smoke and mirrors. You have given us pages and pages of smoke and mirrors so far.

You congratulate Cochran of doing such a good job he was able to confuse not only the jury, but the general public, as well. Despite *clear and powerful evidence, even now Simpson's guilt was in doubt.* Maybe the evidence wasn't so clear and powerful, or maybe you will be a more dazzling lawyer, or maybe you will be shrewd enough to pick a racially biased jury that will want to make a statement for the non-blacks. You begin examining the jury pool along racial lines. How revealing for you to be so interested in the group's racial attitudes. Are you planning to play into this bias, Mr. P? Be careful you don't forget your quest for justice. Too much manipulation could spoil the results. Not the moving of money, but the legitimacy of the verdict. You know, the kind you accused the Dream Team of capitalizing on.

You present all your evidence; the same evidence that was presented in the criminal trial. You assert that you have debunked the two main defense arguments: "...: *planting and contamination of blood evidence.*"[2]

You claim that planting was preposterous. Can't go with you on this one, Danny boy. You claim the police did not have access to O.J.'s blood to plant it even if they wanted to. *"All the blood was observed by numerous investigators* before *he returned from Chicago."*[3] Dan, we all know that our blood does not have our name on it. It must be analyzed in a lab at some future time. All the blood at the crime scene looked alike depending on the stage of decay. This blood is then removed from the scene and sent for analysis. In the meantime, O.J. offers a vile of his blood. From this vile, it is later found, that some is missing. The best explanation is that the vile wasn't filled completely. Swatches were made of blood samples at the crime scene. O.J.'s blood is now available. How do you know for certain that there wasn't a switch in swatches at the laboratory? Do you feel that swatches being switched are too devious? What about the DNA planting evidence that got those guys off death row in Missouri. Are they less devious in Missouri than in California? Show me the study that proves this point. Can you vouch for the security procedures in the lab? How good was the security while delivering the samples from the detectives to the lab? There are a number of ways planting could have taken place. We learn of new ones all the time. If you have a bad cop it is possible you have bad evidence. We have watched the Petrocelli Magic Show, but let me assure you it is amateur compared to the Police Magic Show. Now you see it, now you don't. For you to believe this audience too naïve to accept as true your slight of hand on this issue of "...*is wildly out of the question*"[4] that the police would plant evidence is a major underestimation of our intelligence. You claim that it isn't even plausible that LAPD would plant evidence on O.J.

"The LAPD liked O.J. and had always treated him with kid gloves and reverence usually accorded celebrities in Los Angeles. They had no reason to frame him."[5]

Dan, at times you are impossible to understand and act strangely naïve for a big time lawyer. O.J. was a major trophy. Catching him killing two people would make the careers of all involved. This is a once-in-a-lifetime opportunity for most cops and prosecutors. If they thought he was the murderer all they would be doing is sealing his fate and theirs with justice and prosperity all around.

You claim *"I drew all the obvious and direct links to Simpson"*[6]. Maybe obvious to you, counselor, but you must be hiding something because to me your evidence is suspect. No officer saw a second glove at Bundy. From this you conclude that it wasn't planted at Rockingham. If gloves were in two different spots at Bundy and not together, the police would be seeing one glove at a time. Unless closely inspected how could they know which one they were observing. Beyond that, this could be another case of very short memories. It is more difficult to believe that O.J. peeled off both gloves, dropping one at Bundy and the other behind his Rockingham house. O.J. is leaving two damning pieces of evidence, and when returning from Chicago freely meeting with the police for a several hour interrogation. If he knowingly left behind this kind of evidence along with all the other *obvious* stuff, wouldn't it make more sense to hide behind his attorneys and develop a scenario regarding the murders that would paint him in the most favorable light? He doesn't act like a murderer who left a conspicuous trail of evidence. In fact, isn't he acting like an innocent man?

You believe that you solved the contamination problem by pointing out that no one came forward and confessed they had botched a double homicide. You could not find any evidence of poor handling or swatch swapping. Dan, you have already proven you are naïve, but now I think you would have trouble finding your way out of a closet with a flashlight. Again, you are trying to contaminate the reader and juror's thinking to best meet your intended goal of moving money around.

You build your case with a metaphor.

"…relationship that end up in murder proceeds along a path as prescribed as the Stations of the Cross: history of abuse, history of rage, estrangement, jealousy, and rejection. It's commonsense."[7]

This is not commonsense when looking at a solution to who murdered Ron and Nicole. If your components of murder were obviously the case, imagine how many homicides there would be. Over 50% of marriages in the U.S. end in divorce. How many had abuse, estrangement, jealousy, and rejection? There are far too many divorces to count. Add on to that total all the marriages that don't end in divorce, but are very troubled. You said earlier there are about 2,000 homicides each year between ex or current spouses. There are 35 million people divorced. The amount that ends in murder is so infinitesimal as to be statistically irrelevant. Applying the circumstances surrounding the O.J. case, it becomes less plausible because he had much to loose by being caught. Commonsense says that the less you have to lose, the less you care about the consequences. O.J. had very good reasons to care a lot.

You tell the jury that only Simpson and no one else had a motive to kill Nicole. You feel you have established this as fact. Again, you make an absolute statement that you have no way of knowing is true. You admit knowing Nicole had many affairs. How can you summarily dismiss that one of these men was not angry enough to kill Nicole? How many other men had she rejected? Jason might have had a reason to want Nicole dead. She was after his father's money. You know how powerful that money thing is, Dan. Faye's drug bill could have brought collectors. And on we go. A motive didn't even have to exist; other than a burglar doing Bundy happens to pick Nicole's house. No intention of murder, then Ron shows up, things go bad. When you continually give us a one-note song, O.J. is the killer; you need to back it up with some compelling evidence. No mere proclamations will make us, the reader, admire the way you are handling this case. So far, I believe you have failed abysmally. Though you claim that you demolished his cut alibi, you didn't. Even if you did, you haven't explained how a cut would be on the finger, but not through the glove.

You made some points. You changed the minds of 10 of the 33 mock jurors. 28 of 33 now vote to convict. Three more than you need. Now your partner does his side of the case. He raises many of the points I have. That there were no marks on O.J.'s body didn't make sense. There must have been a struggle. He attacked your timeline. He raised the issue of Mark Fuhrman. Mr. Fuhrman was a bigot who might have been one of those to plant evidence. He points out the Detective Vannatter is running around town with a vial of O.J. Simpson's blood.

You provide a criticism of some lawyers. You make a very large statement here, Mr. P.

"Lawyers can be really deceitful, we can make powerful and passionate arguments that are just totally false."[8]

I am glad you included yourself in this group of officers of the court. So well you should. Lawyers can and do lie. They can be passionate about it. They can be deceitful. Sometimes they are and it's good that you confess to us in your book that you are among this group of protectors of justice. What I have had the opportunity to do throughout my review of your book is to point out those times I believe you are passionately making false statements. I have tried to be respectful throughout my analysis of this book. Each word you give me is taken seriously. As a lawyer you are thoroughly trained in the art of communication. Random House, a prestigious book publisher, publishes your book. That's impressive. You have a best-selling author help you write this book. The subject is very sensitive and important -- **Justice**. This is not a piece of fiction by a lawyer trying to be another John Grisham. Your book is about the lives of people and the accusation is murder. Truth is the most essential element of the process. Now you tell us that you and your colleagues are deceitful and can passionately make false statements.

You have presented the thoughtful reader of your book a serious dilemma. How do we sort out the truth from the fiction? We know there is a lot at stake, money – fame – business – winning. How can we tell where you stop making false statements? The answer is simple. We can't tell. We can't trust you. You are telling us not to trust you. This is ironic. A lawyer confessing that he can't be trusted. He then writes a book we are supposed to trust. We are left to use our own commonsense. Not just you, Mr. Petrocelli, but as you say, "we lawyers". This reader didn't need your confession to know that lawyers will do what is necessary to win and move money around. I was aware of this proclivity before I read your book. The lawyer jokes confirm the popular attitude about lawyers. Too many attorneys are pathetic. The brush that you use to criticize yourself and other lawyers probably

174

paints the civil litigators and government prosecutors more brightly than others. You don't care to make any distinction. You accuse all lawyers. Logic doesn't permit me to go that far, but there is much evidence of the damage lawyers have done to make the case, far too many lawyers cannot be trusted. Since you proudly include yourself in this group, it makes my examination that more telling.

Back to the blood sample hypothesis: the police would not go around planting blood. This may be true. It may not, but that is not the point. All of this blood analysis comes down to the swatches being controlled. Unless you have a very secure system, there is no telling what swatch ends up in what envelope. Anytime, with blood in hand, a rouge cop can discreetly smudge some blood in conspicuous places. You would have to show us, hermetically sealed, security procedures that controlled the movement of the swatches. You give us none in your book. None was given in the criminal trial. If such a secure procedure was in place, you and the prosecution had an obligation to let us all know that the evidence couldn't have been tampered with. Remove all doubt from our minds. By leaving this important subject unaddressed you ask us to guess about the security. With the terrible history in police departments, especially the LAPD, this reader can't automatically buy your statement, that plantings is wildly out of the question and truly absurd.

Your associate partner, Medevene made a totally reasonable case. The motive theory didn't ring true because their relationship was not very different than many others in troubled marriages and Nicole was a woman doing all kinds of wild things. You admitted to Nicole living in the fast lane. He rehashed the material in the criminal trial that produced the *not guilty* verdict. The result of his presentation brought the jury back to their original feelings. 55% thought he was guilty, 45% not guilty.

Now we come to a major factor in this case, racial bias. You and witnesses you deposed have said many times that the *Dream Team* scored many points with the race card. It may have been the deciding factor in the case according to you. Let's remember, Dan, you did not spend anytime watching the case, but somehow you deduced that race was the swing subject. Your own analysis of the public's reaction to the trial and the jury's voting make a clear and convincing statement, you are a bigot. The most insidious type of racist, one that is quick to sell out to anyone in pursuit of money. And sadly you have no clue you are one. You think you are colorblind. If anyone accused you of being prejudiced you would be deeply offended. Some of your best friends are black, Hispanic, Jewish, and Asian. How could you be accused of being a racist? Easily, Daniel (WAP) Petrocelli, you lay it out clearly in your book. With the pen in your own hand you make every black person hold you in contempt. You are a throwback to the racists of old. You confess by your writings to being prejudiced in the same way you confess to being a liar. At least we know where you stand.

During the mock trial you could watch the reaction of the jurors without them seeing you. Something surprised you.

"We assumed, from news reports and widespread anecdotal material, that Simpson was fully supported by the black community. Conventional wisdom had it that he was their champion."[9]

One of the characteristics of a bigot is to deal in generalities. You are under the impression that Simpson was *"...fully supported by the black communicty"*[10] What an insult to them! You are accusing black people of not being able to understand the evidence and the facts of the case, but just blindly back up a murderer because he is black. I guess you thought that blacks are not only dumb, but in favor of murder if is one of their heroes. Your surprise came when you observed blacks listening to information at your mock trial, they reacted appropriately if they thought O.J. was not telling the truth. You interpret this reaction as the blacks defending Simpson as a representative of their race, not as an individual human being. You claim that every black person was only interested in making a racial statement. This is a racial statement, on your part Dan. Do you get it now?

Your arguments only changed the minds of 2% of the jurors. Mathematically this is tricky. You have only 33 jurors. 2% of 33 are less than one person. All that preparation, all the evidence you said was convincing did nothing to change the minds of these people. Since they lived on this planet, they came to this mock trial with preconceived notions probably drawn from the criminal trial. Their minds were made up unless you could give them something new to consider.

Now the jurors are asked to deliberate. Talk things over and come to a final, and in your method, a unanimous vote. You had the forewoman in favor of your position. You considered this an advantage. She could direct the flow of the discussion. Your characterization of the jurors:

"The other white woman on the jury was quiet, reserved, almost intimidated. The Hispanics were open-minded, but leaning toward the defense. The three blacks were adamantly, vociferously, powerfully pro-Simpson..... You know the cops hate the blacks."[11]

How cynical. Blacks or otherwise, Dan, there are people who have lived in the *streets* and have developed an attitude towards police work. Your life, as you described it earlier, didn't take you to the reality of the ghetto or poor neighborhoods. The people that have experienced bad police conduct would be expected to make strong statements. That doesn't make them ignorant. They are dealing with their reality. You admit even if there was some tampering that shouldn't contaminate the other evidence. No, Dan, some tampering does taint all evidence. How can the juror distinguish between the real and the planted evidence? If lawyers can passionately lie, can't police tamper evidence? The answer is clearly, yes, but you insist on giving us smoke and mirrors to cover up the obvious. It's not working on this reader, Mr. P. You see, that for you to succeed in getting O.J.'s money you would have to negate all such hints or implications of evidence tampering or hope to manipulate the jury selection to those who are not as aware of the history of police work in L.A.

You further confuse me with your observation that the jurors were highly influenced by the media. How could this surprise you? You have been going out of your way to get the media on your side. You paid off the L.A. Times with the first look at the depositions to get favored positioning on the stories. You hired a PR firm to make sure you looked well in the press. You worked with Geraldo Rivera in getting information. Now you tell us it will be tough to get an unbiased jury. What a bad joke! You don't want an unbiased jury, Dan. You want the most biased jury you and your money can get. Isn't this what this mock trial is all about? You want to be able to identify, with the help of a top jury selection consulting firm, to load your jury with those that are most biased toward your case. You want Santa Monica because of the large percentage of white residents; or better said, fewer blacks. You are carefully analyzing the juror's response and measuring it against racial bias. This is solely for the purpose of making sure that they are not on your jury if you can help it.

The mock jury did not discuss much of the relationship between O.J. and Nicole. They were more interested in police frame-ups, conspiracies, and racial bias. And well they should be. The relationship between O.J. and Nicole requires a lot of conjecture and there wasn't any news. Remember you couldn't document more than one incident of spousal abuse. The rest of the information was just conjecture, gossip, and unreliable. The main thing these jurors had to analyze was the blood evidence. You accuse the black jurors in particular for being extremely interested in the planting and contamination and whether the LAPD had followed procedures. I don't see what is wrong with this line of inquiry. Sounds like the intelligent pursuit of information. You say that the jurors were treating this like a game, not seriously. Slow down here, counselor. Here you go again attacking jurors for not doing their job. You draw the conclusion that these jurors would let O.J. get off merely because the police didn't follow procedures. This is an awful accusation. You want us to believe that if all the evidence convincingly pointed to O.J. as the killer of two people, the black jurors would vote to have him acquitted just because the police didn't follow procedures. A blatantly bigoted remark again, Mr. P.

You conclude: "We all expected a racial divide; that was the legacy of Simpson's criminal defense."[12]

You are not boiling down this case into a purely racial issue. This is tantamount to saying that it doesn't matter what is presented to the jury, the votes are going to line up, black and white, with Hispanics and Asians somewhere in the middle. Why bother going through any presentations? You are convinced it won't make any difference.

According to you, the three black jurors dominated the discussion. They were fervent, angry, and zealous. They wanted to pay back the LAPD for years of mistreatment. Dan, didn't you consider, even for a moment, that these three people might have been the most aware jurors speaking with conviction, honesty, and life's experience. They might have been getting the truth better than the others. Not because of their skin color, but because they understood the evidence. Three blacks out of thirty-three jurors and they are taking over. You accuse the non-blacks as being weak and the blacks as strong. This may be some form of reverse racism, but racism, prejudice and bigotry in all forms Dan and you point at yourself. Shame, shame, and shame again. But, thank you for reminding us how little progress has been made regarding prejudice even among the intelligencia.

The blacks overwhelmed, intimidated the other jurors. You claim that the others were trying to base their decision on the evidence, but the blacks would have none of that. There three, according to you, would not apply any of the standards of measures of justice. They were only trying to get at the LAPD for past misdeeds and if that let a killer off the hook, so be it. I would like to hear from these three to see if they sold out as you say, Mr. P. You then slander the white, Hispanic, and Asian jurors. "...the case against Simpson did not have the same meaning or the same stakes."[3] You are accusing these people of taking a double homicide, brutal killings, at that, casually; not important; just a couple of spoiled rich celebrities, so what? What a difference do their lives make? The non-blacks argued logic and the blacks were aroused by passion. Mr. Petrocelli, how prejudiced you are, unabashedly a racist. You put this in print for the world to see. The blacks wanted repayment for 200 years of mistreatment and according to you they would sell out Justice and the conviction of a murderer for the cause. Beyond preposterous, the most anyone in this group could accomplish is a statement against the LAPD, one that was already out there and needed no affirmation. There were too many bad cops on the LAPD. It was widely known. The LAPD recognized they had a problem and was trying to fix it. How much has changed, I don't know. I live on the east coast, but it wouldn't take too long to find out. Dan, take a walk through South Central L.A. and do a brief survey. After a few questions you will find out if race relations have improved. Please don't take a copy of this book with you, too dangerous.

"...the non-black jurors were getting blown away. The less educated blacks, in particular the women, were the most vocal."[14] Mr. P you take prejudice to a new level. The female, uneducated blacks were the most vocal to free a murderer? Your more educated non-blacks were weak. They were willing to go along with these three outspoken jurors. You insult the whole group with this analysis. There should be 33 jurors insulted at your conclusion that they were either racists, sheep easily led, dumb, and just easily compromised. Bringing a killer to justice was not that important. It was a game, a joke. Then again, why have a trial? Most importantly, this is a lesson to you that your game plan has to change. If your assessment is correct you better not have any uneducated black women on your jury. Load the deck with educated white folks. They can process evidence better. They can be trusted to give you an unbiased verdict. Doesn't this sound dumb to you, Dan? Not so dumb though, if all you want to do is move money around. As far as I can tell this Lawyer Law of Greed has not been repealed. If anything it is flourishing more preposterously than ever. Some lawyers are even getting a bonus in the money they make from writing books about plundering and stealing, then brag about it.

You go to this jury with a number of specific questions because you don't like the results. You are groping for methods to get the votes to go your way. You found it mind boggling that the African-American women would not accept your evidence. Mr. P they are not accepting it because you have not presented a convincing case that the evidence is reliable. They questioned, and rightly so, the premise of your arguments and did not come up with satisfactory answers. You are devastated. You admit that you were sheltered in your cocoon of depositions, legal research, and interviews. Yes, you were creating billable hours, but from my observation, none that produced anything of real significance to persuade a reader that O.J. committed the crimes. Now out in the real world, you have found the simple truth. Some people believed O.J. was guilty and some did not. The group was split roughly 50/50. Remember, there were only three blacks on your mock jury. So there were some non-blacks that were not buying into your story. To you it was clear, for you to win you simply had to find at least nine jurors that were in the 50% preconceived category. That is three more than the statistical average. The statistical average is 6 since we can't have part of a person as a juror. Now we are into a reasonable risk range for your victory. You have the district, Santa Monica, in your favor. More than 80% of voters are non-black. It is probably more like 95%. You also have your expert jury selection firm to weed out those that might not like your case. You are starting off with a decided edge if your theory is true, that this case is going to be decided along race issues. The blacks are going to defend their hero and the whites are going to carefully and accurately evaluate the evidence you honestly present to them. If you note a strong dose of sarcasm here, Dan, you are finally paying attention.

What did this mock jury experience do for you? In your view, you saw your case unravel, all your hard work meant nothing, it had been reduced to confusion and lies and racial animosity the defense had sown in two years of constant public disinformation. You were drubbed. You felt you had a loser. Smart going you didn't take this case on contingency. You also knew that you have some statistical advantages going into the real trial and you may get lucky. You might draw those jurors who see it your way, but you can excuse all that away by blaming a racist, dumb jury. You still get your $1.2 million. You find a way not to take responsibility for the outcome of the case if it doesn't go your way. Surely, you will take the glory and bragging rights if you win.

You retreated to a bar with your colleagues to assess the damage. You were demoralized and discouraged. "'You got your ass kicked,'.."[15] your partner explains. You need to find a new way to win this case. Kind of late now, but your story did not convince the jury. "...*and crying into your beer.*"[16] Was this part of the billable time? Look back at those records. You drive home woefully depressed. The next day you rethink and decide to retool your whole case. If you didn't have the budget for this mock trial you probably wouldn't have come to the realization that you needed to manufacture a better story. Part of the cost of Justice, eh? DecisionQuest, your consulting firm analyzed the data and prepared the report on the mock jury. The points that worked for you were the blood evidence and testimony of Allan Park, the driver, the gloves, hair sample, and the shoes. That's it. You continue to give us old stuff and weak arguments. Those who voted against felt that there wasn't enough evidence, a possibility of tampering, and lack of time to do the crime. Where is the new and convincing evidence that you promised us, counselor?

You hire DecisionQuest to do a telephone survey of 600 people representing a wide cross-section of the population. Results are about the same as the mock trial. You conclude that it is a racial case, plain and simple. You conduct additional focus groups with blacks to get a better understanding of their attitudes. You are becoming a racist expert. You are convinced it is going to be an issue in your trial. You are discovering that the blacks are speaking from personal experience. They know first hand that profiling does exist. It is not absurd for evidence to be planted. Some bigoted whites are especially upset with a black man who marries a white woman and abandons his black wife with two kids. There are blacks that don't like this profile, either. O.J. was not every black person's hero. Give credit where it's due. I believe that if a black person were presented convincing evidence, despite the fact a superstar, black or otherwise, would fall, they would vote for justice. You present a case filled with big questions, lots of weak presumptions, and known liars. Since this case is going to be tried by lawyers that are suspect themselves it might be difficult for a jury to be convinced of guilt. The criteria you set is one crafted by a prejudiced person. Citing the uneducated black woman as a less qualified juror is purely offensive to any reasonable person. This is a murder trial. The evidence, you claim, is convincing enough to convict someone on a double knife murder. What sort of education would you require of someone to qualify them to sit on this jury? What kind of formal education should they have? A degree in criminology? A law degree? You want to discount true life's experience in favor of some sort of an education that would make someone more qualified to understand the evidence in a murder trial. I'll take the real life experience any day.

The accused is entitled to an unbiased jury. We know this case, because of all the media hype; it is impossible to find someone that didn't have an opinion about the murders. Depending on what reports and when they heard them, people will form opinions, establish some bias. It is natural for a person to relate to the possible discrimination an individual might receive based on history and personal experience. Opinions are formed. When you bring someone into a court of law and make an elaborate presentation you may or may not influence some preconceived notions. When you step back from your racist approach, reason should tell you there were people of all color with varying opinions about these murders. There were blacks that felt strongly he was innocent, or wasn't proven to be guilty and there were blacks that felt strongly that he was guilty. All of these feelings came out of a gut reaction to information from TV, newspapers, radio, and conversations. For you to bunch all blacks as incapable of being reasonable, fair and honest puts you at the head of the class in the Hall of Shame – Bigot Division.

Yes, more blacks are suspicious of police activity and that is not to be criticized. They know more about the subject. There is a long, sad, and conspicuous history here. The LAPD is not an exception. Didn't you wince when Rodney King was being beaten? Hope so, no matter what they thought Rodney did or may do in the future, you say a clear case of racial profiling and evidence of the condition of relations in LA. Dan, if you really wanted a fair trial and justice as the main objective you would not have spent one minute on this race issue. Let the jury selection fall where it may. Trust that some people even with little education can understand truth, can spot foul play, and would vote their best to punish the guilty and free the innocent. You are making sure this is a race war. Let's keep those dumb blacks off our jury. They can't convict a murderer who is black and a hero. Impossible! No, Dan, insist that the jury not be manipulated to engineer a winning verdict irrespective of the truth. You quote several opinions given by the blacks you had polled. One that impressed you was from an educated black woman, very articulate on a number of issues. She admits that when she saw the verdict, she was excited. She was pumped that O.J. got off. She tells you she is not sure if O.J. did or did not commit the crimes. The evidence didn't do it for her. She was happy, however because in similar circumstances a white person would get the same results. You can interpret this several ways, Dan. A bigot might say this black woman was looking for payback for centuries of unequal treatment and this was helping to even the score. I hear the woman say that the white accused could get off if the evidence was unconvincing, but history has shown with the same type of facts the black would be convicted. This is not saying she is convinced that O.J. is the killer and it is a good thing to let him off to even the score. The criminal trial had too many unanswered questions and at least one rogue cop. Black or white, reasonable people would do what O.J.'s jury did, acquit because the prosecution did not prove their case. The blacks have a right to cheer because too often it didn't make a difference if the prosecution presented a good or bad case, the black person did not get a fair trial. Again, look at all the blacks that are being released after DNA tests have established they couldn't have committed the crimes. Every time you hear a slur about Italians doesn't it tick you off? You probably don't hear too many of these slurs in your neighborhood, but blacks are hearing it everyday all the time. It is coming from people like you who don't even know you are insulting, rude, and just plain prejudiced. I believe if you gave your book to a black person they will tell you what a racist you are, Danny Boy.

You list all of the misunderstandings the blacks have about the case. There were many. Why was there another trial? O.J. just won. Acquittal didn't mean he didn't do the crime. Dan, did you check to see what non-blacks felt about these questions? My survey finds the same answers from non-blacks. How could there be another trial? Seems like double jeopardy, doesn't seem right. Just money hungry people playing jury roulette. People were really disturbed there is such a law that allows someone to go through this twice. These questions were reasonable, Dan. What they didn't account for was the law, made up by lawyers that give them an additional bite of the apple, more billable time. You would presume that once O.J. was acquitted it was over. Making this a racial issue, again, you profile black women as more likely to vote in favor of O.J. for protective reasons. Did you even check the percentage vote among non-blacks? You don't show us the numbers. Remember your stats show that the general population was about evenly split on guilty vs. not guilty. You had to make sure no black mother was on your jury. Nasty thinking here, fellow American!

At the end of this chapter you summarize your feelings about the race issue. On one hand you say, *"Race had nothing to do with the reality of the case, but might have everything to do with the result."*[17] You blame O.J.'s defense team for causing this to be a racially driven trial. Mr. Fuhrman was not a figment of their imagination. He was all too real. He perjured himself about using the 'N' word. He was hiding his racism. The prosecution presents a key person who is discovered by the defense to be bragging about the race issues to someone writing a book on the subject. We have an authority on prejudice in Mr. Fuhrman and you want the defense to ignore him. Most people have color TV's these days. The race issue has been a problem in LA back to the riots in the early 60's to currently with the expose of bad police conduct.

You admit there is a problem, but you lay

"the racial divide squarely at the feet of Simpson and his lawyers. In one of the most disgraceful, cynical, and socially irresponsible defenses ever used to set a guilty man free, they created the race issue and exploited it. **White people are out to get this black man.** *Using false arguments, Johnnie Cochran blinded a largely African-American jury with a fervent feeling of racial pride and passion that they let a killer back into their community."*[18]

"...defending O.J. Simpson, black America has embraced a liar, a cheat, a womanizer, and a, butcher."[19]

Remember O.J. never took the stand. So how can you blame him for creating the divide? Also, it was not his lawyer's obligation to prove O.J. was innocent; it was the prosecution's burden to prove guilt, Justice 101. Yes, Johnnie Cochran said, *"'Send a message.'"*[20] The message that I heard him calling for was not to convict this man or any man if you are not convinced he committed the crimes, beyond a reasonable doubt. They didn't say he was innocent; I am not saying he is innocent. That is not what they were charged to do. They were asked to not guess if he could have committed the crimes, but to decide based on the evidence presented whether there was sufficient proof to render a guilty verdict. You want to change the rules that you know so well, Mr. P. You even remind us of them in your writings. This jury did not embrace a liar, a cheat, a womanizer, and a, butcher. That dramatic writing is a huge insult to the jurors, the blacks, and all fair-minded people who deserve to see the laws carried out as intended. O.J. did not lie, he didn't testify. Cheating had nothing to do with the case and butcher wasn't proven. This mock trial experience, your racial profiling, and your proclamations about racism do you and your profession a great disservice. Personally, I think you fought to attend race management classes.

Notes:

[1] Daniel Petrocelli, *Triumph of Justice* (Crown 1998) pg. 326

[2] Ibid, pg. 328

[3] Ibid pg. 328

[4] Ibid, pg. 330

[5] Ibid, pg. 328

[6] Ibid, pg. 326

[7] Ibid, pg. 329

[8] Ibid, pg. 330

[9] Ibid, pg. 331

[10] Ibid, pg. 331

[11] Ibid, pg. 332

[12] Ibid, pg. 333

[13] Ibid, pg. 334

[14] Ibid, pg. 336

[15] Ibid, pg. 336

[16] Ibid, pg. 336

[17] Ibid, pg. 342

[18] Ibid, pg. 342

19 Ibid. pg 342

20 Ibid pg 341

NINETEEN

Something is Very Wrong

Something Wrong

The last thing you do before jury selection is to go over the forensic evidence. This is very important because this is when you hoped to get *dripping knife* type evidence. The criminal trial failed to convince the jury that the forensics was enough evidence to convict. Dr. Henry Lee, a top forensic scientist and O.J.'s forensic lawyer worked together on the case. They concluded that there was "'*Something wrong*".[1] They challenged the legitimacy of the blood evidence. You accuse Barry Scheck of taking this phrase,

"*There is something wrong, There is something terribly wrong about the evidence…you must distrust it. You have to distrust it.*"[2]

and "run(ning) wild with it."[3] It would seem perfectly natural for the defense team to challenge the blood evidence. Vannatter was walking around with O.J.'s sample blood vile and no evidence was presented that a safe procedure for securing or storing it was in place.

You knew from the start that Dr. Lee would not appear at your trial. He testified in the criminal trial in behalf of the defense. His attorney, Barry Scheck, represents Dr. Lee in the civil trial depositions. You don't like this because it sends a message that they are still in O.J.'s corner. Two experts sticking by their prior positions bothers you. You accuse Mr. Scheck of selling out at the criminal trial. Are you saying that Mr. Scheck is one of those lawyers that passionately deceives and falsely represents their clients? He is one of you guys? Yet, you praise him for having formidable skills, special talents, brilliant lawyering and experience. Now you tell us he sold out for O.J. Was it the money? Was it for the fame of being involved in the case of the century? Help us with your theory here, Dan, fame, money or both? Don't let us believe that Mr. Scheck is a man of integrity who earnestly wanted justice to be served. He is just another lawyer staining the flag of America, using his talents to "...*fool a jury*". You must realize how hypocritical it is for you to make such statements. You who are the Crown Prince of selling out for money and fame, the King Midas of turning fiction into gold, the royalty plundering the kingdom at all costs. Here again you want it both ways, counselor. Everyone on the opposing team is a liar and you are the Knight in Shining Armor. All this sounds like a pain in the wallet to me.

Your criticism of Dr. Lee and Scheck's message that *something is wrong* meaning everything was wrong is inaccurate. They were talking about one evidence swatch being wrong, not everything. When you accuse their logic as being faulty you imply that something was wrong with all the evidence, which misleads the jury and the readers. Mr. Scheck and Dr. Lee confronted each drop of blood evidence and provided an explanation to the jury. It did not prove that O.J. was implicated in these murders. Remember, the prosecution had their forensic experts testifying which gave the jury a contrasting story. If the prosecution had established that proper procedures were followed and the evidence was secure that identified O.J. then the jury would accept that. You want us to believe that the jury would not accept it even if it were clear it was convincing. Why wouldn't they? Are you going to respond with the race issue? I hope not because you failed miserably on that subject. Evidence must be convincing *beyond a reasonable doubt*. The job of O.J.'s experts was to get the jury to consider if there could be doubt and they did. You paint this as sinister. I believe the sinister act was to indict a person for the murder of two people without clear evidence that could be presented to a jury no matter how skillful the defense lawyers were; the jury could not have acquitted. Bringing O.J. or any other person in on a murder charge, putting them through the emotional and financial rigors of defending themselves, demand that the prosecution have a *dripping knife -smoking gun*, or similar evidence. The real crime here is lawyers, prosecutors, and police, using the legal system to further their personal agendas. Throw enough against the wall something might stick. Everyone jumping on the feeding train, all a win for them and a terrible nightmare for those charged.

Your observation of Dr. Lee as a charming, incredibly smart, but deadly, is a strategic piece of writing. Who is the good Dr. killing today, your case, perhaps? If Dr. Lee isn't one of the most respected forensic guys in the world, his is certainly up there in the front of the class. Dr. Lee gave a detailed criticism of the poor techniques, shabby equipment, lack of experience and methods of storing evidence. You claim this has nothing to do with the O.J. case. Dan, this has everything to do with it. A jury has to feel confident that the evidence presented is legitimate beyond question. There is no wiggle room here, too many cases of botched evidence sending the wrong person to the electric chair or a life in prison. It happens all too often to say that this is impossible. I know you are a civil litigator, but good heavens, Dan; don't you watch television or read the papers?

You accuse the Dr. of purposely misleading the jury. You now make him part of the conspiracy to get a murderer off. According to you he goes out of his way to not give a full professional objective analysis. All the Dr. did say was the way the evidence was presented did not lead him to a conclusive opinion. It was a "...*the swatches were not completely dry when they were put in the bindle*". He gives no opinion because he is not supplied with enough good evidence. He opines that the evidence in this condition suggests *something's wrong*. Your side has an obligation to say, "No, there is nothing wrong. This is exactly what the tests would be expected to reveal if O.J. were the murderer. And here is why the evidence is exactly right and why we have brought you all here today." It is not Dr. Lee's job to prove the evidence does not point to O.J. It is the burden of the prosecution to make it clear to the jury, irrespective of the defense team's tactics, that O.J. is the killer. Obviously, the government failed to do that. For this failure you accuse the wrong people.

You bring us to another critical part of analyzing the murder - the timeline issues. Whether or not O.J. had enough time to commit these murders goes to the heart of the reasonableness of the accusation. O.J. has a substantiated alibi at 10:50 p.m. If the killing Ron and Nicole took more than one minute you lose. According to you he could not be the murderer. You only have this brief window of time to make your case. Dr. Lee and Dr. Baden both testified at the criminal trial that these murders didn't happen in a short period of time. We are looking at: a double homicide, bloody crime scene, and 58 wounds on Ron all happening in one minute by an arthritic 50-year-old retired football player. To arrive at the possibility your questions come down to if examining if something is possible. You believe that you have a success because "... *Ed got him to admit it could have been as short as sixty-one seconds.*"[6] He is not asked if it is likely or reasonable. You get the witness to say it is *possible*. You then morph what is possible into it is a fact that the crimes to place in one minute or less. You need the discussion focused on seconds, not minutes. Since it is possible it did happen or was reasonable to have happened does not mean it did happen in one minute. You feel you got to push him (Dr. Lee) back to a minute. Why push him? We are looking for convincing evidence and you engage in a preposterous exercise of possibilities. You need to find a way to get the Dr. to say this crime took place in one minute. Desperate lawyering is right out in the light of day. You use your questions and answers out of context to support an essential premise on your part. O.J. had enough time to commit these crimes and get into a limo to go to Chicago. You are proud your team got the Dr. to say that this crime could have taken place in a very short period of time, as little as one minute. You will be able to say to the jury that experts could not deny these crimes could have taken place in a minute. It is very hard for a person that can see lightening and hear thunder to believe that this double homicide took place in a minute. Somehow, you feel you can take this concept and run with it for a touchdown. All I see is a fumble. Maybe with your smoke and mirrors you will get people to see it otherwise. I remember you telling me that lawyers were good at that trick.

Your associate continues to try to paint Dr. Lee into a corner with carefully crafted questions. Dr. Lee doesn't want to speculate as to whether or not something could have happened in a certain way, but merely lets you know there was a struggle. It is up us to apply commonsense to the information available. You claim he doesn't challenge the DNA test results of the hair or fiber evidence amassed against Simpson. One strand of hair in a cap and a few fibers from the Bronco do not conclusively prove that he was on the scene. Son's can wear their father's shoes and their hats. We can't forget that the hat may have been planted. This is certainly more likely than your outlandish theories. *No, Dan, there was not a mass of evidence against Simpson. There were a few items, suspicious at best with each having alternative explanations.*

You challenge Dr. Lee as to whether or not he had any scientific fact to show the LA police planted or did anything cheating with any evidence. The Dr. didn't have any such fact. Why should he? It was not his job to investigate police misconduct. Just because he didn't have any evidence does not mean there was no tampering. You want us to disregard the Dr. telling us that procedures at the LA lab were bad. Vannatter walked around with O.J.'s blood violating police procedures. There was no documentation to prove the evidence was free from tampering at the lab. Who had keys to rooms, file cabinets, and records? Evidence has left storage facilities in police custody before. You want us to believe that this bloody double homicide took place in less than one minute, but there was no way the police tampered with evidence. I can't go down that road with you. We heard from the top two people in the profession that there was *something wrong,* but you want us to ignore this critical observation by the best in the business.

Notes:

[1] Daniel Petrocelli, *Triumph of Justice* (Crown 1998) pg. 343

[2] Ibid, pg.343

[3] Ibid, pg.348

4 Ibid, pg 344

5 Ibid. pg 349

6 Ibid pg 348

TWENTY

Jury Profiling – Racism at its Best

Jury Selection

You have taken us through your understanding of the case. You have deposed all the witnesses and examined all the evidence. The discovery phase is now complete. Only thing left is picking a judge and jury. Unless something dramatic is discovered during the trial, the readers have all the information that will be presented. The book cover and your introduction promised we would learn what happened that night in Brentwood. Your book told us it would prove conclusively, that O.J. Simpson told lie after lie, and that he did indeed kill his ex-wife and an innocent man. You were going to give us the story we didn't hear about and the trial we didn't see. I don't see you keeping your promise to your reader. For someone who watched the O.J. trial, unlike you, I cannot find any new information. Not one drop of evidence.

The following are the main points of the civil trial and your supporting evidence:

1. O.J. had an incident of beating his wife in 1989. You did not find one other incident that you could present at your trial. All you collected in your depositions were rumors there were other acts of brutality. No new evidence here.

2. O.J. did the dastardly deed in about one minute. You did not prove this happened; all you could produce is a statement that said it was possible that the crimes took place in one minute.

3. You produced no new blood evidence.

4. You could not establish that the procedures that made sure evidence was safeguarded and reliable.

5. The Bruno Magli shoes were at the crime scene, but you did not prove who was wearing them. Could have been O.J.'s son or someone else?

Not only did you fail to produce any new information or evidence, you failed to dispel important questions.

1. How do you account for no noise during the commission of these crimes? There was a struggle without anyone calling for help that is unreasonable.

2. What happened to O.J.'s alleged murder outfit?

3. How come there were no bandages on O.J.'s hands right after the crime?

On and on these questions and more, sit out there and you don't address any of them. You have a big problem here counselor; you are going to need to pick a jury that is sufficiently biased to buy into your feeble theories. You need a judge who will give you lots of leeway. You are going to have to suppress logical questions. You will be tested in your use of smoke and mirrors and be at your best in manipulation and deceit. You are going to have to be very persuasive to take this package of old information and put a new spin on it so the jury will buy in. Can Daniel Petrocelli make chopped liver out of chicken feathers? Or the real question: since we know how it turned out, how did he do it?

Taking us through the logistics of picking the judge and setting the ground rules for the trial was oh, so boring. I'll skip over that and follow while you hunker down with your pretzels and M&M's at a hotel in Santa Monica to begin the process of jury selection. Your research showed that the better educated the juror; the better they would be for your cause. They would be more receptive to DNA arguments, less likely to be influenced by claims of wild conspiracies, racial bias or other emotional concepts having nothing to do with the reality of the case. Because of the hardship rules you believe that these were exactly the people who would not be able to serve on the jury. You complain that the jury pool is stacked with unemployed people and government workers. Dan, you seem to be forgetting that we are dealing with a double homicide that was the subject of the most publicized trial in recent memory. DNA evidence is standard procedure in murder cases. Racial bias is not confined to the uneducated, as you have proven. You are racially biased and have a law degree. Do you want to make us believe that all unemployed people are uneducated and dumb or that government employees are not qualified to sit on a murder case? You have just insulted more than 25% of the American population. Government workers out there, Dan doesn't think you are qualified or educated enough to be a juror on a murder trial. Are you saying that working for the government makes you incapable of finding the truth in this case? He doesn't say, but there could easily be an implication that you are racially biased, even you of color. Postal workers, you are pointed out in particular. I would like to see the research that establishes if you work for the Post Office you would be likely to give O.J. a free pass on murder.

You believe that *"The single most important part of the selection process was jury selection."*[1] You then insist that prospective jurors have been influenced by the publicity surrounding the case. You focus on their preconceived notions as being the single most important element of winning this battle. You are forgetting about finding justice, again. Your concerns illustrate your need to find jurors inclined to your theories. Since you assume that most people had a definite opinion as to whether or not O.J. committed the crimes, it will be your job to find those who felt he was guilty. That shouldn't be that difficult since you tell us over and over that everyone knew O.J. was the murderer. You believe that there would be no way to find a fair and impartial jury under these circumstances. Therefore, to win you would need those who would likely agree with your theories: male, educated, whites. You did all you could to influence the jury pool through your positioning in the media. I hope for your sake, they show up.

The judge understood the problem of selecting an impartial jury. He put together an extensive questionnaire to draw out the likelihood of the juror being biased. In addition, you acknowledge your concern about people wanting to be on the jury for the wrong reasons, like exploitation. You fought hard to keep those that felt O.J. probably committed the murders. You kept off those that believed police could plant evidence. Your claim that it is absurd to think that police would plant evidence shows how naïve and out of touch with reality you really are. And you insist that it is rare that an innocent man was framed. Let me refer you to a play *Exonerated* based on 102 people who were released from death row because they were subsequently found to be innocent. In the vast majority of these cases, the police in cooperation framed them with the prosecutors. In many cases these men were black. Black people understand that framing is a reality. You want to rule it entirely out as a possibility. By holding tight to such a limited position you are demonstrating your intention is purely to win and not to seek justice. This is evil in the face of your promises to us.

You assume those jurors that said they weren't sure, were O.J. supporters. Isn't this why we have trials in the first place? A trial is supposed to provide the evidence to convince a juror. The jury was unsure. They listened to the evidence in O.J.'s case and the prosecution did not prove to the satisfaction of the jury O.J. was guilty.

Because of all the suspicious aspects of the evidence, the question of tampering has to be addressed. To demand only jurors who believe tampering impossible instills a jury bias that would lead to an unjust conclusion.

Your jury consultant firm, DecisionQuest advised you to stay away from black women. The told you that you couldn't win with black women on the jury. You do it again, and it hurts my sensibilities. The firm you hire to help you select a jury comes up with an absolutely racist conclusion and you accept it. Are they saying that black women are not intelligent enough, fair enough, or reasonable enough to convict O.J. Simpson? So if you are a government employee or unemployed and a black woman, also, you are not fit to be on Dan's jury. Wow, you are bad, really bad. The hunger for money and fame has made produced a warped thinking person. You admit that race dominated your agenda. That is your doing, sir, and your need. From the other side of your mouth you say you don't need biased jurors to win. You hire a racist consulting firm to help you sort out biases. You attempt to make a distinction to cover up your racism. You would accept a juror, even though black, who was well educated and a real leader if he told you he thought O.J. was "'...*probably guilty*...'"[2]. How intellectually generous of you! This soap doesn't wash away your prejudices however. They still stink. You also would accept a black female law clerk that thought O.J. was probably guilty. That's a big step, but your bias still stinks. The kind of profiling you are laying out is racist and outlines the big problem blacks have with the white community. You are probably shocked that you are receiving this criticism. You feel comfortable in being color-blind. You give to charities that help the black community. You make speeches in favor of integration and associate with blacks in business and as friends, but Dan, when it comes down to when it really matters and your principles are on the line, you sell them out. You stomp on them. You ridicule them. In my opinion you are yelling, "Nigger, you ain't as good as we are!" You are stabbing them in the back while smiling. Do yourself a big favor and take your book to your closest black friend and have him explain to your how sick your thinking is on this subject.

You add to your list blondes as another group who can't think for themselves. O.J. had a way with blondes; you surmise this from O.J.'s demeanor. How as a group would they be helpful to you? Dan, remember he is being accused of killing a blonde. What are you thinking? Your generalities have spilled over into ridiculousness.

You also eliminate any juror who wanted to serve. You were suspicious of their motives. Are you ruling out those that wanted to fulfill their civic duty? Aren't we supposed to consider it our responsibility to serve?

When O.J. saw blacks being disqualified, he left the courtroom. That seems natural. An obvious attempt to keep blacks off the jury is a painful insult showing how badly you need to keep the jury tilted in your favor. Why shouldn't your using the race card be unbearable to O.J. and something he would rather not witness?

Now you insult on all women. They like the handsome attorney, Mr. Baker that would influence their decision regarding O.J.'s involvement in this crime. Unattractive lawyers beware; the cards are stacked against you. Ladies, can you try hard and see past the good looks of the defense attorneys? Accusing O.J.'s lawyers of profiling to have only white, brunette women on the jury, you say, "Baker was very good at walking up to a juror, making her feel at ease, and then cutting her head off."[3] Is this a metaphor making O.J.'s lawyer a lady-killer? A killer using a knife and cutting the lady's head off. Sick, sick, sick!

You sum up weeks of trying to select the jury by concluding,

"Whites favored your side, blacks favored Simpson, we were face-to-face with America's unyielding race problem and it was very demoralizing. Here, in front of our eyes, the case was degenerating into a racial contest, our worst fear."[4]

This is your perception of where the process has taken you. Are you really this racially paranoid? It is all black and white, no room for anyone to be a legitimate impartial juror. All the blacks are wrong and all the whites are right. You have drawn these lines, counselor. This is a sad condition on the face of it, but when it is going to affect the accused it is criminal.

In the middle of jury selection, Mark Fuhrman pleads "...nolo contendre"[5] to perjury. That meant he was not going to try to prove that he didn't commit perjury in O.J.'s criminal trial. This was a devastating development to your case. It knocked the wind out of you. At this point you knew that Fuhrman had been exposed to the whole world as a liar in the O.J. trial. This plea was not news, so no surprise here. You should have been totally prepared for it to be confirmed. The insinuation that his lying impeached him as a detective on this case is correct. The lying was related to the case in several important ways. Since you acknowledge that race could be an issue in regards to the conduct of the police, perjury could be construed as a cover-up for racism. An unavoidable and reasonable concern, you proudly take and use to your advantage. It becomes a tool used to exclude any juror that sees a connection between a perjurer and someone who would plant evidence. This is very shrewd lawyering on your part designed to confuse the jury. You want us to believe policeman who commit perjury or invoke refusal to testify under 5th Amendment rights would not plant evidence. Therefore, your logic says even though Fuhrman was a perjurer because he was a detective he would not plant evidence.

Further you don't believe that jurors should consider it possible for the evidence to be suspect. How ridiculous you are, Mr. P.

Now you confess to a whopper, you have taken this incredible journey to find unbiased jurors. I have had a field day pointing out how dumb that statement is. Now you admit to us the obvious:

"...all this talk about wanting a fair and unbiased jury, that's nonsense; you want jurors who are biased in your favor. You want to win." [6]

Thank you, for stamping the message indelibly in print. You want to win, justice be damned. Find the biases in jurors and exploit them to your advantage. Trample on race, gender, and employment, whatever is necessary to win. Move that money around and make sure that at least $1.2 million sticks on you. Ruin lives, drag people through the expense and humiliation of a trial, see if you can stack the jury deck high enough in your favor to deal yourself a victory. Manipulate, coerce, lie, do anything in your favor to win. Thank you for calling it the way it is, the way you want it, and the way your colleagues want it. Write the laws, litigate, prosecute, and convict. A great business you have created, Mr. Lawyers, which in itself is a crime and a great scam on the American public.

You are so proud of your tactics you have put it in a book to memorialize your victory. This is like reading about the coach that fixed the Super Bowl game bragging about the great win. This is akin to hearing about the businessmen that cooked the books, deceived the stockholders, and boasted how well their company was doing. What has the legal profession come to? This is a clear case of some in an honored profession aiding and abetting a dishonest way of life.

With all of this, you still want your victory to have some people of color on the jury. You believe it would look better. As a disguise for your real feelings, you need to find that rare black person that would believe O.J. to be guilty. Your opponent, Baker, did not display the same paranoia. He stated all the jurors looked fine to him. He passed on the first 12 presented. But no, you couldn't resist playing the powerful race card. You turn around and accuse the defense because they objected to your systematic exclusion of African-Americans from the jury. You were appalled they made you look like bigots. It did and you are! You contend that you weren't excluding blacks because of their color, but because they were biased. Are all the blacks you encounter biased, but whites aren't? This is very, very wrong and instead of being ashamed you are proud of this contemptible behavior.

After fifteen working days you finally settle on a jury. Ten whites, one Asian/Black from Jamaica, and a 62-year-old black woman with some college. You feel you have a chance to win since you only need 9 jurors for a victory. I am confused, Dan, because over and over you state that people's minds are made up about this case and racial bias is too deep to overcome. If you are right there is no reason to have a trial with the decision preordained. According to you, no amount of evidence or logic will make a difference. Is this the jury roulette game? Let's see how the lawyers can load the cartridge and the results have been determined. The trial is just a show to create more billable hours, great PR, and more business for your law firm. The truth is not the issue here and justice isn't the motivating force. Glowing in the spotlight with your $1.2 million, less expenses, is what it is all about. You have eloquently, with the help of a professional writer made the point about what was really at stake going after O.J.

Notes:

[1] Daniel Petrocelli, *Triumph of Justice* (Crown 1998) pg. 363

[2] Ibid, pg. 367

[3] Ibid, pg. 371

[4] Ibid, pg. 372

[5] Ibid, pg. 372

[6] Ibid, pg. 374

TWENTY-ONE

Storytelling Time

Opening Statements

The trial is ready to begin. You are prepared for the experience of a lifetime. You talk about concern as to how to present this case? There should be no reason to worry about the outcome since you are convinced that everyone knew O.J. committed these crimes. You charge the prosecution for bungling the criminal case. I wouldn't expect you to let that happen again. O.J.'s lawyers played the race card in order to win and you are going to trump that play if they try that again. Your path seems nicely laid out for you. Why do you need to complicate the situation? You have a jury with only one black woman to scuttle your presentation. No problem here you only need 9 jurors to buy into your version of the murders. This looks like child's play, unless you have misled us. Except reality says because this case is one of circumstantial evidence there's no telling how the story will play out. There is no dripping knife to help with the verdict. There are many matters that cause doubt. This is going to be a tough case to sell to even reasonable people. You are going to need a strategy. You decided to get the jury to focus on O.J. Simpson. This was his trial; not the LAPD; not the forensics, not the witnesses. Again and again, in the search for justice, why is such a loaded strategy necessary? Simply present your evidence, witnesses, and let the jury decide guilty or innocent. There is really no need for manipulation, engineering evidence out of context, suppressing thought and logic, legal histrionics, attacking witnesses;

all the tools of the trade of lawyer's hell bent on winning at all costs. Leave the tricks at the courthouse door and contribute to improving the standard of the justice system in L.A. I haven't forgotten what you preached earlier. Rather noble sounding, but given the state of the legal profession today, suspect. Please, just insist on fair presentations of the facts and concede that in a battle of circumstantial evidence, there could possibly be alternative causes for the crime. Leave dogma and deceit out of the halls of justice.

The judge didn't go along with your motion to suppress any suggestion of police wrongdoing. The defense would be allowed to examine witnesses concerning these matters. Your first attempt to be an architect of deceit runs into a roadblock. You expected to lean on a California statute stating routine work done by state employees is presumed to be done correctly because you didn't want your evidence to be challenged. You didn't want expert testimony that criticized the handling of the evidence. This may be good lawyering, but lousy pursuit of the truth.

You didn't want any criticism of the LAPD or the jury to hear any of the evidence was contaminated or tampered with so you were successful in limiting testimony to what the state of the art was in collecting and examining evidence. It did not matter how the evidence was collected. It was collected and the procedure could not be attacked. Taking away one of the most vital aspects of this case; you set it up for the defense team to work with both hands tied behind their backs. You found a statute completely nullifying the defense's position. This in turn succeeds in eliminating any discussion of alternative ways this crime could have taken place. I can see from a technical and legal standpoint, this limits the scope of the trial allowing less reasonable doubt, but if your goal is to discover justice then you are heading the wrong way. You are carefully crafting the context of this trial to part Mr. Simpson from his money. The great care however, is the reprehensible way prosecutors create a specific context, not allowing the jury to see the whole picture. Good strategy for winning at all costs, but this justice thing you so patriotically wave in our face is flying upside down.

Still at the beginning of the trial, you are wrestling with "*What is this trial really about?*"[1] You are showing us how confused you are when you ask the question, "*What* was *our case?*"[2] What happened to all the bravado when you claim that O.J. was the killer, it was obvious? The answer therefore must be, "this case is obvious and we will help the jury get it. After all, we are experienced, high priced lawyers trained in communication and presenting clear and unambiguous evidence. Should be easy."

You remind us,

"'This case is about justice.' I said to my partners. "It is not about money, it is not about compensation, it is about justice. Fred Goldman's last chance for justice.'"[3]

Your partner calls you on this. "'People aren't going to buy that. He is suing for money, and I think we should make it clear and not be elliptical about it...'"[4]

"I think to Tom, the whole battle for justice sounded a bit pretentious and candy-ass."[5] Got that message right, Dan. He warned you the jury might not buy into this justice thing. After all, Fred Goldman is Jewish and,

"Everybody knows Jews like money. If he denies he's in it for money he's lying".[6]

Here is a little more racism to spread around; no Jews are interested in justice, just money. Now, if you had said no Jewish lawyers maybe you have something. And while you are at it, why not say: no Italian lawyers are interested in money, just justice. This is all sickening, hypocritical, piles of manure. Finally, you agree to leave this pursuit of justice thing out of your opening remarks. In the name of honesty, you should have left it out of your book.

Confident that you could win the case by getting O.J. Simpson to lie on the stand, you will attack him and make him tell demonstrable lies, following with a parade of witnesses who would reveal the rest of his deceptions. Then you will close with Ron and Nicole's families. Your strategy is to avoid the details and get the witnesses off the stand in a hurry not to educate the jury too much. Certainly your portrait of the killer, confining all your thinking to the building of the story, the circumstantial evidence will lead to O.J. What you scrupulously avoid is the same evidence would also lead to other possible murder suspects. The evidence does not conclusively point to O.J., but it will, if you really reach and make a number of unreasonable assumptions. This is your business, as you directly state:

"When we read a good book, it tells a compelling story. When we go to the movies, we want a story that engages us. …I tried to tell the jury a story they could understand easily. I was a story about two people and how their lives ended tragically, together, in a murder."[7]

You are indeed telling a story, but not one of fact, rather one of fiction, a fairytale. This is a yarn that could be believable. I agree that O.J. could have committed these crimes, but this is not the point of our legal system. What could have and did happen are two very different situations. Jason could have, a drug dealer could have, another Nicole lover, any number of possible candidates. The problem with your story is that it has too many holes in it. Understanding this weakness is why you have to strategically develop guilt out of context. You are not willing to admit there are any other possibilities of how these crimes were committed. This is the tunnel vision that lawyers have developed to help them win cases; your story, no others. This is a contributing factor in the breakdown of our justice system; lawyers engineering laws, facts, and showmanship to force a result.

Facing the jury you begin to tell the story as if you were there with all the details from your imagination. You start off with Nicole putting her children to bed, then filling the tub with water and lighting some candles to get ready for a relaxing evening bath. This is too much to believe, right from the start. You don't know that she put her children to bed. That is a guess and an important misdirection. Then you have Nicole answering the phone at 9:40 pm. It is her mother asking her to get her glasses from the restaurant. This we know is true, because Mrs. Brown can verify the fact. The kids and the candles in the bath is your conjecture. You didn't tell the jury there were dozens of candles around the bath leading one to question if a guest was expected. Could a lover be expecting to share this bath, comes upon Ron and something terrible happens? This lover brings a knife because it is one of his love playthings or maybe it's a weapon. Since this lover doesn't like her sleeping around with other men, he gets upset. Maybe he gets in a rage because he believes Ron to be another lover. They have words, Nicole comes downstairs, steps outside, sees the two men going at it, tries to stop the argument, and things get out of hand. Testosterone was raging! Or maybe Nicole brought the knife from the kitchen for self-protection. The killer knocks Nicole down and hits her head. The men go at it and the killer takes the knife, Ron puts up a great fight, but ultimately looses. The killer has to get rid of Nicole because she would be witness. This is one of a number of imagined possibilities and although it sounds like a piece of pulp fiction, it is made of the same clothe as your story. I feel awkward making up stories, don't you? We both have the same set of facts and evidence. Mine is better because my killer has the opportunity to dispose of the murder weapon and bloody clothes, O.J. didn't have the opportunity to get rid of evidence.

You have Nicole calling the restaurant and speaking to a friendly waiter. No, no, Dan, Nicole knows that Ron works there, she has gone dancing with him, and so she specifically asks for him. Were the candles meant for Ron? Even though there is no specific evidence that Nicole and Ron had a relationship up to this point, relationships do start somewhere. This could have well been the opportunity Nicole was waiting for. Ron fits the description of the type of guy she is attracted to: young, handsome, in good physical condition. Maybe the invitation to Ron was fortuitous for Nicole. The problem with this visit is Ron comes upon a drug dealer (new supposition) and they get into a tangle. Ron leaves the restaurant at 9:50 pm, walks to his apartment to change. It would be likely that he showers also, since he just finished working, unless he was expecting a meeting in the bath tub. This is important because the timeline is critical in this case. Even you admit this, Mr. P. Let's calculate how long it would take to get to his house, shower, dress, and get in his girlfriend's car to drive to Nicole's. This should take about 25 – 35 minutes to me. This takes me to 10:30 pm. At 10:40 pm someone hears a male voice say, "*Hey, hey, hey!*"[8] You presume this is Ron. That is misdirection on your part. We don't know for sure that it was Ron's voice. It could have been the killer or one of his accomplices. These are important assumptions you are making for us. You want to pin down the time frames and build your case around faulty assumptions. This is not fair, counselor. The *heys* could have been someone else, not Ron. Even if they were Ron's, your story is still badly flawed.

Trying to appeal to the jury's emotions you set up another neat scenario.

"'Ron Goldman's life ended because he agreed to do a friend a favor, only to come upon her rageful killer and his. He might have run from danger, but he did not.

Ron died, ladies and gentlemen, with his eyes open.'"[9]

This is quite a story you are conjuring up for the jury. First, he didn't get killed because he agreed to do a friend a favor. He got killed because he was in the wrong place at the wrong time or he was part of the problem. Second, Ron may have provoked the killer. We don't know for sure what happened between the parties. You know that a dead man is not attackable and we all feel sorry for Ron because we assume he had nothing to do with the cause of the killings. Unfortunately, he may have. Not that he planned anything, but he got caught in a bad situation and did not back down. Being protective of Nicole or just plain confrontational with whomever was in that walkway ignited a tragic explosion. Ron may or may not have had any participation in all of this, you can't know for sure. What disturbs me is that you don't allow for any other circumstances leading up to the murder. We know we don't know what happens and the improbable can take place. Sometimes things get out of control and you look back shocked that such events could occur. You try to get us to believe a simple story consistent with ones we have read about or seen in the movies.

Dramatically you conclude that Ron died with his eyes open. He witnessed the killing of Nicole and the person he saw commit the crime was O.J. Simpson. We don't actually know what Ron saw, this is just more of your fanciful imagination. He may have seen nothing. He could have been attacked from behind, spun around by one of the killers while he was being knifed to death. He may never have seen Nicole or O.J. This dramatic presentation is intent on appealing to the sympathy of the jury. You have taken literary license to write this story and are selling it to the jury with passionate conviction. Is this an example of *lawyers lying passionately*? Since you were not at the murder scene and there are no eyewitnesses, this portrayal is pure fiction, yet you tell it as if you are a reporter at the scene. What is the jury to think? Why would this nice attorney lie to us by making up such a story? Your law degree, your credibility, your wordsmanship, and your presence are selling this story. It all comes down to whether or not you are believable, not whether O.J. is the killer. The best storyteller wins!

You have promised the jury you will prove O.J. was the killer. Just like the cover of your book promises the reader will be convinced O.J. was the killer. So far all you have been able to do is make big promises. Let's take a look at how you fashion your story so the jury will buy a ticket. You tell the jury,

"...all the evidence identified Simpson as the killer, and there was no one else in the world with an apparent motive of killing"[10]

Let's analyze the evidence as you present it. Your second proclamation is gross speculation. You don't know positively there was no one else who wanted Nicole dead. She had many lovers. How do you know that one of these was not hurt and angry with Nicole? Could they have felt rejected and pushed to the point of rage? People with promiscuous lives run the risk of breaking hearts. Broken hearts can produce murderers. Jason may have had several motives: a chance to do something for a father who was tormented by this woman or he may have had a crush on Nicole and been rejected himself. There are a number of possibilities. Take your pick or add to the list. You misdirect the jury by making a declaratory statement that only O.J. could possibly have a motive. Lie number one and counting.

You will prove that O.J. Simpson could not, would not, and did not tell the truth. First of all, O.J. did not testify in the criminal trial. The lying that you are referring to would have to be during the depositions taken by you. We have already gone through them and you didn't prove conclusively that he lied. You didn't like his answers, but you didn't prove he was lying. The main points of the cuts on his hands and how many times he hit Nicole were not subjects with good evidence. The story about the Bruno Magli shoes was too weak and irrelevant. So what exactly did he lie about?

If he knew who was the killer, most importantly if it was his son Jason, for that reason he may have structured his answers to be uncertain. You will not concede that any of this is possible although you have not proved it is not possible. It is important for the reader and the jury to read between the lines at what was not asked. You didn't have the guts, honesty, or integrity to ask Jason where he was the night of the murders. Your avoidance of Jason is clear evidence, Mr. Petrocelli; you wanted to skip any questions that could throw doubt on your story.

Your next lie is to claim that there is no basis for believing there was police tampering involved in this case. This is naïve of you and a blatant misrepresentation of a highly likely possibility. This completely eliminates any semblance of dealing with the truth since this case is solely based on circumstantial evidence. You explain that most of the police working on the case were home in their beds asleep. Fuhrman didn't get to the crime scene until 4:00 am. You claim that it would take dozens of people to pull off a framing conspiracy. I take exception to those statements. We have a glove and a few smears of blood. Big questions surround these two pieces of evidence. It all cries out to something very wrong with both of the theories you present, but you state emphatically there is only one possible explanation. This reader can't see by what you have presented so far that this is true.

If as you state, O.J. were a police favorite, why would they want to frame him? This is a gross assumption and generality on your part. You provide no proof that he was a favorite. To me it sounds like he has been a nuisance several times. You forget the bounty for catching a killer, especially a superstar; promotions, lifetime recognition, career making. The higher up the celebrity ladder, the bigger reward for the catch, as you know, Dan.

You want to explain away the eight-hour delay of processing the crime scene. There may not have been any sinister intention, but it did present an opportunity for foul play. Someone could have put a glove in their pocket unnoticed. Experts claim that contamination of the evidence was possible. This brings up confusion for the reader. Since we don't know the procedures, for an expert to tell us the evidence was mishandled and procedures faulty, gives us reason to wonder how much to trust their conclusions.

You spoke to the jury for three hours! You insist that it is obvious that O.J. was the killer and the only thing that had saved him was the race card. The thought of listening to three hours of storytelling is dreadful. O.J.'s lawyer's opening remarks were confined to telling the jury what a great person and athlete O.J. is. You criticize this, rightfully. He should have attacked the evidence. His trashing of Nicole also proves his poor performance. O.J. needs you, Mr. P, as Baker continues to do a lousy job. This confuses me because Baker is intelligent and experienced. He is a very successful lawyer, how can he fail to defend his client effectively? I am really sorry for O.J. You can see through it, in the pursuit of justice, why would you not ignore the shortcomings of his attorney? You have been well trained to be a predator and drool at the missteps of your opposition. He is handing you the weapons to slay his client. How nice for you, but how cruel to O.J.! You point out that

"...*these few strong words buried Simpson. Baker was staking his entire case on proving the photos were a fraud. He left no room to wiggle. If Baker failed on this one issue, by his own reasoning and his own words, his client, O.J. Simpson, was a killer.*"[11]

the case on discrediting the photos of the Bruno Magli shoes. If he failed to prove they were a fake, he was calling his client a killer. What a travesty! He was basing his case on a narrow point and not a good one at that, but maybe O.J. was misdirecting you. If he knew who was wearing the shoes that night, was he purposely forfeiting to protect his son? Is there any amount of money that would prevent you from protecting your son thereby saving his life? Ask any father what they would do? Is money more important than the life of your son?

Baker did an awful job in his opening remarks. This is not the first time that a lawyer has failed his client. There is a whole body of law that covers this crime. There are convictions that have been reversed due to ineffectual representation. Very sad and happening too often. People rely on lawyers to defend them and rather than pass on the case due to inexperience or lack of time to adequately prepare, they just take the money and fail to do a proper job. This is yet another part of the legal system that needs addressing. Lawyers accepting work they are not capable of handling and misleading clients while grabbing the money. What you have done by effectively critiquing Mr. Baker is put a question on the validity of the outcome of this case.

Notes:

[1] Daniel Petrocelli, *Triumph of Justice* (Crown 1998) PG 380

[2] Ibid, pg.380

[3] Ibid, pg. 381

[4] Ibid, pg. 381

[5] Ibid, pg.381

6   Ibid, pg. 381

7   Ibid, pg. 384

8   Ibid, pg. 395

9   Ibid, pg.385

10   Ibid, pg. 385

11   Ibid, pg. 394

TWENTY-TWO

The Case of Smoke and Mirrors

The Case-in-Chief

You call your first witness, Mr. Heidstra. He was walking his dog about 10:30 to 10:35 when he heard another dog barking. What I'm hearing is Heidstra is not exactly sure of the time. In this case, a few minutes difference of the happening of any event can lead one to believe very different results. You have admitted that O.J. had only one minute to kill his victims for him to be the killer. Since every minute that is accounted for is critical, should Mr. Heidstra be mistaken by only a few minutes, there goes your case out the window. "About two minutes later he heard 'a clear, young' male voice say, *'Hey, hey, hey!'*"[1] Again, he isn't quite sure about when and he estimates *about* two minutes. Did anyone test Mr. Heidstra on his ability to tell time without a stopwatch? Does he have any special training that would make him qualified to do time estimations accurately? Each moment is so important, yet you take this casually. Why is Mr. Baker not challenging these estimates? Heidstra testifies it was all of 15 seconds between the "Hey's" and a door slamming. 15 seconds to commit a double murder? He also hears a young voice yelling. How does he know that voice is a young man? What is his experience in evaluating the age of an individual that he does not see? I have some forty-year-old friends with voices like teenagers. More importantly, how do we know that this is the voice of Ron Goldman? It could have been the murderer or someone else. Maybe even the murderer's accomplice. You

211

know Dan, there is too little noise associated with these killings. Such little noise strongly suggests that there was more than one killer. I'm not alone on this subject. There have been other careful analysis of the crimes that concludes that it is highly unlikely for one person to have accomplished the awful murders. It is more likely that it was necessary for someone to hold the victim and cover their mouth and another person doing the stabbing. Two victims, brutally beaten producing no noise for neighbors to hear, do not make sense. Baker should have challenged this aggressively.

Heidstra also identifies a *"'...white kind of Jeep with tinted glass ... 'for one moment' and then sped away south on Bundy, away from the murder scene.'"*[2] You try to reconstruct this time pattern as fuzzy as it is, between 10:35 and 10:40 pm contradicting Heidstra's claim that it was (... *"'Exactly. Around that time.'"*) *..in an attempt to move him closer to 10:45 pm"*[3]. Baker does challenge the problems presented by this testimony. We are dealing with estimates in details that call for precision if this timing is the basis for the case against O.J. We don't have minutes to throw around and still account for all of the activity that must have taken place that night. Your theory has O.J. leaving Bundy at 10:45 pm, driving back to his Rockingham estate, scaling the wall, dropping a glove, banging into Kato's wall, changing his clothes, running the washing machine to get rid of the evidence, cleaning up after the bloody mess, getting dressed, pulling his luggage together in order to meet his chauffeur, Mr. Park, at 10:55 pm, including the drive back home, all taking place in 10 minutes. How can you really believe it happened this way? Kato isn't sure when he heard the thumps; it could have been 10:40. This would kill your timeline altogether. Even at 10:50 it doesn't make any sense. Five minutes to do all I have listed? O.J. is fast, but not that fast. No one I know is. The only thing that proves to be fast here is a lawyer's golden tongue making up this fantastic story.

Another resident, Mr. Karpf, walking a dog near the crime scene heard barking between 10:45 and 10:50 pm. His original statement to the police put the time of the barking between 10:50 and 11:00 pm. All of this gets you to conclude that Ron and Nicole were dead by 10:40. This timing is necessary for you to stick to your theory of the one-minute - double homicide with a knife. According to the forensics experts, Ron's struggle and all of the blood caused by the crime could not have happened that quickly. In order to have bloody footprints, blood would have had to leave the victim and get all over the walkway. A quick killing doesn't suggest this possibility. This whole timeline thing is in the land of guessing. We have to deal with what is possible and probable. One of your nifty tools is to take the nearly impossible and present it as probable. This is crafty, deceptive, misleading, and just plain dirty legal work in the quest for money.

Mr. Karpf says, "*He heard no struggle going on at that time.*"[4] This is very important; a witness that says there was no noise, none, nada! A double homicide in the open with no sound of a struggle! Doesn't this just scream at you that there was more than one person committing these crimes? A knife murder, a struggle, with no noise, must be someone with their hands over the victim's mouth. Unless you can give me another explanation, it doesn't make sense to me.

The police were called after midnight. The police and you are fuzzy about this timeline. Since time plays such an important roll in your fanciful account, wanting us to accept this loose estimate is reprehensible. Preparing to put the police on the stand, you show us your legal fangs. You debated on this strategy "...*long and hard*".[5] You must have felt this testimony could hurt you. In order to mitigate any damage, you needed to plan this out precisely. You decide to limit the amount of witnesses so as not to have contradictory stories. You want to keep the testimonies brief and limit their scope. You would block the defense's cross-examination and control their ability to insert their story into yours. You will do what is needed to engineer what the jury will hear. Don't let the defense tell its story. Don't let the jury hear of other possibilities. Stick with your context, your fabrication, and your passionate deception. That is what you are being paid for. This is a lot like two sport teams competing. Each does all he can to manipulate the rules, get away with as much as possible, cheat whenever... load the deck, if you will. Then insist that the opposition abide by the rules and makes it okay even if the team is not competent enough to be on the field. After the victory, you beat your chest and write a book about how you won!

Officer Robert Riske and Miguel Terrazas were the first to arrive at the murder scene. It is very important to you to establish that all the evidence is found before Fuhrman arrived at the scene. This was shortly after midnight. It was dark. There was landscaping in front of Nicole's condo. Kelly tells us he found one glove, a hat, the pager, and some various items lying next to the bodies. He also sees some blood droplets along the alley going away from the victims. Some blood was on the back gate. He describes how they secure the crime scene. He doesn't say that he did an inch-by-inch inspection of the scene, only that he observed the evidence. The other glove could have been in several different places: on the property, but not in clear view, under the victim, off the property, in a policeman's pocket, any number of places. You cannot definitely say that O.J. dropped the second glove at the back of his property. This theory gives the reader reason to seriously question your logic. Why and how would this tightly fitting glove end up on the lawn behind his house? Your explanation asks us to believe that O.J. would drop a critical piece of evidence in a place that would direct the police to him. He might have just as well provided a full confession. He didn't return from Chicago and go to the police station as a man who had left incriminating evidence behind. One would expect that he would have had legal representation while speaking to the police.

When the defense asks the officer if he called for any assistance in tracking the murderer(s) with police dogs, you objected on the grounds that the police didn't have to explain their actions. They didn't have to explain that at no time, in any way, did they take the action to find another suspect, other than O.J. The detectives had made up their minds there was no other way these two people were murdered. That doesn't sound like good police work to me, Dan. Your insistence that this not be questioned, questions your motives. The whole thing stinks! You even criticize Judge Ito for permitting the trial defense team to question the actions or non-actions of the police. These are all relevant questions in the quest of justice. You insist on tunnel vision. Evil work, Mr. P!

When O.J.'s lawyer asked, "*Give me your best estimate of when Detective Fuhrman arrived... Where did Detective Furhman go first?*"....[6] You object to the question, of course. You did not want the jury to know what Fuhrman could or would do. After all, he is a perjurer in this case. Oh, I am sorry; you don't want the jury to be reminded of this. Officer Terrazas sees blood on the back gate at 12:15 am. This is an hour and fifteen minutes after the crimes were supposed to have been committed. Has the blood dried? You don't tell us what experts consider being the drying time for blood droplets. If the blood had dried then how did the officer know this blood was associated with this crime? Mr. Fuhrman claims he was asleep at 1:00 am. How can we be sure about this? You believe his claim, but none of O.J.'s account of where he was that evening. Fuhrman may have told people he was asleep, but in fact, wasn't. Did he have any witnesses to verify this? The pictures of the blood on the back gate were not taken until three weeks after the murders. THREE WEEKS! What were the criminologists thinking? Of course you don't want O.J.'s lawyers questioning the procedures of collecting evidence. Without photos taken at the time of the murders, how can you be positive there was no tampering? Three weeks later they get around to photographing a piece of evidence that you consider critical. I submit that based on the fact there were no cuts on the gloves it was not likely a way for the murderer to leave any blood behind. O.J.'s cut is on the top of his hand. How does a drop conveniently get from the top of his hand onto the gate without being smeared? You never established that O.J. was bleeding that evening. There were no bandages, no bloody autographs, and no witness seeing evidence of cuts on his trip to Chicago. How then did O.J.'s blood get onto the crime scene? Finally after three weeks and very dry blood, they get around to photographing a droplet. How can you date when exactly the blood got placed on the gate? It could have been months before the crime or days after. How do we know it wasn't Jason's blood? No one even tried to match it with his sample for all we can tell. Your blood evidence theories are lawyering at its worst. What I am witnessing are smoke and mirrors, the weapons of a crafty lawyer, being used very well.

The officer's testimony gets tainted when he is asked to identify the blood he saw that evening. Looking at the pictures he has identified rust spots as blood, also. Yes Dan, *"Terrazas had made a mistake, it happens."*[7] You have to admit that your assumptions with this testimony were wrong. This causes a fury and you had a major fiasco on your hands. You call it a little mistake and accuse the press of blowing it out of proportion. Dan, if the officer confuses rust and blood during the night, only if the blood was still wet could we believe that he made a worthwhile observation. If the blood was dry, his testimony is worthless. Rust, blood, no problem, you say. It is a problem all around. You learned something from this mistake, I hope.

You continue to pound the blood and the missing gloves theme. You now pull your race card. You are a piece of work. You have a black police officer testifying that he saw blood on the street outside the Bronco and inside Simpson's compound. First of all, what was he doing inside O.J.'s property without a warrant? Again, at what time did he observe the blood and was it dry or wet? If it were dry, when did they get there?

You believe a non-black jury would consider white officers capable of lying and planting evidence, but not an impressive looking black officer. You have prejudice oozing out of every pore, Mr. Petrocelli. Your generalizations are the basis of most prejudice. You believe that black people, especially postal workers and females would be biased in favor of O.J. Daniel, this is sick thinking all the way around.

According to you O.J. dripped blood all over Rockingham. This is another time you use hyperbole. *"The crime scene was swimming in blood."*[8] Dan, no! There were a few suspicious drops. That can't be described as *all over*. You claim the all over proposition to debunk the racial theory, because this officer said he saw some drops of blood. This was the dead of night, by then the blood would have coagulated, even if it were left at 10:30 p.m. He would have no way of knowing when the blood got there, if it was blood, or to whom it belonged. There are far too many variables for this officer to make any conclusions.

You have Officer Thompson taking extensive notes as to whom and when the police arrived at the crime scene. Except, Thompson left the crime scene to go to Rockingham so he could not have tracked what was happening at Bundy.

Mr. Phillips is your next witness. Phillips is Fuhrman's superior. You hope he will vouch for the information Fuhrman provides was, *"Solid and unassailable, he was our preemptive answer to the defense strategy of* Fuhrman, Fuhrman, Fuhrman.*"*[9]. We need to take a close look at this point. What is so special about this man that makes him so believable? Who knows what Mark may have on him? This is more of your naiveté. Remember President Nixon and the problem caused by bosses cover for their employees. What is it he will vouch for that will dispel the implications of perjury? Will you tell us, Dan?

It is a preposterous theory that the glove may have been planted, according to you. This is a very important part of the case. One has to wonder how the glove ended up on O.J.'s lawn. It didn't seem likely that he would leave it there if he were washing the other bloody clothing he wore during the crime. Your theory is that he did washing before he met his airport driver. This is what is unbelievable to me. What a time to do a washing. Funny if there was less at stake here. You list five reasons to support your claim of the glove being left on the lawn by O.J. Let's look at them.

First, no one ever saw a second glove at Bundy. This poses several problems. It didn't necessarily have to be at Bundy. It could have been in the street. No one may have seen it because it was hidden in the bushes or overlooked due to the darkness. It was possible a police officer could have picked it up unnoticed. Gloves fit easily in a pocket. You flatly state that it was impossible and I take exception to that statement.

Second, there was no reason to believe that Fuhrman suspected O.J. because the police were canvassing the neighborhood for witnesses and information. Wrong again, Dan. Fuhrman was involved with O.J. and Nicole years earlier during a complaint about a domestic dispute. He was aware of on-going problems between O.J. and Nicole since their 1989 incident was on the airwaves. He could reasonably assume that O.J. was involved in the murders and finding crucial evidence would certainly enhance his career. He really had nothing to lose. He would get kudos for discovering the glove on O.J.'s property. If O.J. had supplied an airtight alibi, then the glove would be out of place, but who would really care? No one would have known he was the one who planted it behind O.J.'s house in the dark of the night; a very simple act without much risk. Yet, you suggest that he would have gone to jail for life if O.J. was proven innocent. Not very likely, Daniel!

You ask how Fuhrman would have known who the killer was. He had enough circumstantial evidence to suggest that it was O.J. He didn't have to be highly inspired to come up with that. This was a good bet with enormous upside potential for his career. You do know how police promotions work, don't you?

You believe that he wouldn't have planted the glove because he didn't know if it was O.J.'s blood. That seems highly unlikely to have stopped him. Why did he go to O.J.'s house in the first place? He must have thought O.J. was involved in some way. If it were just a politically correct visit to inform him of his ex-wife's murder, he was in the wrong. The correct ones to be notified would have been Nicole's parents or sister since O.J. was divorced from Nicole. Knowing their history, one would assume that O.J. was involved in the murder in some way. Ex-spouses are natural suspects. It would be reasonable that Fuhrman would have wanted to seize a career opportunity by being involved in solving the case. After all, a little glove planting is not such a big deal.

Your final point repeats the last two points. What if O.J. had a good alibi, wouldn't that get Fuhrman in deep trouble? He merely found a glove. That doesn't mean he planted the glove. It would not act as a deterrent to believe he thought he might get in trouble. There was not much likelihood of that.

All five of your proofs that Fuhrman could not or would not plant the glove are flawed. Based on the information he had the opportunity. It is less likely that O.J. would have left the glove there. The reader is left wondering how a glove would have ended up in such an improbable place. At best, these were tight fitting gloves that wouldn't have just fallen off indiscriminately. This would not have been an accidental dropping unless he had removed them at Bundy.

If he had removed them at the crime scene then he would have been carrying them in his pocket while driving back to Rockingham, possibly along with the knife. He would have to get back onto his property while covered in blood. Did he scale his wall carrying the glove and the knife? Not a good bet since he most likely would have left blood evidence. You don't present any evidence there was blood leading up to where the glove was found. No shoe prints or blood drops were found there. Yet, you want us to believe that O.J. was bleeding all over the place. Unless, O.J. Simpson, as Peter Pan, magically flies over a wall, drops a glove, gets to the house and leaves no trail after committing a very bloody murder, the theory doesn't work.

There are no real answers to your questions. They are flawed and your conclusion is absurd. If O.J. fell against the wall of Kato's apartment after dropping the glove there would have been additional blood evidence. How could he not consider it a high priority to get to the glove before leaving his property to go to Chicago? If he were the murderer it would be a confession. If it were an oversight, knowing the glove were left behind, it is not likely he would willingly offer himself to be questioned by the police without an attorney present. He didn't act like a man guilty of a crime especially knowing he had left incriminating evidence behind. Mr. P, you do nothing to dispel the possibility the glove was planted. Mr. Fuhrman is the most logical suspect here. It would have been helpful to all if he didn't hide behind the 5th.

Mr. Phillips, Fuhrman's boss, tries to help you cover the story by saying Fuhrman was not out of his sight the entire time they were at Bundy. This seems highly improbable. It would have only taken a moment for the glove to be slipped in a pocket. I am trying to visualize Fuhrman's boss looking only at him. Was Phillips doing anything else other than watching Fuhrman? Another officer may have slipped him the glove in a quick second. Fuhrman would have then owed him one.

The explanation you give for them visiting O.J.'s house is to give him V.I.P. treatment regarding the evening's events. The police wanted him to hear of his ex-wife's murder personally and not on the media. Give me a break, counselor. In the middle of a murder investigation, a crew of policemen goes over to O.J.'s house to tell him about the murder. One officer, not a posse, could have delivered this news. They jump over walls and begin to inspect his property. O.J. was being treated like a suspect from the onset. Fuhrman and his band of detectives believed they knew O.J. committed these crimes since it all fit to them. Prior spousal abuse, a black former football player who was arrogant, all added up to: *We've got the bastard this time!* This is the more likely scenario.

Phillips calls O.J. in Chicago and tells him Nicole was murdered. Phillips felt that O.J. acted unusual by not asking the usual questions that he hears after making these kinds of announcements. Is Phillips telling us he has made hundreds of these death notifications over the phone? Phillip's couldn't see O.J.'s reaction, yet he is making these important assumptions. He had to make many assumptions, all of which he concludes to be a confession that he committed the crimes. The assumption Phillips tries to promote is that since O.J. didn't ask for details he must have been aware of how the murders took place. This is a ridiculous reach of logic refuses to travel with this observer.

Detective Tom Lange is your next witness. You cleverly limit his testimony to two topics: the evidence collected at the crime scene and the quality of the data. You don't want the defense to go into the subject of why the officers went to Rockingham. Good strategy to not have the jury hear that evidence could have been planted or contaminated. If there were other reasons the police went to Rockingham you certainly didn't want your jury to hear them. No, you only want the jury to hear what you think will form the decision in their favor. I fully expect you to continue to use every deceptive tool in your arsenal to blow the defense out of the water. Cut those obstacles to victory to ribbons! Victory equals money and fame. Victory, Victory, Victory, the gods of lawyer's fortunes!

Lange confirmed there was blood at the scene and footprints leading away from the crime. This is not new information, Dan. Lange wanted to give us the impression that he was unaware of the domestic disputes and violence between O.J. and Nicole. That doesn't wash. O.J. and Nicole's problems were out in full view of the public. It would be likely that someone at the crime scene would have pointed that out as important in the solving of these murders. For Lange to hold up the story of going to Rockingham as a goodwill visit is another sad example of treating the jury and your readers as dumb and naïve. It makes a lot more sense to believe that they were suspicious of O.J. from the beginning. That would be good police deductive reasoning, ex-husband, celebrity, past record of spousal abuse –let's go get him! Collaring O.J. could be a great feather in their cap along with the raises, promotions, and fame that all come with being associated in solving a high profile double murder. There are just too many benefits for the players to pass up. If O.J. has an alibi, then, no harm, no foul. At the end of his testimony there is still nothing new. This story still has a bad aroma to it.

Now we move on to Vannatter, the other senior detective on the case. You claim that Vannatter was subjected to the wildest and most vicious accusations regarding the possibility of planting blood evidence.

So you decide to severely limit the scope of his testimony. You decide to run this risk even though there is a chance that the jury will see through this tactic and suspect you have something to hide. You have many things to hide, we know. Your strategy should work. Vannatter says that he did not open the envelope with the blood samples or put them in his pocket. Were there any witnesses to verify this claim? Carrying around blood of a suspect and failing to deliver it directly to the laboratory immediately makes this observer suspicious. You insist nothing foul was done here. You make this too easy, Mr. P. This is a complicated case with much at stake accept such simple analysis. Mr. V had an obligation to his profession to not permit this type of confusion. He should never have taken the chance there could be an accusation of foul play. This is a double homicide that required the most careful of police work. Lives are at stake and justice is threatened. There is no room for allowing doubt to enter a juror's mind if in fact there were nothing to hide. Loose police procedures can't be overlooked, especially in a murder trial. If you need to confine his testimony in the pursuit of O.J.'s money, then do your lawyer thing, but don't try to blow the smoke and use mirrors to minimize sloppy detective work from the most seasoned veterans on the force.

Notes:

[1] Daniel Petrocelli, *Triumph of Justice* (Crown 1998) PG 395

[2] Ibid, pg. 396

[3] Ibid, pg. 396

[4] Ibid, pg. 396

[5] Ibid, pg. 397

[6] Ibid, pg. 399

[7] Ibid pg. 399

[8] Ibid pg. 401

[9]. Ibid. pg 401

TWENTY-THREE

Shut Up, Please!

The "Gag-Free Zone"

The press jumps on Judge Fujiski because it appears that he was booting off blacks in the jury selection process. The jury was being stacked with whites. It was, and you were the cause of the problem. You state over and over that you didn't want uneducated black women on the jury, nor black postal workers, etc. You want the jury to buy to your point of view and the judge was accepting your challenges. You were in the middle of the war for winning the press. You did all you could to get the press to buy into your version of the case. I can resist recalling that you were appalled that Johnnie Cochran played the "race card". And here you are working it to the hilt with the jury selection. I yell HYPROCRICY and you yell MONEY. You believe that most of the reporters believed that Simpson was guilty. Have you forgotten that the press lives off bad news? You know, planes crashing, not landing type news. O.J. being guilty is far more interesting than him being innocent. Their living depends on bad news, ask Geraldo Rivera. If it is found that O.J. has an airtight alibi, there would be no case and therefore, no media coverage. They had a feeding frenzy on the circumstantial aspects of the case. Since the jury was not sequestered, you're concerned how they will react to the press coverage. Weren't they told by the judge not to listen to these programs? The press was confused as to why there was a second trial. So were many of us that felt it was double jeopardy. You did explain to us that the law permits an additional lawsuit based on different standards. The public, rightfully so, believes that the criminal trial is held to the highest standard and if someone is acquitted that should be the end of it. The reverse may happen, civil to criminal, but not the other way around. O.J. didn't get back money he spent defending himself. There are no refunds even though you are found not guilty. Now he has to ante up again. What if he is victorious? The accused get more legal bills despite the outcome. This process just doesn't fit with our image of *Justice*. All we see is more money being spent on lawyers. Is there anything wrong with that, Mr. Daniel Petrocelli, Esquire, partner at MSK?

According to you, if you can show the blood was not tampered with, they lose. This is a large statement to make in a high profile murder case. I disagree with the base assumption in any regard. You did not eliminate the fact that the blood at the scene could have been Jason's. The father-son thing changes the odds regarding similarity of blood type and DNA. You didn't eliminate the possibility blood collecting swatches were tampered with. You didn't deal with the fact that O.J. visited Nicole's condo in the past and may have deposited blood at that time. You didn't address the fact that the blood found on his walkway could have happened previously. You can't give us the dating of the time the blood was deposited. You are only guessing. O.J. was at these two locations many times before. Is it not possible that at other times and in other ways his blood was deposited at these sites? You also don't explain how a gloved assailant (remember no cuts on the gloves) gets to bleed through bloody gloves in a way that leaves conspicuous drops. No cuts on the gloves, no blood on the ground or the gate. The cuts described on O.J. were on the top of his hand. How does that blood, one drop, get on the gate? There were no other cuts on O.J. No, Mr. P the case doesn't merely rest on whether or not the blood arrived at the lab without being tampered with. There is a lot more to this case than you wish to reveal. Too many unanswered questions gracefully avoided. You are very slick, Mr. Lawyer.

Matheson, the scientist with the LAPD lab said upon initial analysis he did not see blood on the socks found in O.J.'s room. He did indicate that the socks should be examined closely at another time for blood. If Matheson, a trained in forensic evidence, picked up the socks, examined them, and didn't see any obvious signs of blood the first time around that says a lot to me. He was looking for blood. The blood could still have been wet. It would seem like it would be hard to miss the many drops found later on. You want us to cut slack for the police and detectives on this case. You claim that just because there was some faulty procedures and contradictory testimony, we should look at the big picture. I fail to understand how in such a high profile double murder case there was so much incompetence. The police work on thousands and thousands of murder cases. We, the public, in order to respect them, have to believe they really know their business and are scrupulous in collecting evidence. Lives depend on the accuracy of their information. We would think that the LAPD sent their finest to this case. The evidence collection should have not become an issue. There was no room for error here. There is no room for error here, Mr. P. You ask O.J. to account for each minute during 10:00 pm and 11:00 pm the night of the murder and your policemen can't tell the difference between blood and rust.

We are told that Ron and Nicole's blood was found in the Bronco. Where were these stains? How many were there? How would O.J. manage to deposit their blood? Was it from his hands, his clothes, or the gloves? You don't explain the way the blood got into the Bronco. This blood wasn't discovered until September, three months after the murders. Where was the LAPD in the meantime? How could they not immediately be going over the Bronco with a fine-toothed comb? This is outrageously poor police work and has all the signs of foul play.

Your point that no other person's blood was found at the scene is incriminating evidence against O.J. This doesn't make any sense. Why is it now a prerequisite to being a murderer that you must leave your blood traces behind? The man who impounded the Bronco said he inspected it for blood and did not see any. This witness is blowing apart your theory. There definitely could have been blood planted in the Bronco. You call him a minor witness. Certainly, you are consistent. All witnesses for the defense are minor and can be ignored. Your witnesses, on the other hand, are all truthful and cannot be challenged.

Dennis Fung, LAPD criminologist is the next witness. He testified in the criminal trial that "*...it was a mistake*"[1] to put a blanket over

225

the victim. This was yet another setback in your contention that the science in this case was handled properly. You dismiss Fung as

"… naïve, and totally guileless…. He is easily led, and as a result, is fully capable of saying things he doesn't mean."[2]

This is great. The man in charge of gathering and preserving the blood and physical evidence is incompetent and unreliable. He wasn't a professional witness. Too bad, but whose fault is this? Do you want us to give the prosecution bonus points for incompetence? Why should this be O.J.'s problem? The prosecution made it his problem and a very expensive one to defend himself against these flimsy charges. You point out that the defense lawyer, Scheck, tore through Fung. It is easy to question the validity of the evidence. Contamination should be simple to sell to the jury.

Now we look at the gloves. Testimony is presented by a salesclerk at Bloomingdale's stating Nicole bought two pairs of similar gloves in 1990. What happened to the other pair? Were they given away, perhaps by Nicole to one of her many lovers? Maybe Jason received a pair. There are too many options to merely pin the gloves on O.J. These are also cashmere-lined gloves. Rather a poor choice to wear during the summer planning a murder. Again, if at best they were very tight fitting for O.J. you will need a good explanation of how and why the gloves came off and were dropped where they were found. From all the descriptions the gloves would have to be pulled off since they were so tight fitting. This would have been a conscious decision. Dropping a bloody glove in plain view would be the same as a confession. This must happen frequently during the panic of the moment and thankfully leads to criminal blunders and honest arrests.

Not only do you want us to believe that O.J. made this critical mistake at the crime scene, but he also repeated it at his own home. Was he leaving breadcrumbs for the police? If O.J. were the killer he would obviously been reviewing the events of the evening and weighing his options while on his trip to Chicago. Would he then return to LA and allow the police to interview him unescorted? It is more likely that he would be hiding behind his many lawyers and concocting a story that would make him the victim. I will present more on this later.

For O.J. to drop two bloody gloves and yet artfully dispose of the weapon and the bloody clothes he was wearing doesn't make any sense.

If he had an accomplice in disposing of the bloody clothes, he would have included instructions to find the glove on his property. He would also have asked the co-conspirator to pick up the socks on his bedroom floor. At the least there would have been a search through the house for incriminating evidence to dispose of along with any traces of blood. A co-conspirator would want to go over every step of the crime scene to take away any evidence, because if O.J. is caught, he cooked also as an accessory to the crimes. O.J. would somehow be in touch with this person, or persons to make sure everything was fixed. This wouldn't that hard to do considering the vulnerability of the evidence. Gloves, possible fingerprints, footprints, socks, clothes were all available for a while before the police arrived at the murder scene.

The consequences for an accomplice in this kind of case are severe. Let's say for a moment that someone did indeed cooperate with O.J. in disposing of the knife and the clothing. They would be putting themselves at O.J.'s mercy if he was caught and tried. At any moment he could rat on his friend and this person would be looking at life imprisonment. You suggest that it could be Mr. Kardashian, O.J.'s friend and attorney. I say no way; these people are too smart to get involved in this way. You tell us if he were the killer he needed help in disposing of the incriminating evidence. If he didn't have this help, he couldn't be the killer. Isn't this so?

The more believable story would be after committing these crimes, O.J. would say to Mr. Park, the limo driver; "I'm sorry, but I feel awful, I am going to have to postpone my trip to Chicago." then send the driver away. He had more important business to take care of, more important than a public appearance in Chicago. He would have to clean the house, get rid of the evidence, clean the Bronco, and work on a plan to avoid being a suspect like setting up an alibi. This would be more likely to have happened with his friends than the prospect of them cleaning up blood and evidence. It's more likely to have someone to vouch for his whereabouts at the time of the murder. You have admitted how easy perjury can be, but bleeding on the way to the airport, bleeding on the plane, bleeding in Chicago would just not fit the image of the *Juice*. Leaving the scene of the crime in this condition would not have been an option because it was an invitation to being caught, but he did leave because either he had no idea the murders took place or he was told by the killer and the best thing he could think of to do was to *get out of Dodge*?

Leaving the crime scene with all of the incriminating evidence just doesn't add up. It would have been too easy for O.J. to change his plans and clean up the mess, return home, and await the phone call of the bad news. I submit this as being a more plausible option if O.J. was the killer. Option A: stay behind and cover the tracks you know you left or Option B: Leave town and hand deliver all the signs you are the murderer. Option A wins hands down. O.J. did not act like someone who just killed two people and left much incriminating evidence behind. Then, we must ask, how did the evidence get there? Those trails would lead back to whoever would profit from catching O.J. as the killer. You insist there was no reason for any law enforcement officer to plant evidence for lack of motivation. You are forgetting that there is a political machine set up in the law enforcement agenda much as in the justice system. Career advancement and getting justice as they see it is plenty of inspiration. This case had all the ingredients to inspire foul play; famous players, racial innuendos, double homicide, previous abuse. What more could a policeman want that was trying to make his mark forever?

You go through the pains with the manufacturer of the gloves to explain why they did indeed fit O.J. Simpson. I never doubted the gloves fit. Cochran did a masterful job with the gloves at the trial. Why not? It was the prosecutions obligation to prove the gloves fit. Your smoke and mirrors games utilize a theme. If you can prove that theme you consider it a victory. Time and again your themes are irrelevant. Even if the gloves fit that doesn't mean O.J. committed the murders, but you are so pleased with yourself that you can get someone to say the gloves fit. O.J. therefore you are guilty. Nowhere during this fitting exercise did you show the cuts on the gloves where blood could have passed or them matching the cuts on O.J.'s hands. What I need to see is a corresponding mark or cut on the gloves that correspond with the major cut on O.J.'s hand. Something that confirms the cut could have taken place during the commission of crime. This is the same nothing you had with the shoes. You have yet to add one scintilla of new evidence in this trial that would convince the jury or this reader that O.J. is the killer. You are running out of pages and I am running out of patience. You don't even plan on keeping your promise to me, do you? Where is the evidence that convinces me that beyond a shadow of a doubt, O.J. is the murderer? Actually, the opposite effect is happening. Examining the evidence this closely is making it clearer than ever that it was not reasonable for him to be the killer, but on we go with your shrewd tricks to win this civil case and get this money moved around. Maybe there will be some knockouts in the twelfth and final round; a lucky punch or two and the defense go down for the count. We'll see.

Dr. Huizenga returns to the stand. He is the guy that examined O.J. after the murders. He was looking for cuts and bruises associated with this crime. He testifies that O.J. was physically fit enough to commit them. I'm not a doctor, but it doesn't seem that O.J. was examined thoroughly enough to come to that conclusion. It takes a lot for an almost 50-year-old guy to subdue a fit young 25-year-old when all he had is a knife. If Ronald puts up a struggle, which is what seems to have happened, what information do we have that this aging athlete could handle the aerobic demands of killing two people? Wouldn't they have had to put O.J. through some stress, mobility, and strength tests to determine if he was up to this kind of battle? Golf, this is not! There is no evidence that O.J. was doing anything special to keep himself in shape to whoop on 25 year-olds. He didn't have a motive to be in a rage over Ronald. What would get him to that level of anger making him take on a strong young man? As a competitor all his life, you would expect O.J. to pick his battles wisely, especially when his freedom is at stake. Yes, he may have lost it and believed he could take on this young stud, but, under the circumstances, if Nicole were truly his target, once Ron got on the scene, it is more likely he would pass. The absence of testing O.J.'s stamina makes me doubt the accuracy of your speculation. Put O.J. on a stress machine and watch his heart rate or do something to verify his ability to accomplish this crime. Again, you give us too much guesswork.

On June 17th the doctor examines O.J. again and finds three cuts and several abrasions on his hands. This is five days after the crime. What is everyone waiting for? What happened to his hands in the meantime? O.J. claims he gets cuts "'nicks and stuff'" from playing golf and the ' *I bleed all the time*"[3]. I just play racket ball and I get cuts all the time. Look at your hands right now lawyers, any cuts?

Now you bring us through a journey that demonstrates a bit of the game of lawyering. One of your partners was to handle the part of the proof that O.J. was the killer. He was taking on the spousal abuse history and was prepared to put on experts that would testify that O.J. profiled as a wife killer. These guys had a mountain of credentials. They believed that O.J. committed a revenge killing. An amateur killed Nicole; not a Colombian hit man. You insist on removing the possibility that there was a bad drug collection deal going down and want to introduce the absurdity of a Colombian cartel guy. No, Dan, if Faye Resnick owed some money to her drug dealer or Nicole was getting a delivery and Ronald came on to the scene accidentally, nasty stuff could have happened. It did not have to be a murder planned out in Cali, Columbia by some drug lord, just a plain local collection gone awry.

There are redundancies in my critique of your analysis, because you insist on repeating similar theories that are silly, dumb, naïve, and or deceptive. I am following your book, page-by-page, argument-by-argument, and responding to each. The repetition is of your making. I feel I have an obligation to comment each time you make an absurd statement, otherwise, by default, it could be assumed I accept your arguments. Each time though, I try to add an additional look at how attorneys work their points and either wears down the adversary or hope if they repeat a point enough it will sound like the truth. This is wearing on me, but not causing me to back down.

Notes:

[1] **Daniel Petrocelli, *Triumph of Justice*** (Crown 1998) pg. 417

[2] Ibid, pg 416

TWENTY-FOUR

Where to Deposit the Thermometer

More Degrees than a Thermometer

You dress up Kato in a tie and succeed in limiting his testimony or he may backfire on you as a key witness. You carefully present the trip to McDonald's as an attempt to set up an alibi. I fail to see what kind of alibi this created except for your re-digging the hole of premeditated murder. There are problems with that theory. If the killings were more than a spontaneous rage and had planning, then we have to consider if the plan made any sense. With the time constraints that O.J. would be facing if he were planning to murder Nicole as you insist, going off for a hamburger would be a very bad plan. There are too many things that can't be controlled when timing is critical. You know how slow a fast food place can be. Long lines, customer hold ups, things to straighten out on an order, and any number of possibilities. O.J. would certainly have picked a more reliable alibi that he had more control over if he had masterminded this murder. This is why your story about how all this happens seems nonsensical. Can you imagine O.J., saying, "Come on Kato let's go have a hamburger." and then thinking, "That will certainly convince people that I couldn't have committed Nicole's murder." The great hamburger alibi! It makes you wonder if he could have thought that up all by himself or stole it from a cheap novel.

All you are able to get from Kato is old news. Kato merely repeated what we already knew; thumps at 10:40 to 10:50 and seeing Park at 10:54. Useless information if you are seeking hard facts that O.J. is the killer. You have no theory regarding the thumps. Do they incriminate or exonerate O.J.? The thumps mean nothing by themselves. What was O.J. doing banging on a wall three times? What explanation do you have for them? A staggering killer on the run? Kato's time recollections are so imprecise as to be at best, useless. They show that O.J. didn't have the time to commit the murders. Yet, you put this lightweight on the stand as though he has something of value. I guess you are hoping by insinuation, since you want him as a witness, he must be telling something of value.

Because he has yet to take money you want us to believe he is a valuable witness. I don't know what he would have of value that isn't already out in the public. If he is hiding something then what kind of witness is he? Is he saving the *big story* for another day and some big bucks? You and I don't know, but to feel he is a more valuable witness because he hasn't received money doesn't tell me anything of value. Hamburger, thump, clock estimate. What a story!

TWENTY-FIVE

Not So Simple

BLOOD SIMPLE

Mr. Petrocelli you are feeling confident before O.J. was to take the stand. You feel that your forensic evidence was *"...unassailable"*. This is a strong description, counselor. Other than the Bruno Magli shoe inference, your forensics were the same as the criminal trial. The experts said *something was wrong* and yet you want to dismiss any questioning. Are you trying to tell your readers that nothing was wrong? Only the experts were wrong. You have not brought me there with rehashing the old evidence.

You take exception with O.J. wanting to finalize his custody hearings and delay your proceedings. Criticizing a father for wanting custody and suggesting it was part of the overall strategy to portray O.J. in a better light is not winning over my vote. A favorable ruling in O.J.'s behalf on the custody matter would imply that the judge did not see any risk to the children being cared for by their father. So be it. You call the custody matter a strategic move on O.J.'s part and he is just playing games. The judge resolved the matter and scheduled O.J.'s testimony.

You put on your witnesses to establish that the forensic evidence pointed clearly to O.J.'s guilt. They testified that the hair fibers found in the cap was similar to O.J.'s. You didn't tell us how similar or if they could have been similar to his son's or how many other hair types were also similar. The blood evidence on the gate, Simpson's

233

socks, and the Bronco all suggest O.J. was the killer according to your interpretation. Not enough information here to work with other than gross speculation, Mr. P. Cotton fibers on Ron's shirt, Simpson's socks and the gloves at Rockingham all subjects that have been addressed before and reasonably challenged. You don't want to believe there are any other explanations. The reader of this critique has heard many reasonable explanations, all of which should not have escaped your logical mind.

You insist that the socks with the meager amount of blood found in O.J.'s bedroom was highly incriminating. I have several serious problems with this supposition. For O.J. to be wearing $40 dress socks with a sweat suit and Bruno Maglis doesn't fit. The amount of blood and getting through a sweat suit is questionable. But, you have no problem with these issues and no explanations. This is your evidence and you have the burden to make it clear that there are no questions regarding the conclusions they provide. You want O.J. to explain why these are not appropriate. How did that become his burden? You do offer some DNA degrading explanations, but again this is part of technology that experts have trouble finding agreement. All along you insist that there was no planting of evidence. The socks give a good example of the confusion. When first examined there were no sign of blood, only later was blood found and in a strange way.

We do know that 1.5 cc's of blood was missing from the vile that can't be explained. Again, and again all of this was gone through thoroughly at the criminal trial. That jury wasn't persuaded the evidence was enough to convict. I don't know what happened that night in June of 94 and unless you were there, at best you only have guesses. Since it is not unheard of for the L.A. police to have problems with evidence, I don't see how, with the suspicious nature of what has been submitted, that one could summarily dismiss the possibility of evidence tampering. You say that the blood was found before O.J. returned from Chicago, therefore there was no blood to spread around. You don't show us the logs of collection so how can we just accept your statement. The casual manner you present your arguments demand more backup data to be convincing. The contamination of the blood, possible switching, even if inadvertent, and or poor handling of evidence all lead to confusion and something not smelling right about what we are presented.

You know that O.J. isn't going to accuse the police of planting. His best strategy is to answer with is "I don't know". Since this is your evidence, it is your responsibility to explain how blood got there, O.J. shouldn't be required to answer questions that require speculation on his part. He did not plea the Fifth Amendment, as Furhman did in the criminal trial.

It is time to turn to Kato's testimony. You believe that his testimony regarding the timeline was crucial. Since Kato comes off a bit flaky, whatever he says is hard to take seriously. His accounting for time assumes many important factors. Was his clock accurate? How good is his memory? If the thumps were at 10:40 O.J. is innocent. Kato's estimate was that between 1 and five minutes. That's a wide spread under the circumstances. Kato says the thumps were between 10:40 and 10:50. That means Kato could be giving O.J. the out if you use the 10:40 and there is no reason not to do so since it was possible according to Kato. At 10:50 O.J. would only have 10 minutes to get cleaned up and ready to meet Park the driver who was in the driveway waiting for O.J. None of these time frames makes sense. Because amount of time, or the lack of time is an essential ingredient in the murder trial. The reader can plainly see that Mr. P. isn't going to nail O.J. with Mr. Kato.

When you promise simple answers you want us to go along with your theories. The blood evidence, time frames and motives all are very complex issues and require careful analysis before arriving at any conclusion. So far your evidence hasn't permitted me to be convinced O.J. is the killer.

Notes:

[1] Daniel Petrocelli, *Triumph of Justice*, (Crown, 1998), pg. 440

TWENTY-SIX

Bust

Alibi Buster

Allen Park, the limo driver, has nothing more than old stuff to offer. He did not see the Bronco parked on Rockingham between 10:23 and 10:40. He saw Kato at 10:54. The thumps happened at 10:51 according to your version of this story. Let's subtract 6-7 minutes for O.J. to get from the crime scene to Rockingham leaving us at 10:45. The *heys* were reported at 10:40 so that leaves five minutes for the dirty deed to begin and end. Given this time line, O.J. has six minutes to shower, change his clothes, do the wash, clean up all the blood, gather his things, and get downstairs to leave for Chicago. With all this racing around, killing, cleaning, dressing, thumping, packing, O.J. is signing autographs along the way to Chicago without a bandage on his bloody multi-cut hands. My fingers have trouble tying this gibberish together. How does your mind and mouth handle processing all the garbage? You must have good training to scale mountains of intellectual manure.

Park claims he sees a black man walking across the driveway. You want us to believe this is O.J. How do you know it wasn't Jason or someone else? You don't want to go there. Jason fits the description Park gives. You also have the challenge of dealing with conflicting testimony from Park as to which side of the driveway he saw this man go up. You had to put a special spin on Park's testimony so he doesn't appear confused.

Now we come to the missing "…*small, dark bag*"[1]. How small was it and what could it have contained? You want us to believe that O.J. was in control of the bag and that it contained the murder clothes and the knife. Was it big enough to hold these items? Did anyone ask either Park or Kato these questions? I can't find any evidence that the size of the bag was determined. It seems better for you and the prosecution to leave the details alone and let our imagination take over. If the clothes and knife were in the small black bag then they couldn't be in the Louis Vuitton bag. If they were not in the LV bag then he didn't need anyone to help him dispose of the evidence. He carried the stuff on to Chicago with the challenge of disposing it somewhere along the way, unnoticed. This would be very dangerous for he certainly wouldn't want to be caught with it on his person. He must have done a great job of magically making the small bag disappear. You want O.J. to be a magician just like you, Mr. P. Not likely, he doesn't have the advanced training like you.

I am not as certain as you are that Park didn't see the Bronco. He may have, but didn't recollect. People do miss seeing things, especially when distracted with an important task or just plain don't notice. He could be right because the Bronco was gone, being driven by Jason. Ever hear of a son driving his father's SUV? He admitted during the criminal trial he wasn't looking for a Bronco, that could explain why he didn't see it. You criticize Marcia Clark ever posing a question to him in that fashion.

Despite your insistence that evidence presented on the blood, hair, clothes, shoes, gloves, photographs, and witnesses prove that Simpson was the killer; I still don't see it. Dan, aren't you puzzled about a knit hat being worn in the summer in Beverly Hills by O.J. Simpson? What's the sense in that? This makes a feeble and suspicious disguise. It would have looked strange to Nicole seeing O.J. dressed up in a knit hat, gloves, and a black sweat suit in summer being invited to come out and talk. Picture O.J. ringing the bell, (Oh, sorry, I forgot it wasn't working) knocking on the door and waiting for Nicole to answer. There was probably one of those intercom systems in this million-dollar condo. Nicole comes to the door, peeks through and sees O.J. in this outfit. Quite a sight! Now what happens? Would she ask him in or even open the door? I highly doubt it.

If she did, we can imagine the episode going something like this.

"O.J. what are you doing here at this hour and what is that outfit you are wearing?" exclaims Nicole.

O.J. replies, "Open the door, I need to talk to you."

Nicole, opening the door, "What do you want?" We now have to imagine O.J. forcing himself behind her, pulling his knife and slitting her throat. Sometime in the middle of all this Ron shows up with the glasses and gets attacked by the *knit hat killer.*

This scene is too improbable for this reader to believe. It is too hard to get behind someone in a doorway, too difficult to imagine Nicole stepping out of the house and exposing herself in that way at this hour of the night. If this bizarre plan was on O.J.'s mind, how would he deal with the possibility the children might be awake? Would he plan to go to the house and kill Nicole with the children inside? She might scream and frighten them. There would be blood all over the house. That is not a real life scenario. Mr. P you have not given us one reasonable premeditated plan befitting even an enraged killer. You have not walked us through how you thought O.J. might have planned a murder with the intent not to get caught. All of the elements here, including this outfit, the time, and the place are not conducive to getting rid of an ex-wife.

If you asked a group of school kids to write a murder mystery, I would be disappointed if they came up with such a lame murder plan. They would all tell you that if this is O.J. or anyone considering a plan they would be just plain dumb. He may be arrogant, and even lie, but not that dumb, Dan. No one is that dumb, at least when it comes to premeditated murder. Sorry, not exactly no one, but you get the point. I was slipping into your world of hyperbole. Shame on me!

You finish up the physical evidence with FBI expert William Bodziak. He establishes that there are Bruno Magli shoeprints at the scene. Okay, we have given you that, but you haven't told us who was wearing the shoes. It could have been Jason or one of Nicole's many lovers. The more you avoid the examination that someone else could have been wearing the shoes, the more you show how desperate your quest for legal victory has corrupted any chance for justice.

You call the shoe evidence "...*pristine*".[2] What a nice vocabulary you have, but it is lacking a vital element, whose feet were in them and when? These are hollow victories. You denied us the answer when you had the opportunity to ask Jason. You never asked him where he was that night or any questions that might have implicated him in the crime. There may have been several motives for Jason to do it and we know he had the opportunity. O.J. might be protecting him and cannot tell what he really knows. He is a possible suspect, but you didn't show the moral courage to ask the important questions. I am left wondering why. The only answer I can come up with is that you were afraid. Afraid his answers might ruin your opportunity to move money around. Each time you bring up these questionable pieces of evidence doesn't your conscience tell you that you are betraying the law and its purpose? If it did, you probably wouldn't hear it with all the noise from the outside saying "Way to go, get the gold, no matter what it takes". It is obvious the truth has lost its chance to come forward.

The Juice is now in your crosshairs. You can't wait to put him on the stand and "...dismantle"[3] him. You want to catch him in lies and convince the jury he is the murderer. Since you know he is not going to confess, you need to stack enough lies and suspicious behavior to get the jury to believe he did it. In researching other opinions of this case, I read Vincent Bugliosi's book, *Outrage!* He is an LA prosecutor that has won 105 of 106 cases including the Manson murders of Sharon Tate and friends. His book is very critical of how Clark and Darden handled the case. He is also critical of how the *Dream Team* performed, despite their victory. He makes an important point when explains that any good attorney can make someone look like a liar. This is a powerful and far reaching observation. He devotes many pages instructing how Marcia and Darden should have cross-examined the witnesses. It is scary to know that innocent people can testify in their own behalf and a skillful lawyer can make them look like a liar. Unfortunately, he is right. A powerful cross-examination can confuse people, put them on the defense, and effectively paint a very incorrect picture for the jury. This is why many lawyers will not let their clients testify. Not because they are guilty, but because they are easy prey for a bulldog attorney going after the jugular vein. Add this on top of the possibility in this case that the witness is protecting a son and you get a situation that distorts the truth for all the wrong reasons. Yet, you are waving victory banners and beating your chest over subjects that are likely not what they appear to be.

Notes:

[1] Daniel Petrocelli, *Triumph of Justice*, (Crown, 1998), pg. 466

TWENTY-SEVEN
Manipulation Day

Examination Day

You are feeling good today, counselor. Your guess is the judge will permit you to execute your strategy of positioning your presentation so that the jury will be under your direction, your analysis, and your verdict. Positioning is a good thing. You elbowed your way to the front of the line. There is no way your opponent will have the last word possibly influencing the jury against you. Your next position statement sums up how you see your mission.

"More than anything, I wanted Simpson's first appearance before the jury to be on our terms, confrontational, accusatory examination in which we would throw everything we had at him."[1]

That is a mouthful. Break this man down with your legal weapons. You wanted this more than anything. This is a confession that nothing is more important than breaking this man down to appear a liar. You sound like a lawyer in a rage; a rage that puts decency aside, truth aside, justice aside. You remind me of the lawyers you spoke of earlier, ones that passionately deceive and lie. These are great weapons in the conflict of confusing a jury. You have been preparing for your Super Bowl and you are in the locker room getting pumped for battle. You can't wait to rip the head off your opponent. A little cheating here and there is no big deal. The winning is more important than anything.

You get help from your partner, Peter. Together you prepare an outline because you want to *"...attack him hard"*[2]. O.J. has not yet testified and you are counting the lies. Your "*…steamroller of impeachment*"[3] forecasts this for you in advance. You are going to "'…*Fuhrmanize*"[4] Simpson. What a novel concept! You use one of your key witnesses as the role model to make Simpson appear a liar. If you can get O.J. to look like as big a liar as Fuhrman, you might win this case. We are left wondering if you can get O.J. to the level of perjury or using the 5th.

In preparation for the examination you get hold of O.J.'s phone records. You find what you consider a "*…piece of gold*".[5] I am not impressed because you have given other evidence similar evaluations and they ended up more like fool's gold. You find that at 6:56 pm on June 12th, O.J. called his message answering system and retrieved a message about 5 minutes long. You conclude this is the message that Paula Barbieri left; one of those "*Dear John*" messages. You need this to contribute to O.J.'s motive and state of mind. There is no way to know for sure it was Paula's message he listened to or someone else's. You don't know anything else, except that he received some message. This is unimpressive thinking and obvious molding of evidence you are serving up today.

Another advantage your team prepares is having your assistant, Yvette, handing you documents for presentation to the jury like a nurse handing instruments to a surgeon. You plan to do some cutting up here; slicing your witness into little pieces. Suppose you got a good laugh conjuring up this analogy? It's no surprise that your writing is getting sleazy.

Fred Goldman gives you a pep talk before you start. "*I know you are going to kill the son-of-a-bitch!*"[6] You both have murder on your minds. You head to the execution chamber from your office and encounter a media feeding frenzy. Things are working out just as you planned. Lot's of publicity with you in the spotlight. Legal history being made and you are front and center. You must have been pretty proud of yourself.

Before the trial, O.J. and his family and friends said a prayer. This upsets you. What's the problem? Maybe their prayer was that you be honest, fair, and seek justice. Maybe he hoped that this wouldn't be reduced to a spectacle for the purpose of making money. What a callous nature you must have to scorn his right to say a prayer before this ordeal was to begin.

The big moment is upon you. The world was waiting for O.J. to take the stand. Would you be able to prove he was guilty? The next half hour was all-important to your career. You were going to be judged. You start thinking about the possibility of failure and how ugly that would be. You make this very personal and I give you that right, but it speaks to an agenda that is not strictly in the interest of justice, only the consequences of winning or losing and how it will make you look.

Notes:

[1] Daniel Petrocelli, *Triumph of Justice*, (Crown, 1998), pg.472

[2] Ibid, pg. 472

[3] Ibid pg. 473

[4] Ibid, pg. 473

[5] Ibid, pg. 473

6 Ibid. pg 475

TWENTY-EIGHT

Show Me the Pack

A Pack of Lies

We have arrived at the essence of what this trial is all about. O.J. is going to testify. He didn't have to, but he decided to take the stand. This act of testifying has an implicit message because it was voluntary. This witness, more correctly, the accused has nothing to hide. He is willing to be questioned knowing that you will be in his face, unrelenting, and using all your weapons to distort the truth. Not testifying silently implies guilt or at least hiding something. We know most lawyers do not like their clients on the stand, unless there is a very good reason. This is a war of words, strategy, interpretation, delivery and speculation, a battle between the lawyer and the accused.

Since Mr. P has promised to expose O.J. committing lie after lie, I have been waiting all these pages for this crucial part. I want to take all your claims of lying and analyze them. After evaluating whether it was indeed a lie, I will determine if the lie has value in incriminating O.J. as a killer. Now we are faced with defining what a lie is. There are *white lies* that are not necessarily evil. "Darling, that was a great roast you cooked this evening." It may not have been great, but the effort put in cooking it made it great. On the other end of the scale is perjury. A clear lie with unassailable proof it is untrue. "I was at the diner at 8." Yet six sober, solid citizens, with good eyesight and no reason to lie, saw you at the crime scene. This is the evidence we would like to have. This doesn't happen often, so most of us must make a judgment regarding whether the witness is lying or not. Even good and wise people can disagree based on their perceptions of the witness. There are different skill levels of liars.

In this case, O.J. has been through all the accusations many, many times. He has had a chance to rehearse the answer to each and every possible question thrown at him. Bright, experienced lawyers on how to answer each question have coached him. O.J. is aware of what might be asked that could incriminate him. He is prepared to the best of his ability to answer your toughest questions. Before O.J. got on the stand he must have been both nervous and confident. I don't believe for a moment that he thought he could say something that would remove all cause for doubt that he was guilty of these crimes. I don't think he was convinced you could make him look like the killer; either because he was so well rehearsed, innocent, or both. His lawyers must have felt the same way or they wouldn't have let him take the stand. He is aware of the possibility of losing this case, but not because he confessed or said something convictable. This is a classic battle. You are prepared to totally destroy O.J. and his willingness to face you to have a jury decide what really happened.

I am going to keep score. Each of your claims of a lie is going to be evaluated based on its incriminating value, relevancy, and as part of the whole picture. Let's go, I am ready. Let's see how well you fulfill your promise.

First question: You start by attacking the area of spousal abuse. You ask O.J. to give you the details for the beating in 1989, three years prior to the murder. The abuse was public knowledge and Nicole's picture with all the bruises was shown to the world. He had publicly apologized for hitting his wife. You want to establish that O.J. is a violent person and had serious problems with Nicole. You specifically ask O.J. if he got physical with Nicole. He didn't like your choice of words and challenged you. He said he "...*touched*"[1] Nicole. You don't like his choice of words. Both of you are debating the degree of contact O.J. had with Nicole. Everyone agrees there was contact, but you are now debating how to characterize the contact. O.J. denies he punched Nicole. Nicole told the police that she was punched and her hair was pulled. To back up your questioning you ask, "*Nicole had to go to the hospital, right?*"[2] O.J. claims that he suggested Nicole go to

248

the hospital. You don't like the implication of that statement. O.J. further states that it was Cowlings and himself that suggested Nicole go. You flatly state that O.J. is lying. This is lie number one. Unless you get Cowlings to confirm your contention that O.J. did not share in the suggestion, your first claim is not backed up by facts. This whole exchange does not even rate in the world of incriminating lie. Score: O.J. – One, Dan – Zero.

You now ask O.J. if he went to the hospital that night for treatment. This is a low sarcastic question. You are trying to disprove that Nicole also hit O.J. You know that she could have hit O.J. and even provoked the incident without O.J. ever having to go to the hospital.

You show another picture of Nicole a few days later with bruises. For dramatic emphasis, you make sure the picture stays on the screen so the damage would sink in to the jury's mind. You now claim "...*for half an hour all he had done was tell one lie after another about her.*"[3] You have only shown us one example of what you consider a lie. Did O.J. advise his wife to go to the hospital? She did go to the hospital. You have no proof that he didn't give that advice. Are you hiding this half hour of lies? Since I expect you would reveal them to me, I went back and reread your last pages to see what I had missed. Since you can't get him to say such slop you put words in his mouth. This is despicable. Can't you just stay with his testimony and not invent what you hoped he would say? (I just caught you in a lie, which should give O.J. another point!)

You ask a nasty dilemma question, "'*So, in your mind, you weren't battering her that night, were you?*'"[4] He frankly answers that at the time no, but based on what he has learned, yes, he did batter Nicole. He admits he was battering, no denial, and no lie. You consider this a sly answer.

Even though O.J. did not lie to you, you admit, "*Nevertheless, I was setting him up.*"[5] The jury is shown letters for O.J. to Nicole trying to win her back. You characterize these letters as apologies for the beating. O.J. doesn't accept your definition. What difference does this make? O.J. wanted to get back with Nicole. You want the letters to be apologies and he calls them something else. Is this really going to lead us to believing O.J. is the type of individual that would kill? These word games don't fall into my category of incriminating lies. Did you produce a *gotcha confession,* NO. They won't even be added to any pile of information to be processed. You go on to point out one of the strong reasons that I believe O.J. did not commit the murders, the prenuptial agreement. In the letters he agrees to amend the prenuptial agreement to stipulate he would forfeit half of his net worth if he ever hit her again. It is this agreement that gives suspicion to Nicole's claims of being hit. If she were to be hit again, all her frantic money problems would be solved. We have been on this subject, but I am surprised you reintroduce this concept to support your contention that O.J. is the killer. Are you dumb or what? Thanks; in my book this line of logic is helpful to O.J.

At this point I am catching my breath. You are a man of smoke and mirrors. You are giving out a whole lot of smoke here and are polishing those mirrors. You point out that all the prenuptial agreement said was O.J. would never hit Nicole in the future. You congratulate his lawyer for the careful wording. Now, when O.J. is asked if he agreed to tear up the prenuptial agreement if he ever hit her again, he says yes. Your conclusion is that O.J. finally admitted that he beat Nicole. Dan, he said he *hit* her. He took responsibility for the bruises in the picture, but you want all this elevated into an admission that he *beat* her. You chastise his attorney for letting his client admit to hitting Nicole. These are nonsensical word games. I still fail to see where you caught O.J. in a lie that is incriminating. Score: O.J. – Two; Mr. P Nothing.

Because O.J. wouldn't admit that the letter he wrote to Nicole was an apology you want to add that on to his lie pile. The intent of the letter is in the mind of the writer. What evidence do you have that his intent was other than what he claims it to be. Remember, innocent until *Proven Guilty.* I am giving this one to O.J., also. Sorry, Dan. Score: O.J. – Three; Mr. P – Zero.

The next trap you lay to catch O.J. in a lie is in respect to how important was the preservation of his image. You quote from a book he co-authored that he confesses to being image conscious. O.J. agrees that at the time the book was written that was true. What a stroke of good fortune for O.J. to admit his guilt, you crow! I don't get the point. What does this admission have to do with confessing to murder? You ask about other references to preserving an image. He doesn't specifically recall the passages. You refer to him saying,

"'The ghetto makes you want to hide your real identity from cops, from teachers, and even from yourself. And it forces you to build up false images – humble, swaggering, casual, or tough…'"[6]

You take this as a damning admission. I don't see it that way or the point you are trying to make. If he wrote a book admitting taking steps to not hide being from the ghetto, it implies he is past the problem. It is no longer a game that needs to be played. You want it to put everyone on notice that you can't trust the actions of the person you are seeing. A book confessing this weakness does the opposite of what you imply. It is saying that O.J. doesn't need to pretend anymore. You try to get O.J. to admit to a jury that he is not currently honest with the image he is portraying. Your line of attack confuses him. You want the jury to read into all of this that O.J. hides his true personality and shouldn't be trusted. This is all a bunch of dribbling, legalized posturing. Nowhere does it speak to the reason we are traveling through this book. Did you catch O.J. in a lie here? Even if you did, it's a bad question. No points for either side just a lot of wasted time for the reader and jury, but billable hours for you. After reading this book, don't you dare hide behind your editor, Peter Knobler. Every word in this book is your responsibility, right? O.J. takes responsibility for his book and so must you.

After you get O.J. to acknowledge that he is capable of lying and has lied you want to use this as a basis of condemning him as a liar through this whole interrogation. This is a nasty piece of maneuvering. You need to ask yourself if you have ever lied or are capable of lying. Now does that make you a lying attorney? You admitted it to us earlier that lawyers like you will lie. This subterfuge does not get to the facts of the case. Ask O.J. your questions and let's evaluate the answers, forget the legal Nintendo for the moment.

You continue to press the point about Nicole's beating to get O.J. to admit he hurt her. He doesn't accept your description once again. He agrees she was bruised, but you want him to say she was hurt. You call his denial of your description a lie. In my book, it is merely a disagreement on terminology not a lie. The picture of Nicole is easily worth the 1,000 words; all this banter is semantic wrestling. I just can't count this as an incriminating lie, Dan. You claim your prowess at showing O.J. as a liar in front of the jury. As far as I am concerned, you have yet to land one in the strike zone. We have merely gone over old turf and the spectators have been fully exposed to Nicole's injuries at the hand of O.J.

Around you go again; you will not let up on this subject. Because O.J. talks about the beating on a sports show you believe he is downplaying the seriousness of the incident. You equate that to lying when it is necessary to protect his image. He doesn't disagree with you. Then you twist this admission into meaning that he felt Nicole's bruises were no big deal. O.J. admits it was a big deal to them. Remember they went to court over the incident and O.J. agreed not to do it again. O.J. testified that he believed this was not a big deal to the audience watching the sports show. This is a matter of opinion, not lying. No one likes to hear of anyone hitting their spouse, especially if it is an important icon, supposed role model. Sadly, there are so many reports; one of them is not a big deal. Sorry you missed an opportunity to nail O.J. even harder here by accusing him of lying to the American public. Shame on you, counselor; don't feel too bad, though. Life would have still gone on as usual even if you were quicker on your feet. Your team congratulates you for a great job of breaking O.J. down.

Now you want to catch O.J. lying to Frank Olson of Hertz Corp. He told Mr. Olsen that the charges were brought because he was being used as a scapegoat. O.J. doesn't remember saying that. You claim you have a witness that would testify to his using that word. This is another instance of so what! O.J. admitted he was concerned about his public image. He said that he would put a spin on things to protect it. We are only talking about a small incident that is already firmly planted in our minds. O.J. hit Nicole hard enough to produce those photographs and he accepted responsibility for his actions. You are so intent on establishing that O.J. is a liar and a violent man capable of planning and executing a knife murder you will distort the obvious, over and over until it becomes your truth. This is a consistent theme in your lawyering, pound, pound, and pound some more. After enough pounding someone might break. What is really broken is a desire to get at the truth and any reasonable conclusions. Your analysis of this first round was equivalent to a knockout round. You had O.J. reeling against the ropes. All I observed was old information, done and redone at the criminal trial with no new dimension. You give us nothing in the way of catching O.J. in a serious lie that helps one believe that he is capable of a double homicide.

The history of domestic abuse in O.J.'s case was important to you. The criminal prosecution didn't do a good job in this area according to your critiques. Judge Ito specifically barred testimony in this area because it was dated and hearsay. You want to work this information in your case. Spousal abuse is a subject that has so many variables. When, why, what was the provocation, was there appropriate future conduct, the degree of the abuse, the questions are too many. After you try to find out the answers, you have to then draw the difficult line to murder. You state, however, this line of questioning was more for a demonstration that O.J. would lie than to prove abuse led to murder. You didn't prove either point so far.

During the next round of questioning you want O.J. to admit that he was upset at losing Nicole. He turns it around on you. O.J. says that it was Nicole that was pursuing him. O.J. insists that friends and family all knew that Nicole was pursing him. To trap O.J. you produce a letter from Nicole that confirms she was looking to reconcile. Two months later they were back together. You use proof that O.J. was telling the truth about her interest in getting back together and turn it around to a document that angered Paula. This anger is supposed to have triggered a breakup call the morning of the murders. Again, you want it both ways. You produce proof that O.J. was telling the truth about Nicole wanting to reconcile after you challenge him on the subject. This proof now becomes a weapon in your arsenal that Paula is going to dump O.J. The major problem is the letter is dated March of 1993, months before the murder. You produce no evidence that Paula saw it or what her reaction might have been to the letter.

The subject of who dumped whom is important to you. O.J. says he wanted to get back with Nicole, but on different terms. He was concerned that it might take some time for Nicole to change her ways. He told her he would want to try reconciliation for a year to see if things would change. You produce an article in _National Inquirer_ that tells of O.J. begging Nicole to come back. He tells you the story is false. You won't accept that they might be wrong. O.J. insisted 9emphatically that the story was wrong. You interpret this as an example of lying. Pushing his, buttons on this made you feel effective. From this you conclude that O.J. is lying under oath and we should rely on a report from the *National Inquirer* instead. I don't see where?

You then turn to a 911 tape recording nine months before Nicole's death. She sounds afraid. " *'He's going to beat the shit out of me!'*" she cries. O.J. says that Nicole was putting on an act for the police. Why do you not think this possible? Do you really believe every 911 call is legitimate? Don't forget the prenuptial agreement of $15 million if he abuses her. In Nicole's words, is her *shit* worth $15 million? O.J.'s actions in the past do not make it very likely that he would be a threat again to Nicole. Perhaps he likes his $15 million too much. Perhaps he likes his lifestyle too much. Remember according to you he is cunning and calculating. Why would he blow all those millions for the satisfaction of striking Nicole? He's gone through too much bad publicity and too much hassle already. Whatever he might be thinking, it is unlikely he would risk the cash and bad press to hit Nicole again. Because you can't find a lie in his argument with the *National Inquirer* you create a new charge of him coming up with a "*...wise ass..*"[8] answer. This part of your book is hanging out in vulgar territory. You lose your grip when you ask O.J. if he acquired "*...an animal-like look*"[9] when he got angry. He answers that he never looked in a mirror when he got angry. That sounds sensible to me. Do you look in the mirror when you are angry? This is a silly line of questioning. Will it help you convict O.J. that he looks scary when angry?

O.J. insists that it was Nicole who wanted back into the relationship. You would not hear of it, but you think it was Nicole's financial problems causing the difficulties. She was bouncing from one man to another. She had an abortion and no prospects of earning any money. She seems to have loved the lifestyle that O.J. provided. He had the money and was generous with her family and friends. Why wouldn't she want that lifestyle back? O.J. was riding the dream life and she got to enjoy the benefits of celebrity and money. Centerfold models on his arm, movie roles, golf, and travel, adoring fans were all on his balance sheet. Nicole had custody of his kids and O.J. wanted them back. All you want us to see is a deeply disturbed man so tormented that he is willing to give up a life of fame and success to beat up and kill his ex-wife. It is easy to understand that this couple had a lot of tension that lead to nasty encounters that sometimes turned physical.

If O.J. could truly not control his rage, there would have been more than just bruises. Yes, at one time he did the wrong thing, but there is no evidence that he consistently lost control of himself and acted out his anger.

You felt the jury was not buying O.J.'s explanations. You had crafted your questions well enough to make him lose believability. You were good at making O.J. squirm. You prove to us how effective legal bullying can be.

It is a big victory for you when Nicole's diary is permitted as evidence. You consider this critical for establishing her state of mind. Nicole's entry on May 22nd was "*We've officially split.*"[10] O.J. says they broke up on May 10th. The expression, *officially split*, is incorrect in that it implies some legal imprimatur. It doesn't make any reference to whose idea it was to split. With all of the back and forth going on in their relationship it is hard to know what is real. Another tantrum, another kiss and make up. What we have here is O.J.'s word versus an entry in a diary. A diary kept by a 30-year-old woman who could be the beneficiary of a prenuptial being rescinded. There are too many variables to definitively say what the truth might have been. You must prevail on getting the jury to believe that O.J. had a reason to be angry. You say this anger proved he had a motive for the killings. I do not see the links strong enough to make a connection. The evening of the murders contained just one of many similar occurrences that were negative to all parties. Not unusual behavior at all in the life of O.J. and Nicole Simpson from what we are told.

Your introduction of O.J.'s letter telling Nicole not include him in her lie to the IRS give you an attempt to show the nasty side of O.J. You state this letter provoked a "*...vile arguments*"[11] O.J. denies your claim. You make up a story that O.J. threatened Nicole over the letter and he was going to report her to the IRS. He denies that and says the letter was merely a request for her to straighten out the problem with the IRS and leave him out of the deal. You insist that Nicole hung up on O.J. and this angered him. According to your version of the story, he didn't care for her treatment and retaliated in anger. O.J. claims he did not feel that way. It sounds like you are just making this story up to fit your plot. In asking the questions that way O.J. is put on the defensive. This is not an exercise in finding the truth, but a show to manipulate the juror's impressions.

Now you read from Nicole's diary quoting O.J. saying, "'you hung up on me last night. You're going to pay for this, bitch."[12] O.J. says this is "*Absolutely false!*"[13] You shout at O.J. asking him if he told Nicole, "'*you are holding money from the IRS. You're going to jail, you @#$%%%!*'"[14] O.J. replies, "'*I have never used that phrase, ever, with anybody in my life!*'"[15] You don't believe O.J. This is your opportunity to prove that he pulled a *Mark Fuhrman*. Mark said he never said nigger and the Dream Team proved he was lying. Since you never produce proof of his saying this, O.J. wins this round.

Nicole's diary goes on to quote O.J. cursing numerous times. You shout, get into his face, make up stories, and go off in a huff when he denies your fairytales. Nicole has impeached herself in so many ways with her lifestyle there is no good reasons to believe her diary entries are true. She committing a crime against the IRS and trying to drag O.J. into it causes this whole episode. He wants nothing of it. Yet, you want to crown her the sweet princess of truth with diary entries that can't be challenged.

O.J. is denied the opportunity to face his accuser here, which is a fundamental right in our justice system. Without exercising that right, we are left guessing who is telling the truth. You play into the sentimental power of the written word of a beautiful young woman that was brutally murdered leaving two children, friends, and family behind. Calling her a liar or portraying her as someone setting a stage to collect $15 million is not politically correct. Our consciousness would consider this dirty play because she is not here to defend herself. You are bullying O.J. because of the delicacy of this situation. O.J. has prepared a letter under the advice of his legal counsel to go on record that he isn't part of her scam to rip off the IRS. Remember we carry the burden of those who cheat the IRS. You spin this to mean he is being vindictive and wants to hurt Nicole. Now you set up O.J. for the kill. You state that the phone conversation on June 2nd prompted O.J. to have the letter hand delivered. O.J. disagrees with you. You tell us that this denial destroyed all his credibility. You put words in O.J.'s mouth insisting it was an angry conversation. I don't understand how you can be so outrageous. You weren't there and you cannot produce a single witness to confirm your theory. Yet you quote from a conversation as though it were factually correct. O.J. denies your version of the story and so you conclude this makes him a liar. He denies there is any truth to Nicole's entries regarding abusive language directed at her. You ask if these entries are "'...*a pack of lies?*"[16] O.J. answers, "'*Yes*'."[17]You turn your back on him in disgust, "...and let his answer hang in the air".[18] You leave the courtroom breathless and stunned by your great showmanship.

We need to study the entirety of Nicole's diary to get a sense of what purpose it was serving. Was it a journal, a fantasy, a combination of dreams and thoughts or a recommended practice to set up prenuptial attack? Without a thorough analysis it is difficult to make conclusions regarding the accuracy of its statements and their meanings. We all know that out of context, entries in a diary can be misleading. This is one of the big injustices brought about by the current legal strategy in both civil and criminal cases. Lawyers have become masters of drawing conclusions out of context. They artfully give a jury a small fact and the magically construct a story to fit a desired conclusion. This powerful tactic wrongfully puts innocent people in jail. People that we pay tax money to keep interred.

O.J. has just left the stand and I have yet to find one lie. All of the facts Mr. Petrocelli represents in his book are just word games. There were no disagreements on the facts, only disagreements on how to characterize the facts. Arguments as to what said and how it was said between two people, one being dead so unable to agree with or deny the other's claim. No witnesses were produced and there was no opportunity for cross-examination.

Notes:

[1] Daniel Petrocelli, *Triumph of Justice*, (Crown, 1998), pg. 483

[2] Ibid, pg. 483

[3] Ibid, pg. 484

[4] Ibid, pg. 484

[5] Ibid, pg. 485

[6] Ibid, pg. 486

[7] Ibid, pg. 494

[8] Ibid, pg. 494

[9] Ibid, pg. 494

[10] Ibid, pg.494

[11] Ibid, pg. 495

[12] Ibid, pg. 496

[13] Ibid, pg. 496

[14] Ibid, pg.496

[15] Ibid, pg.496

[16] Ibid, pg.497

17 Ibid, pg 497

18 Ibid, pg 497

TWENTY-NINE
Undeniably Deniable

Denying the Undeniable

O.J. returns to the stand so you can search for more lies that will incriminate him. You promise us that you will catch O.J. in lies regarding conversations he had with several people. He denies that he had an *argument* with Paula before a party at La Quinta. This must be a misprint since are describing what Nicole said. O.J. says he remembers Nicole say she was leaving. Your version of the incident is that she yelled at O.J. that he was stealing her friends. You admit Nicole was "...*out of control*".[1] According to you this is an escalation of their problems. You are just guessing at this useless and confusing reasoning.

This mission now is how to set the stage for O.J. to be in the killing mode by June 12th.

"*Wednesday, June 8: Had another letter delivered to Nicole, stating that she was not to use his housekeeper, Gigi, as 'emergency cook, baby-sitter, or errand runner'*"[2].

You think this indicates a growing hostility. What I see is Nicole abusing her friendly relationship with O.J. She still wants the benefits of being O.J.'s wife and he is not happy with being taken advantage of. The princess, Nicole, expects O.J. to be providing her all these niceties that is an indication she has not let go of him and the grand lifestyle he provides. She gets huffy because O.J. won't continually reach in his wallet. Simpson states that the only conversations he had with

Nicole in the week before the killings were about the kids and the dog. Your version of the communication is they had ugly word exchanges escalating in anger and intensity with each day. Where do you get your verification of this assumption? This is irresponsible speculation that is a desperate fabrication to give a desired effect. This is akin to lying. So far you are the one busy misleading people. You weave a tale with no concrete facts, not one witness, using dead people's testimony and inventing conversations. So far, this trial reveals the lawyer as the one abusing the truth.

You try to pin O.J. down with a conversation he had with Bobby Bender, a friend from Long Island. In your version of the story he was so depressed over Nicole he couldn't get out of his chair to play golf. O.J. admitted he felt badly at that time, but it was over his swollen hands and knees from playing golf and a flight he had taken. You believe he wouldn't admit that he was upset about breaking up with Nicole. That might be so, but O.J. is probably careful about what he says because of too many wagging tongues. Your conclusion is that he is lying because he wasn't honest about the problems he was having with Nicole. This is another *so what* episode. It is not surprising for men to be ambivalent about their ex-wives. There are the good memories and then the bitter times. There are times they feel glad for a chance to be free of the problems that led to a divorce and other times they long for what could have been. This social chitchat is meaningless especially in conjunction with a murder case. It says nothing compelling that would lead a reasonable person to believe murder was brewing in O.J.'s mind. O.J. had been playing golf for about two weeks straight. So neither the swelling nor the depression was all that bad. Maybe it was the effect of the plane flight. I see no discernable lies being told here. Through this whole testimony there is yet to be one noticeable lie. Keep pitching maybe you will find the plate, but as of now, you are well out of the strike zone. Still you are pounding your chest with pride about how the spectators are impressed with your performance. This trash talk is not impressive.

The next lie you try to establish is O.J.'s denial that he had a fight with Paula over her desire to attend the dance recital for Sydney and be included in Nicole's family gathering. O.J. says he did not fight with

Paula. Paula might have felt rejected by not being invited, but surely she understood that mixing the family was not especially fun for O.J. This is not an uncommon scene in messy divorces. No one is happy in these circumstances, but murder is not normally the expression of upset about not being able to please everyone. Both of these women, who seemed to be vying for his money and attention, were the ones having the problem, not O.J. He was doing his best at feline behavior control.

O.J. denies several of your accusations: telling his friends that he and Paula had a *beef* the night before, picking up a *"Dear John"* call from her, or having a near confrontation with Baumgarten on the golf course. Are any of these denials lies? I don't get clarity from the information testimony you give. It could be that some of these casual conversations were forgotten. How substantive are these issues anyway? Can you prove he picked up the phone call from Paula? He did pick up some messages. The phone records prove that, but exactly what he listened to or how he interpreted it is a matter of opinion. Some say the golfing incident was no big deal. All of this does not add up to proof that O.J. was acting unusual.

We can prove that O.J. did spend twenty minutes in conversation with Kato's contact, a Playboy centerfold. This would have been a delightful attitude adjustment when you are having problems with two other women. Better than a Tylenol. O.J. claims he took a nap after the phone call before taking the red-eye flight to Chicago. You then present an argument that represents what is so disturbing about your arguments as a whole. You state the following to show that O.J. is lying.

"Nobody takes a nap before hopping on a transcontinental flight, and I wanted to show that it wasn't sensible for Simpson to be dozing off between 10:15 and 10:45 which was a major portion of his alibi."[3]

What survey did you take to establish this fact? Nobody means nobody and so establishes that O.J. is lying? This is a most absurd argument. Taking a nap right after a dreamy conversation with a beautiful woman, following a long and trying emotional day, before going out into the public eye on a midnight flight is a sensible thing O.J. could have done.

O.J. gives you considerable detail regarding the dance recital. The dance recital was crowded and Nicole saved a seat for him. He tells us some of the people who were sitting near him. You quote a renowned threat expert, Gavin de Becker.

"...a liar will fill his answer with a jumble of unrequired details to create a buffer of credibility and truth around a core lie. This was a classic case."[4]

I don't know if you are talking about your presentation during this trial or about O.J.'s. It seems the former fits better than the latter. You use a picture of O.J. with his arm around his daughter to show that he didn't have any cuts on his hands at the recital. Since he claimed that he got the cuts in Chicago there are no lies revealed here.

Back to the messages that were picked up on that evening. He claims he never picked up Paula's message. You begin your assault on Simpson's lie that he never picked up Paula's message dumping him on account of Nicole. You do not have proof to back up your claim. He insists that he never picked up the message. You ask again if he picked up a message at 6:56pm that lasted five minutes. He denies it again. You give him the chance to change his mind, but O.J. sticks to his story. He was with Kato at that time. The only proof you have is someone picked up a phone data sheet showing a message at 6:56pm. There could have been a technical glitch, but I will give you this one. After not lying throughout the trial why would he suddenly lie about this? It is a long reach to go from hearing a message leading into raging vengeance against Nicole. In between all of this he makes a date with a Playboy centerfold. It appears as though he was able to take most things in stride. Trying to connect his failing relationship with Paula to a premeditated murder of his ex-wife is not solid enough evidence to convict this man for this observer.

The call that O.J. made to Nicole at approximately 9:00 pm,

"In my view, was a conversation that led to murder. Nicole had it with him – throwing her and their kids out of her home, jeopardizing her financial security, pulling every string and using all he held over her –the IRS threat was the last straw."[5]

This sounds like a list of why Nicole would want to murder O.J. not the other way around. She was angry with O.J. because he wouldn't participate in her scam on the IRS and was tired of feeding her lavish lifestyle. Where in this is there a motive for murder? Nicole is being her selfish self and O.J. is not playing along. You do not give us any real substantiation of facts that might drive a man into a murder rage. O.J. has far too much experience with this woman to risk his life on these petty concerns that are for him an everyday occurrence.

You add that he wasn't invited to have dinner after the recital. They were dining nearby on his money and yet without him. Could this have been the clincher? He had a rough day on the golf course, his girlfriend is giving him trouble, and his family snubs him, so he decides to have a burger with Kato. He corrects you when you try to call it a "'...date".[6] The jury finds this funny and that bothered you. You accuse O.J. of clowning around. This is no time for jokes. This is serious business. You establish they get back about 9:35 pm. Your time references are too precise to be accurate especially from recollections. It is obvious you need this special timeline to support your story. He tells you why he parked the Bronco on Rockingham after the burger run. You don't like his explanation so come up with your own reasons; after a murder you park your Bronco somewhere other than its usual place. How does this make sense?

Observing O.J.'s body language on the stand and his eyes fluttering overtime - you equate to lying. Right in O.J.'s face you press him hard about going to Bundy to murder Nicole and Ron. This is pretty bold of you. Did you really expect him to break down and confess the murder under your forceful interrogation? Absolutely not! What you were hoping for though was his body language to indicate that he wasn't telling the truth. I am reminded of skillful attorneys who can make a truthful person appear as though they are lying by applying pressure, asking loaded questions, and making them squirm on the stand. By your account of O.J.'s demeanor, he looked and acted uncomfortable. At one point when you were leaning on O.J. especially hard, he turned to the jury and answered one of your questions, "*That's absolutely not true!*"[7] You admit this was a scary moment for you.

You describe this as the defining moment with the victory of the case at stake. You continue to accuse O.J. of filling the day with lies. Still, I can only account for one O.J. lie, the rest are yours. You worry that if the jury looked into O.J.'s eyes and saw the "*...truth*"[8] (whatever that look is) it would be the end of your case. For reason or star power *"it came down to this moment."* You are powerfully dramatic, right in the same genre as Jack Nicholson in *A Few Good Men*. Twelve jurors looking into O.J.'s eyes and being able to discern whether he was telling the truth. Is this part of their jury instruction, what did you see in his eyes at the moment he was asked the deciding question? Tell us whether he was lying or telling the truth. You are relying on fortunetelling more than truth telling. Look into their eyes and you will find the truth that you need. Case over!

The same dramatic question is asked regarding Ron Goldman. *"And you killed Ronald Goldman, sir, did you or did you not?"*[10] You didn't expect a confession; your objective was to have O.J. deny his role in the murders, yet something in his denial would send a signal to the jury of his guilt. The look in the eyes test again. How far was the witness stand from the jury? How was the jury's eyesight? Silly questions yet appropriate for your absurd notion. Somehow in O.J.'s eyes or body language was the confession you needed for a victory in this case.

Your observation was that he delivered the denial poorly. The jury wasn't buying it. Further, you surmise that he was mechanical, contrived and clearly rehearsed. He must have said over and over again, *"That's absolutely not true."*[11] He may have been overexposed to the question and the answer certainly became mechanical. How could you expect him to be spontaneous, after all that had transpired? He was asked the question so many times; it is understandable that he would not sound natural. You seize upon this opportunity to challenge his ability to sound innocent. This is not what justice should be about. Where's the evidence?

The next question to O.J. is *"And you got on to your property, sir, and you bumped into a wall on the side of your house at 10:50, 10:51. True or untrue?"*[12] Same analysis on your part. A rehearsed answer and your conclusion,

"No innocent person would repeat such a mantra: he'd be screaming in outrage! Simpson was straining for sincerity, delivered his empty line and failed."[13]

This exchange blows you out of the park, water, courtroom, wherever. Looking closely at the question, I have several problems. Kato heard three thumps. Why didn't you ask O.J. if he bumped into Kato's wall three times? It would have been a strange question to ask because there is not a reasonable explanation for the three bangs on a wall. One maybe, although I have some difficulty with that, but three? No! How do you explain why someone would bump three times against the wall of a room that was occupied by a houseguest? You then try to pin the time down to 10:50 or 10:51. Even if it were so, how would he know the exact time? You didn't say about 10:50. If you concede it was 10:51, that gave O.J. exactly four minutes to get into his house, take off the murder clothes, pack them, or as you said earlier, put them in the washing machine to get the blood off, clean up, dress and get downstairs and out the door where Park sees him at 10:55. Quite a guy, this O.J.! You have him killing two people in about one minute and in four minutes doing a Superman quick-change act. Somewhere in all of this he has to stop the bleeding for the cuts on his hands. No bandages seen. Athletes tend to sweat easily, I would have liked a detailed description of what condition O.J. was in after committing a double homicide, scaling walls, bumping into a wall, and changing clothes in the impossibly tight timeframe you have outlined.

You then accuse O.J. of putting items in a bag and leaving them behind in his Bentley. The next accusation is that at 10:55 he walked diagonally to his house so the driver wouldn't see him. O.J. denies that this happened. You state that O.J. dropped a bag, and point out the spot. Dan, where did O.J. get a bag? What could possibly be in the bag? You have him racing from the crime scene and within a short period of time doing many things and now you added on the bag drop. I can't visualize this entire happening. The camera is rolling too fast.

Now you ask if O.J. dropped blood near a cable in the back of his house, near the wall, where he ran into the wall (the three bump episode). Even if all this were happening as you are imagining, how would he knew that he left a single drop of blood on a cable? And now you make the standard overstatement. *"And you bled all over that driveway and in your Bronco, didn't you, sir?"*[14] O.J. answered, *"'That is absolutely incorrect'."*[15] Dan, O.J.'s blood was not ALL OVER THAT DRIVEWAY AND HIS BRONCO! A few suspicious drops, consistent with the amount missing from the sample that he gave the LAPD were found. For you to ask if his blood was all over the place demanded a truthful answer, "No, counselor, absolutely NO!" How could you ask me such a question when you know very well that the evidence that the police collected were random drops of blood, very little blood? Any blood found on O.J.'s property would have to be time stamped and you know that didn't happen. You are infecting the jury's mind with this image of O.J. pouring incriminating blood evidence all over the place through several cuts on his hand. Give it up lawyer. You are making a mountain range out of a grain of sand. Help me out here. Give me a good phrase for the kind of BS you are shoveling.

You had enough of O.J. for one day, poor Dan. You should be exhausted. No incriminating lies. One Paula phone call mystery and a pile of your accusations that O.J. is telling one lie after another. I'm keeping score and I have yet to see one piece of incriminating testimony that is clearly a lie. Other than scorekeeping, I wouldn't want to be in a card game with you, Mr. P. I would have to watch too closely. It would take all the fun away and your sleight of hand would scare me. The press was all over your performance. What an acting job on your part. You are getting a taste of the celebrity that this brings to you and your firm. Keep up the good work. The payoff will be just like being a rock star.

Your next round will be with the physical evidence. Your partners chastise you because you are not being tough enough with O.J. You wanted to destroy him on the second day. *"This would be the fun part..."*[16] You insist that you had an encyclopedia of damning facts and Simpson had no innocent explanation of any of them. You have lined up your dominos and they going to fall like bricks. You have my attention, even though you have promised me over and over that you had convincing evidence and failed to deliver. You are like the ball player that is in a hitting slump. You are overdue. Badly overdue. You entered the courtroom determined to be tougher and more confrontational. This sounds more like Wide World of Wrestling than a court of truth and justice. Pump those biceps and triceps, Mr. Olympic lawyer.

You are getting ready for the battle. *"'Argue with him. Don't give him his pat answers.'"*[17] You're giving in too easily. Fight harder, Dan. You were surprised that when O.J. returned to the stand he looked tentative. *"'...he might be playing possum. Where was 'O.J.'?'"*[18] I hear the sound of paranoia here, counselor. Maybe he is just tired of being the target of a raging attorney asking preposterous questions.

With the phone records you are prepared to *"…hammer Simpson with confidence."*[19] You take us through the Paula Barbieri phone records again. Before we listen to your tirade about what calls were taken and what was heard, let us not forget whether or not there is any value in this line of questioning in the first place. You are trying to establish that O.J. received a call from Paula that disturbed him. This call in some way added to his motives to kill Nicole. You are using the sum total of rejection as your theory that would drive him to want to kill Nicole with a knife. If you could establish that he heard a call from Paula that she was dumping him, this would help incriminate O.J. and lead us to the conclusion that he was the murderer.

From O.J.'s perspective what motive does he have to lie about receiving a call from Paula? Why would he want to cover up this call? Any reasonable person would not make the assumption that listening to a Paula phone message, even if it were a *"Dear John"* one would help ignite the flames of committing a murder on another person. I am having a lot of trouble finding a reason of O.J. to lie about receiving this so-called infamous call. He and his lawyers must have gone over this point ad nauseam. His lawyers certainly would have reminded O.J. to be truthful about a piece of information that although irrelevant must be handled honestly. If O.J. admitted taking that message, what real damage is there to his defense? Little to no damage caused here because there is not enough evidence to draw a conclusion. Yet, O.J. is digging his heels in and insisting that he didn't take the message.

You are using phone records and treating them as though they are infallible. Tell that to the many companies that have a prosperous business finding incorrect billings and charges made by the phone company. The phone company's records are notoriously flawed. Most people don't want to go through the trouble to check their phone bill, but companies hire phone consulting firms to do exactly that and they pay a percentage of the errors they find. Yes, most of the records are correct, but they are not infallible. Just like your checking account. Most of the time the bank gets it right, but you know that from time to time they do make mistakes.

You ask if O.J. picked up various messages and he denies doing so. Is it possible that someone else might have picked up the messages? He has a secretary and other people that may have access to his phones:

maids, children, whomever. If O.J. is protecting his son or someone he knows his answers may be part of the shield. There are all kinds of speculation, but you want to accuse someone of murder over these disputed phone calls. I already gave you a maybe here, but you really need something more substantive to claim a real victory in the realm of finding a confession from O.J.

This line of questioning continues, painfully, including Dr. Lenore Walker, another *renowned expert* that O.J. told about the phone derby with Paula that day. At this point you accuse O.J. of lacking even the

"...*faintest pretense for obeying the oath.*"[20] This is the oath to tell the truth on the stand. You observe, "*The lies just came pouring out. I became very loud and challenging.*"[21]

Pouring out, Dan? You should lighten up here. The only thing that is pouring out is your bluster. You have O.J. stuck on one simple point and it is taking us nowhere. Fourth and 9½ to go for a first down. Forget about touchdowns here, you haven't even gone the first 10 yards and you are raising the victory banner. It's called *trash talk*.

You go on with this assault. O.J. gives his explanations. You characterize them as blatant lies coming from a witness that was falling apart. At this point you try to make your connection between O.J. covering up receiving the calls and his knowledge that these calls would send a message to a jury that his state of mind would be leading to a murder. You sense that the jury is not caring about what O.J. is saying. He has lost credibility. You may have won on this point with them, Mr. P, but I see it as a tainted victory. It is just more confusion. This is not real evidence that convicts a murderer.

Continuing, you ask O.J. if he was in his Bronco at 10:03 calling Paula. I meant to ask you earlier, Dan, did all these people have their watches and clocks synchronized. You are trying to build a case around specific minutes that are estimated by many people. Unless all their watches and clocks were precisely aligned it would undermine the testimony. Telling O.J. where he was at 10:03 is silly. You didn't ask him where he was. Asking if it is true he was in his Bronco at a specific minute accomplishes nothing. He could have been the killer and have been in the Bronco during that specific minute. All you have is a cell phone record. That call could have been made from anyplace, in or out of the Bronco. For him to say that he wasn't in the Bronco during that minute could be the truth and he could still be the murderer. He could also be telling the truth and was not in the Bronco and was not the murderer.

You then say, *"If he answers, yes, it's tantamount to a confession."*[22] If he answers "no" you call him a liar. Either way he is guilty by the way you have structured the question. Clever semantics, but just more lawyer trickery. I don't believe that either a *yes* or *no* answer to this dirty question incriminates O.J. We also have to remember a big point, counselor. You didn't want to go near the *Jason is the killer issue.* If O.J. is continuing to protect his son and all he has to lose in this trial is the appearance that he was the killer, most of this is irrelevant to him. Money would not be a major issue to O.J. for two reasons. There is no price that is too high to save a son and there are ways to be judgment proof, which his lawyers had probably told him. These questions and answers must have been discussed over and over with his lawyers. O.J. must not commit perjury, but other than that he has little to lose over this trial. Those people who believed he was framed will most likely stay with their opinion. Those that think he did the dastardly deed will stay where they are. All that will change here is that you will get paid for all the histrionics and Fred can say, "I told you so" to an empty audience. Good for the lawyers and expensive to the citizens of the United States.

O.J. is then accused of lying to the police, but he insists that the changes in the account of the phone call are only making them more accurate. He admits that it is a change and you bark back, "'It's different! Isn't it?'"[23]O.J. agrees. He repeats that he didn't get in the Bronco and drive to Paula's and call her from the phone. From all of this you declare that he has been impeached.

"he'd been shown to be a liar over and over -- and in this case, more than a liar: a killer! The damage has been done."[24]

Dan, I have been following the questions and answers very closely, as you can see. Where are all these lies? All we have is O.J. insisting he wasn't in the Bronco when he called Paula. We know the phone records don't tell us where the calls took place. It could have been in the Bronco or out of the Bronco. We weren't there, there were no witnesses; it is just his word versus your guess. Your guess is not evidence. With all that, the call to Paula doesn't mean anything anyway because you can't connect the making of a call to committing a murder. This is all an enormous amount of diversionary tactics. O.J.'s lawyer should be apoplectic by now. He does object and the judge agrees, but you got the questions in fast enough and are proud the damage was done. It is not easy typing this and holding my nose to avoid the stink at the same time.

I have an additional question about the cell phone being in the Bronco. O.J.'s testimony is that he went to the Bronco to pick up the cell phone accessories, not the phone itself. This makes more sense to me. People generally keep their cell phones with them. Although it is done all the time, it is not the most likely scenario to leave your phone, unattended in your SUV's. Phones can be stolen and that causes a lot of grief. You keep your cell phone with you. That's the whole point of having a cell phone. In O.J.'s case if he were waiting for a call from Paula that would be another reason he would keep the cell pone with him. You have him leaving the cell phone unattended and I don't like the assumption. Given the commonsense you want us to use, that cell phone is not in the Bronco as you claim, but with or near O.J. For him to get some of the accessories before a trip does make better sense. O.J. then clarifies the statement he gave the police about what he retrieved from the Bronco. He claims that it was not the cell phone. He claims it was the accessories. You don't like this version. Therefore, you want to chalk this one up as a major incriminating lie. This referee can't call it that way, despite your ranting and raving.

You yell at O.J. in outrage that he is insisting his version of where the cell phone was between 10:00 pm and 11:00 pm destroys his alibi. Baker objects and the judge agree, but you had slammed the point home.

You get really pumped by what you consider success in your interrogation of O.J. You have your version of the reason O.J. killed Nicole and it is time to drive them home. You accuse O.J. of going to Bundy, desperate and alone, calling Paula. He says this is untrue. It is embarrassing for me to hear you ask these kinds of questions. You want O.J. to admit he was desperate and alone driving to the murder scene at 10:00. Remember, Nicole's house was about five minutes away. That would bring O.J. to Bundy at 10:08, driving around contemplating this premeditated murder? You give him time to think things over.

According to you he would be in this killer outfit, sweat suit, $40.00 business socks, Bruno Magli shoes, knit hat; getting ready to unleash a rage that has been building up since the morning. Bad day on the golf course, rejected to go to dinner with the family and a girlfriend telling him to get lost. A very bad day, O.J. Can't control this rage. A murder inspiring day. "Let my life be at risk to get all of this rage out of me." Is the kind of emotion you want us to believe O.J. was experiencing. It should sound ridiculous to you Mr. Petrocelli. It sounds ridiculous to write.

O.J. would think further. "Let's see if I remember all my training while doing the SEAL movie. Can't forget I have to get into the house, behind Nicole, and kill her quietly. Don't want to wake the kids, too messy. I'll have to get back home and clean up and be cool when I meet my limo driver in about 45 minutes. Let me go over this again. Is their anything I forgot that might cause a problem later and make the police suspicious of me? I really don't want to get caught. That Playboy model that I spoke to seemed like she would be a hot date. Don't want to blow that. Maybe a better solution to the grief the women have given me would be to trade them in for new models. I still do get those "let's go to bed" smiles from the ladies."

You're not letting go with your pet theories. Pit bulls pay attention. This is the way that it should be done.

O.J. is reminded that he told the police that he went to the Bronco to get his phone. The phone would then be in the Bronco at 11:00. And by your reasoning in the Bronco at 10:00 and therefore O.J. is in the Bronco at Bundy at 10:40 killing two people. O.J. says he misspoke that it was accessories he retrieved from the Bronco. How is it that until this moment, no one, including the detectives, the prosecution, and all the sleuths not solve the murder using this issue? How could everyone, but you miss this one? If the phone was in the Bronco, O.J. is the killer. That is possible, but as every logical exercise, one possibility does not a conclusion make. You claim, "*It was crystal clear. The phone was in the Bronco at 11:00*"[25] Clarity is in the eye of the storyteller. You claim that it has been established that every time that day it had been in the Bronco. With this logic it is therefore impossible for O.J. to have made a call to Paula from his driveway. You say this is not possible; calls are only made from Broncos. We all know you need to win with this foolishness.

O.J. claims that he was trying to reach Paula for a possible lift to the airport. You say that this is not possible because O.J. knew Paula had left town and a driver was ordered. O.J. could have thought Paula left, but wasn't 100% sure and was giving it a demeanor on the stand should not in itself confess to lying. You are admittedly pounding this man with questions. He is answering them, but the protocol doesn't allow him to fight back. If he considers your questions preposterous it is tough for him to challenge you. You know you have that advantage and are playing it to the hilt. This is an example of a lawyer using his ability to make a truthful man look like he is lying. You accuse O.J. of stating that all of his prior testimony and the records people took were contradictory and you use the tactic that generalizes the situation. O.J. does take some exception or wants to further clarify a statement; you twist that around to being a claim that all their notes are false. Of course, when you ask the question that way and the witness is trying to be specific and you turn it into a generality, it will sound like a bad answer. The witness is also in a position in these matters asked to reconstruct details of an evening that would otherwise be uneventful. There was no reason to remember the sequence of phone calls or the actual conversation. We generally have a good overview and probably a different look that someone else might have about the same situation. Now years later, you are being pressed to remember times, details of conversations, personal activities. Yes, O.J. has gone over all of this in his mind and has reviewed this with all his attorneys. If he were the murderer, I believe he would be less likely to give a story you could pound so hard. He is acting soft on some details in the way a person would naturally act. The guilty person carefully rehearses answers to obvious questions. In O.J.'s case all these questions are more than obvious. Did you hit your wife? Did you have problems with Paula? Where were you during the times of the murder? How do you account for blood on your property? How do you account for blood in your Bronco? How do you explain the thumps on Kato's wall? Did you wear Bruno Magli's? The same old lineup, the same old accusations and the same old answers. Really no surprises, Dan. Your dramatic presentation does put a showmanship flavor into all of this and you're having success in rattling O.J. This doesn't spell confession to me counselor. Just good trial tactics.

You continue to go over the same turf. You are really tearing it up. O.J. continues to deny your allegations. *"'because you were desperate and you were alone that night, true?"*[26]He denied all these assumptions. You sensed that nobody cared what he was saying. That's sad, but really what happens when a witness is pummeled by an attorney and doesn't have the courtroom presence to fight back? That does not spell g-u-i-l-t-y. It spells bullying.

As you are grilling O.J. several thoughts go through your mind. You wished there could be cameras catching the interrogation. You wanted the world to see O.J. squirming. You believed that there would be *"...no doubt in anyone's mind about the depth of his guilt."*[27] Again, the body language and the verbal jousting give O.J. away. He can't hide his guilt. Beauty is in the eye of the beholder, Dan, so it isn't that body language subject to the same definition? You want to read into it what O.J. is telling you, the jury and the world, he is guilty by his mannerisms. He is not saying he is guilty by his words. He didn't confess and the Paula, Nicole cell phone exchange does not convince a jury. So where is the evidence? At best you can only establish he might have been in a bad mood and could have been at Bundy at the time. Too many *could haves* and no proof.

You look into your ego mirror of self-approval and give yourself a big *atta boy*. You had the material mastered, absorbed every piece of evidence and all the nuances of the case perfected. You are thinking O.J. must be very impressed by all your *"...intimidating, spitting his own words back at him verbatim without looking at a note."*[28]

O.J. gives you testimony as to what he was doing at about 10:00 p.m. He hit a few golf balls and called Paula from his driveway, went to his garage to get a club, swung a bit. You are sarcastic in observing that he knew more about the golf clubs than anything else in the case. You have some verbal jockeying back and forth with O.J. So I'm not the only sarcastic one in the crowd.

You attempt to undermine O.J.'s account of that time frame by insisting that he fabricated going back in the house at 10:20 because he knew the driver was there at 10:23. O.J. wasn't expecting the driver until 10:45. How would he believe that he would be in the driveway at 10:23? The judge objected to your fanciful guesses, but O.J. answers anyway, over the objection of his attorney. You felt O.J. was coming apart. You smelled blood. That killer attorney instinct was surfacing. You just love seeing all that blood you can shed. Your metaphors are so corny in light of this case, but more than corny it tells the reader what this is all about. You smell victory and victory spells money. Lots and lots of money. Oh! What a good feeling in lawyer land. You felt powerful. And powerful you are, armed with tricky questions, misleading subjects, and a stage presence in the courtroom that is convincing. Especially with a carefully selected jury, how can you miss? Closing in for the kill, *"I was in control of the courtroom."*[29] Good observation, Mr. P., you wrenched it away from Lady Justice and put it in your wallet.

Notes:

[1] Daniel Petrocelli, *Triumph of Justice*, (Crown, 1998), pg. 498

[2] Ibid, pg. 498

[3] Ibid, pg. 500

[4] Ibid, pg. 500

[5] Ibid, pg. 503

[6] Ibid, pg. 503

[7] Ibid, pg. 505

[8] Ibid, pg. 505

[9] Ibid, pg.505

[10] Ibid, pg.505

[11] Ibid, pg. 505

[12] Ibid, pg. 506

[13] Ibid, pg. 506

[14] Ibid, pg.506

[15] Ibid, pg.507

[16] Ibid, pg. 507

[17] Ibid, pg. 507

[18] Ibid, pg. 507

[19] Ibid, pg. 507

[20] Ibid. pg. 509

[21] Ibid, pg. 509

[22] Ibid, pg. 511

[23] Ibid, pg. 511

[24] Ibid, pg. 512

[25] Ibid, pg. 514

26 Ibid. pg. 514

27 Ibid pg 514

28 Ibid pg 514

29 Ibid pg 516

THIRTY

Explanations

No Explanation

When grilling O.J. about what he did when he went to the Bentley, he said to his own doctor, that he went for his black shoes. O.J. appears to be changing his story. O.J. had the misfortune to say to you that he and the doctor were trying to "'...*figure out*'"[1] the evening. This was the same to you as to a boxer whose opponent just drops his hands and says "punch me as hard as you can!" Your interpretation of *figure out* was the same as lying. That is a possible explanation, but by no means the only explanation. Events took place during a time they were meaningless to an innocent person. The kinds of things you do automatically, without necessarily putting into your memory bank. Where did you have breakfast yesterday morning, Dan? The usual place? How many people were in the restaurant? What did you eat? Was the waitress black or white? There are so many details in our life that in the context of when they are happening are rarely committed to memory. If you are asked to reconstruct that breakfast or other inconsequential events in your life, an aggressive in-your-face attorney could make you very uncomfortable. This is just a rhetorical question from me, counselor?

The problem I have with this phase of your in-your-face questioning is the questions themselves. Even if you got the answers you were gunning for they would tell you nothing incriminating about the murders. If O.J. said, yes, I beat Nicole badly and didn't regret it.

Would that say he is capable of murder? I say "not necessarily so." Politically incorrect—shocking, but if true could still mean nothing. It would be a vile and inexcusable act, but does not confess to a murder. If O.J. were to tell you got the Paula "*Dear John*" message and it upset him greatly. The answer would not help your case. Upset with Paula, okay O.J. let's go murder Nicole. Or, I'm too upset, this is too much to take, I'll kill the mother of my children. If O.J. said he was in the Bronco at 10:00 calling Paula, that doesn't, even with all else added on, brand O.J. the killer. He could have parked the Bronco at 10:05 at Rockingham and at 10:20 Jason gets in Dad's Bronco and drives over Nicole's for a visit. Dad's leaving town, Jason knows it and uses the Bronco. You didn't ask Jason if he was in his Dad's Bronco that evening. You had the chance, but carefully avoided the line of questioning that was begging to be asked. Anything regarding the possibility of someone else being the murderer was to be avoided. There was too much at stake. So far, the questions asked of O.J., even if answered in the most incriminating way, do not add up to a conclusion of guilt. You make a big deal out of his inability to answer coolly. That, my lawyer, observably is not the evidence of guilt. You have such a controlling personality with the ability to upset a witness even in trivial matters. You can get the implication of O.J. lying with just a whole lot of *what difference makes* questions.

You milked the *figuring out* comment. You wouldn't let him get away with it. Your spin is he was trying to figure out an alibi to "… explain the world of incriminating evidence".[2]

The questioning gets intense. You are toe to toe slugging it out in the middle of the ring. Challenge after challenge of the details of O.J. getting ready to take the limo to the airport. Where were you standing? Where did you put your bags? Were you on the left or right side of the driveway? Remember, Park wasn't sure which side of the driveway he was on and changed his story. You dismissed this as a simple mistake. With O.J. it is a confession of killer. Now you volunteer that you believe he laid down his bag containing the bloody knife and the shoes and darted across the driveway to get into his house. Your convenient theory made from whole cloth; vivid imaginings with nothing to back them up. You need to fill in all the missing pieces so you invent explanations. Back and forth you go. Were you near the

Bentley? Were you near the benches? His recollection was that he was near the benches. All of this could be true, but so what? Benches, Bentley, bags, do not tell me anything.

The subject changes, thank goodness, to blood. O.J. says he saw some blood on his pinky, but couldn't explain where it came from. He can't account for any bleeding that night, but doesn't rule out that it could have happened. My small survey says that people find cuts on their hands and arms all the time that they can't account for. Scratches occur all the time, somewhat mysteriously, nothing strange about that. We reach for things in places that have sharp edges, get paper cuts, all sorts of ways we get scratched. You position this whole inquiry in a way that any unexplained drop of blood is clear evidence O.J. is the murderer. He is not giving you good explanations for the few drops of blood and you conclude that the jury should understand this lack of recall as incriminating. I just can't by the logic. This is too much of a reach. Especially after a double homicide that you claim took place in about 75 seconds. You have O.J. with gloves on, yet you want him to sustain cuts. I have to rub it in again, no cuts on gloves that you took the trouble to point out to me. If the murder took place so quickly, how did O.J. sustain any cuts? A murder doesn't have to cause cuts on the killer's hands. If O.J. were an expert and quick in subduing his victims, what would cause the cuts? You haven't given this reader a reasonable explanation as to how and why O.J. should have cuts on his hands in the first place considering how fast the crime took place according to your theories. You need him to have the cuts so they would match and explain the few drops of blood found. You don't give me any trace of O.J.'s skin under Nicole's or Ron's fingernails.

You get O.J. to admit that he might have been wrong about his assumptions as to the cut on his hand when he spoke to the police after the murders. You remind him that this was a crucial question and he should have been more careful when talking to the police. He claims that he didn't feel that there was anything critical about the question. How could he, Dan? He wouldn't have known that they were planning to put some of his blood at the crime scene and at his house. Oops, a slip-up here on my part, but an innocent man has no reason to believe there was incriminating blood evidence. If he thought for a moment that the question was leading to "we found your blood at the murder site and your home", he would have given an answer that might possibly cover as an innocent explanation. After all, blood found in small quantities at a place you spend a good deal of time is not out of the question. You insist "*We've found blood all over the crime scene*;[3] ... Dan, they found a drop on a fence in a suspicious manner. A few drops does not make *all over the crime scene!*

O.J. admits he saw a drop of blood on his pinkie and on his counter, but couldn't explain its origin. You say this is a preposterous story and demanded it be reduced to absurdity. You are succeeding. Because O.J. cannot account for two drops of blood, the gallery at the trial shook their heads in disbelief. The media said the questioning was a painful experience. You were accused of piling it on. How true, but I think you missed the point. No piling on of the truth, but piling on the effect you so wanted for the jury to see.

O.J. explains he broke the glass in his hotel room in Chicago. The broken glass was found. He didn't remember the details of exactly how he broke the glass. The man just got a call from L.A. that Nicole had been murdered. This was going to be tough to deal with. His kid's mom just got murdered. O.J. will be in the spotlight, maybe a suspect. It is fair to assume that O.J. was in a flustered state. He is seeing his life turned upside down; publicity hounds, reminding him of his difficult relationship with Nicole; investigating reporters trying to turn his life inside out. O.J. better than we, could quickly see his life was about to become chaotic. Upset for many reasons, it should be understandable that he is not paying much attention to irrelevant details. This whole glass episode sends out the wrong message. You again demand detailed recall of incidences that happened years ago; things that would not be important to an innocent man. A guilty man would be very concerned about details anticipating questions. O.J. provides the best recall he has regarding any cuts on his hands. You are critical and conclude he is not only lying, but also essentially confessing to being the murderer. I can't be with you on either count. You don't know what caused the cut that the police photograph the next day. You are only speculating and speculating forcefully as though you are certain of what you are saying. It has to be impressive to the jury. You come off with confidence. You are in control and O.J. is fumbling. The problem here is this referee sees a personal foul being committed and the penalty is against you, counselor. You have been running the ball in the wrong direction with no progress in sight. You cannot show us anything in O.J.'s testimony that constitutes an outright incriminating lie. All you give us is some confusion over minutia. Critical to this whole line of questioning was to establish that it was reasonable for O.J., if he were the killer, to have sustained cuts. Based on your time line, no cuts on gloves, no blood underneath the nails of the victims, the difficulty of removing gloves that are tight fitting, and O.J. being the assailant completely in charge of the encounter, tell me Mr. Daniel Petrocelli, attorney with prestigious law firm, what could have caused the cuts? From what you presented to this point I can't come up with a simple answer that would incriminate O.J. You give me no cause for cuts and the only explanation is the glass shattering in the Chicago hotel room, I have to go with O.J.'s story over your guesses. Score in the lying department: one about Paula's phone calls, possibly and nothing else. Where are all these lies you are referring to? You made an emphatic point of showing that O.J. would lie about everything and thereby convince us he was the murderer.

Now we come to the battle of who is being logical. You accuse O.J. of being illogical because he points out that when the police examined him they only photographed one cut. You claim there were other cuts they missed. Now the essence of how you manipulate. You don't want O.J. to claim the police did a reasonable job of examining his hands because you have him accusing the police of being bumbling, stumbling cops who processed the crime scene wrong, missed important evidence and could not identify what evidence they did find, they were corrupt, racist, morally bankrupt, and generally contaminated everything. This is another big lie on your part, Dan. Shame on your conduct, again, counselor. It is important that we remind ourselves that O.J. never testified in the criminal trial. O.J. never made any of these accusations. You are putting these words in his mouth. They are your words and they seem to come from the conclusion that was made by expert testimony at the trial, not, by O.J. Are you listening, Dan? Not by O.J.! Therefore, he is not asking you to believe that they have been incompetent, as you charge. He is merely saying that you should look at the pictures and the record of what the police made when they examined his hands. They only showed one cut. Not all the others you are alluding to.

These are your competent detectives and nowhere did O.J. say they were otherwise. He is not attempting to have anything both ways. Big lie, again, on your part.

The questioning now is trying to determine cuts found on O.J. days after the murder. Scratches are noted. He says they could have happened playing with his son, Justin. This angers you. You accuse O.J. of "...*shamelessly blamed Nicole's death marks on their young child. I pursued him angrily.*"[4] These *death marks* as you call them need to be explained. How could they have happened if O.J. was wearing gloves? Did you do any tests that would show a person could receive these types of cuts with gloves on? What was found underneath Nicole's nails? Just elementary questions Mr. P. Do you have any evidence to back up these accusations? O.J. admits he isn't sure, but is indicating to you that this was a possibility. We are still in the land of explaining events that are rarely noticed except when you are in court and a lawyer places special importance on them. This is another example that if you could establish that O.J. had those cuts before he left for Chicago, you still didn't connect the dots as to how as a gloved, knife murderer, he got the cuts. When is this going to end? We are traveling in circles and not getting any closer to proving O.J. is definitely the killer.

Oh, thank goodness you are leaving this subject. We now go on to the murder wardrobe. O.J. tells you that he changed clothes in his hotel room and put on black pants and a white shirt for the return trip to L.A. This is what he was seen wearing. You have testimony form a Hertz employee and a passenger and they said he was wearing a blue jean outfit, the same as Allen Park had seen the night before. O.J.'s explanation was that he "...*threw up on the pants*"[5] on the plane and had to change his pants. He also remembers bleeding on the plane. You also recall that he asked the hotel receptionist for a Band-Aid. Just about the right time for him to do so if he just cut himself. You don't like this one though, do you? You tell us that no one on the plane recalls seeing him change his pants. No one said he didn't change his pants either, did they Dan? We are now given your guess as to what happened. More story telling. You believe that O.J. bled on the jeans on the plane when he put his fingers in the pants pockets. When he got off the plane in L.A. he changes sometime, somewhere before arriving at Rockingham so that he would not arrive at Rockingham with stains on his jeans. "*...Imagine how that would look.*"[6] I do imagine how it would look, Dan and to me it would look totally innocent because he cut his hand in the bathroom in Chicago. For the blood to be incriminating you would have to suppose that he wore them during the murders. You don't want to go there, Dan. There was no reason for O.J. to change pants other than his explanation; he threw up on them. A shrewd and clever guy would actually want blood on his pants. Wouldn't this be the way an innocent man would act? Your entire exercise regarding what O.J. was wearing coming back from Chicago is an additional waste of time. No lies from O.J. on this one, tiger.

O.J.'s trip to the airport the day after the murders is now in your cross hairs. It is O.J.'s testimony that he was just taking a ride with his friend, Kardashian and then decided to go to the airport to pick up his golf clubs. "*I was trying to kill fifty minutes waiting for my kids.*"[7] You believe that Mr. K. and Skip Taft will testify this is a lie. If you are right, and we will wait and see, what's the point? What does this have to do with implicating O.J. with the murders? You seem to suggest that there is something sinister hiding in the golf bags like the murder knife and maybe some bloody clothes. This is nothing more than wild speculation. As a lawyer aware of the consequences, Mr. K. would be especially sensitive not to become an accessory to a murder. He would be taking a terrible chance of getting into big trouble if he helped hide evidence. Since both of these men are now being closely observed, how do you think they would plan to get rid of the evidence? Far too risky for Mr. K. Another pointless excursion for you.

You decide to get back to the blood evidence. In critiquing your efforts I have felt an obligation to follow each and every claim made by you and offer my reaction. Though you have taken us over the same territory over and over, and I have had to repeat my comments, this seemed like the only ethical thing to do on my part. I didn't want to be accused of leaving out any point made by you that could help support your claim of proving O.J.'s guilt. At this point, the fingers are weary of typing the same old questions and criticisms about the blood evidence. Here we go again. The tactic you employ is demanding that O.J. explain how drops of blood were found at the murder scene. He doesn't have an explanation. Why should he? If at some time when visiting Nicole, a drop of his blood was deposited why would one expect him to know how it happened? He could have stopped by Nicole's after some golf. There was a cut on his hand and a drop of blood was left on the gate. Since it wasn't time stamped, how could he tell you when and how that took place? Do you know how the sample got back to the lab for analysis? You know that as an innocent man, the only guess O.J. would have is some of the blood the police took from him was planted. He's not going to accuse the police of planting without proof. Aren't you somewhat uneasy about Vannatter traveling around with O.J.'s blood? This permits a skeptical person to wonder why a seasoned detective would ignore basis rules of handling evidence. You dismiss the possibility of planting because no one turned in a dirty cop. Just because there was no rat or witnesses doesn't mean the switching or planting didn't take place. There was no witness to the Nicole and Ron murder. That doesn't mean it didn't happen. No one confessed. Planting and tampering take place too often. Murders are unsolved too often. If you are applying logic to one situation you invite the same logic to be used in a similar situation. Sometimes bad people and bad events don't get connected, yet they still happen.

O.J. can't explain how blood drops got on his socks. Neither can you, Dan. How could blood from Nicole penetrate O.J.'s sweat suit and land on a pair of $40 business socks? Dress, business socks don't usually get worn with a sweat suit. A killer slitting a throat from behind a victim is not necessarily going to get smatterings of blood through a sweat suit on to the inside of dress socks. Doesn't compute, Mr. P. Of course, O.J. can't explain how a pair of socks was found in an otherwise neat bedroom, sprinkled with some of the victim's blood. During the criminal trial the forensic expert questioned how blood drops could have gotten on the socks from the inside out. Maybe the killer had the socks on backwards. I remember wincing at this piece of evidence at the time, too suspicious.

You are now going to cover the murder clothes. "*This was going to be fun, because we could dress him from head to foot;....*"[8] Wardrobe inventory time:

"*'You owned caps like that as of June 12, 1994, correct?'*

"*'I could have, but I don't know.'*"[9] You now declare, "*He was destroyed as a witness by this time, his answers were just words.*"[10]

284

I guess you could stop here Mr. P. You would have us believe that after a soft answer there's no reason to believe him on anything else. Good interrogation, attorney. But, I'm not yet convinced. Let's go further.

You show a picture of O.J. in a Playboy exercise video wearing a sweat suit. He says that it was Playboy's sweat suit and he believes he returned the suit to the crew after the shoot. According to you the best part is the shoes. Bruno Magli must be smiling at all the free exposure they are getting despite they were used in the commission of a murder and O.J. doesn't like the style. I don't suppose Bruno spent any advertising capital on the benefits of wearing their loafers in committing a crime. Now they are being coupled with wearing a sweat suit. Normally, sweat suit wearers prefer sneakers. I would find it unusual for someone to wear a sweat suit with loafers, especially if I know that person is fashion conscious. Surely it happens, but it would be the exception. A sweat suit represents activity. Loafers represent relaxation. Not a choice I would expect someone to make when planning to kill someone with a knife. Tough to get the blood off suede and slip-ons that may slip-off during a battle. Bruno, I wouldn't expect a rush of business from the elite crime set.

You give us three objectives in questioning the shoes. First, he owned a pair; second, he would lie about owning a pair; and last, O.J. asserts that the photo in _National Inquirer_ is a fraud. O.J. denies owning these shoes. He is either lying, honestly mistaken or there is an entirely different explanation. If he is the murderer, he has a reason to lie because of the footprints at the crime scene. If he wasn't the murderer, maybe he lies because he knows his son Jason has access to his closet and may have been the one wearing the shoes. The shoes definitely look incriminating, but there are more than two explanations for who possibly could be wearing them at the time of the murders. O.J. analyzes the photo and claims many things about it doesn't look right though he doesn't deny that he could have been wearing the items shown. We have gone full circle, Daniel. So what? With digital photography and expertise in altering photos they could have been doctored. Your expert says no, yet O.J. believes it is a fraud. To the best of his recollection he wouldn't have worn a pair of these shoes. So it seems that O.J. is wrong. I am going to concede that you **may** have a point here, Dan. O.J. should have conceded that he might possibly have been wearing these shoes. I still don't believe that the photo makes O.J. the murderer.

You accuse O.J. of "*Two days of solid lying*".[11] I don't know what you mean by that, but it does sound like a bad thing to do. In analyzing the last sixty plus pages of your book, I haven't found these so called lies. You challenge O.J. on an assortment of silly details that have nothing to do with the commission of murder or confessing to the crimes. Did he have the key to Nicole's condo? Why did he have a fake goatee? Did the police take $7,000 from his closet and then put it back? You didn't like his answers. The last question you submit as proof the police are honest.

O.J. admits that he took off when he heard the police were coming to arrest him. He had to admit that! Millions watched his slow ride on the L.A. freeways. From this *chase* as you prefer to call it; you want the jury to come to a conclusion that this was a display of guilt. You want them to believe that "*If he was fleeing, that was extremely incriminating.*"[12]

Fleeing he wasn't, so how could it be incriminating. Your videotape must have been moving on fast forward. If this was an attempt to get away from pursuers by one of the fastest men ever to have run on a football field then I am an Olympic Gold Medal sprinter! Dan, he wasn't fleeing, he was crawling along the freeway at 40 miles per hour, illegally slow. If anything, he should have gotten a ticket for impeding traffic. Another reason, according to you, was the indication that he wanted to commit suicide. He had a gun and could have pulled the trigger at anytime before the police arrived. Let's not confuse contemplating suicide and committing suicide. In analyzing O.J.'s motive for suicide it illustrates why it is not reasonable that O.J. would kill Nicole.

You ask,"*…why would O.J. Simpson, with all his wealth, orphan his children and kill himself in grief over a woman he said he had stepped beyond?*"[13] Committing a poorly planned knife murder is tantamount to committing suicide. The chance of not getting caught is very slim. He would be the natural suspect. With the power of modern forensics it is tough to get away with murder. The plan you attribute to O.J. is clearly designed to get him caught. Blood evidence, tight time line, many opportunities for being recognized, on and on as before. With the highest risk for getting caught and your insistence that this crime was premeditated, O.J. for all intents and purposes is committing suicide. Since he did not opt to commit suicide with your logic applied here he would not likely commit this crime. You add on the question of why would he orphan his children and kill himself for this woman at this time. Very good question, counselor! The reasonable answer is he wouldn't and nothing really says that he would. The bad hair day he was having really wasn't that special: not such a good golf morning, being excluded from a post recital dinner, current girlfriends saying, "...*his life as 'O.J'. was over...* "[14] don't add up to the elements needed to plan a knife murder. It is committing suicide, and yes, Dan, over what? Now if he knew or thought his son killed Nicole and this would drag him into the mess, well that might be the stuff to confuse a man and lead to the decision to take this strange ride away from the police. In O.J.'s case, fleeing would have been the viable option in Chicago, realizing how much incriminating evidence he left behind. France, here I come, where there is no extradition for murder. He would have been on the phone with his lawyers planning some sort of defense. He would be wiring millions of dollars to a safe haven. O.J. would have lamed out of Dodge when it hit him that he was the only logical suspect, had he left too many crumbs behind. It seems that only an innocent O.J. would have returned to L.A. and gone to the police agreeing to be questioned without an attorney present. Only an innocent O.J. does not have a need to commit suicide.

O.J. agrees to take the stand in his own behalf in this trial. All he really risked was losing money that his attorneys told him could be avoided and has been. He did risk being made to seem like a killer by a crafty attorney. He trusted the jury system. He would only agree to testify if he was innocent. There is a popular belief that attorneys tell their clients, *No matter how innocent you may be a good attorney can make you look like a liar.* Mr. Bugliosi, a former prosecutor with an amazing record, makes that point in his book confirming the belief. Mr. Bugliosi writes in his book that O.J. was definitely the killer. He and Mr. Petrocelli are on the same page. I could not find anything in *Outrage* that helps Mr. P. and his claims of O.J.'s guilt. I found the same arguments and the lack of proof. People really don't want to believe these things can happen in America. Your partner stated, and you agreed, that lawyers in America would passionately make false statements in pursuit of a courtroom victory. O.J. still insisted on telling his side of the story.

Your suicide theory makes me believe O.J. is not acting like a murderer. Strangely enough, the opposite of what you would have us believe. Why do you have so much trouble hearing your own words? Which is the more convincing argument? Commit suicide by planning a flawed murder or not commit suicide when you have a lot to lose? Do you plan to commit suicide or kill your ex-wife when you are about to catch a plane to Chicago to make a guest appearance to play golf after you have just made contact with yet another Playboy model? Mr. Dan, don't look now, but you just stabbed yourself in the foot and it's a bloody mess. Despite all the evidence you have this jury so confused by your aggressive tactics, you may have gained ground. Just more evidence that the legal system has its predators in the skillful wordsmiths creating stories with such conviction the truth slips away. You prove to be an All Star at this game. You could fool a lot of people that this was your first murder trial. Making up lots of yards because your fouls are undetected and you are proud of it. I am glad all lawyers don't play as dirty as you do. The small cadres of your teammates that want to win at all costs ruin it for the hundreds of thousands of ethical lawyers providing good service to their clients. I am proud to know many of them. I also know others like you and am sad to see them thriving.

Pressing on, you ask O.J. has he ever accused the police of planting evidence. He says he didn't. The implication of this is that by not accusing the police of foul play he couldn't use this as a defense. I don't get it, Dan. At the point that you expect him to ask this, none of the evidence was analyzed so why would O.J. have been concerned. Blood at the scene would be expected. This was a knife murder, remember?

You now turn up the volume! Telling O.J. that he was the one who went to Nicole's that night and murdered her and Ronald. Wow, a movie moment! The leading attorney yells at the witness accusing him of a double homicide. What answer did you expect, Dan, a total confession?

Yep, you got me there, counselor, I did it!"

You were obviously doing this for effect. This is a far cry from your insistent claim of seeking the truth. You finish with the accusation of leaving "'..with his eyes open, looking right at you. True or untrue?'"[14] O.J. says, "That's untrue."[15] You have no further questions. A sigh of relief from me.

Notes:

[1] Daniel Petrocelli, *Triumph of Justice*, (Crown, 1998), pg. 517

[2] Ibid, pg. 517

[3] Ibid, pg. 529

[4] Ibid, pg. 528

[5] Ibid, pg. 529

6 Ibid, pg. 530

7 Ibid pg 530

8 Ibid pg 531

9 Ibid pg 532

10 Ibid pg. 532

11 Ibid pg 537

12 Ibid pg 538

13 Ibid pg 538

14 Ibid pg 540

15 Ibid pg 540

THIRTY-ONE
Will the Real O.J. Please Stand Up?

The Real O.J.

As you return to your seat you assess your performance.

"And I had taken him apart I had exposed Simpson as a liar, deeply flawed liar, a man with no conscience."[1]

O.J. did not go into a rage on the stand and you concluded this helped destroy him. You really like the rage concept. Rage, of course, has all types of expression. He didn't physically attack you. You showed rage and you accuse O.J. of killing in rage. It all depends upon the degree of rage, right counselor. You claim O.J. was confessing guilt because

"He seethed where he should have been calm; he was disturbingly calm in exactly those places where he should have raged."[2]

That body language again, revealing guilt. Be damned the testimony, just look into the witnesses eyes, observe his breathing, look at him squirm. That's all you need, dear jurist, to determine guilt or innocence. Way to go, Dan! You got the confession the world was looking for in a look, squirm and a puff. The ultimate lie detector test! This skill could save the justice system a whole lot of money. Put the accused on the stand and have the lawyer scream questions and then evaluate the witness's body language and you can have your verdict. Evidence, logic, forensics, are a big waste of time. The Petrocelli method is far more efficient. Taxpayers of the U.S. thank, Dan.

A juror acts inappropriately, admiring an attorney's tie; another wears an inappropriate tee shirt to court stating, "'*Let's bump into the night*'"[3]. How about three bumps? Another buys candy for all the attorneys. The judge dismisses the wardrobe jerk. You are not happy. She was one you thought was on your side. You look at the alternates and don't want the Afro-American as a replacement. When they pick the new number out of the hat, you were relieved it wasn't her. Your ugly bigots head is surfacing again. When I am reminded how racist you are, it turns my stomach into an even tighter knot than your hypocrisies.

You worry about O.J.'s lawyer cross-examination, fearing the jury would get a different picture. I am sorry, Mr. P. that is the process. You get your stabs and he gets to defend himself. You are confident that after "...*two days of scorched-earth devastation, there would be no chance O.J. could be rehabilitated.*"[4] Patting yourself on the back again. You devastated O.J. with a phone call that he denied receiving. Making lemonade out of lemons?

The court rested with six and a half days off for Thanksgiving. Upon returning it is your time to put on impeachment witnesses. You pare the list down to the best few. Deciding not to call Faye Resnick despite all the stuff she gave you during depositions. You bore the reader with imagining what might have been said despite your taking them off your list. This is just another example of your ability to waste our time with useless imaginings. You call over 20 witnesses in rapid-fire succession over four days. There were only two that seemed to offer testimony that needed to be analyzed. The other witnesses confirmed that O.J. and Nicole had a stormy relationship, he may have hit her, he used the restroom a few too many times on his way back from Chicago, O.J. was upset over the divorce, he argued with Paula, he was angry while playing golf the morning of the murders, he minimized the 1989 incident to a Hertz employee. Nicole may have reported to an abuse center she was being stalked by her ex-husband and he threatened to kill her if he ever caught her with another man, her diary had entries of brutality, and Paula thought O.J. had picked up her "*Dear John*" message that morning of the murders. A wardrobe stylist form Playboy video shoot testified that they gave O.J. sweat suits that matched fiber similar to that found on Ron's shirt. You cause us to remember the killer's outfit was never found and all this is speculation. You presume it was a sweat suit based on some flimsy theory about a thread of cloth used in sweat suit making. There are so many simple explanations possible. Did Ron own his own dark sweat suit? Maybe he was doing laundry earlier that day. Another killer, other than O.J. could have worn the sweat suit. I own about five of these outfits. Jason could have been wearing it. Maybe even his Dad's. If he helps himself to his Dad's shoes and hat, why not the sweat suits also? You know Dan, Jason the son you deposed and would not ask him where he was the evening of the murders. The same Jason that your partner believed was a possible suspect; the same Jason that met his Dad after the freeway chase; the same one who got fired for wielding a knife at his employer; and the one who would lose if Nicole got the prenuptial rescinded. This is the same boy who watched his dad be tormented by this *ho*. O.J. owning a dark sweat suit says nothing concrete about his participation in the murder. Would it even be plausible to suggest that O.J. would keep track of his gifts of shoes and clothing? He was a $30 million man. I wouldn't call him a liar if he failed to remember the contents of each and every thing in his closet.

The testimony of a passenger sitting next to O.J. on the flight back form Chicago reveals that O.J. told him Nicole and a man had been killed in a garden by the street where Nicole lived. You pose this as a problem because O.J. was not told that it was a double homicide. You claim that the only way O.J. could have known this was first hand information. Many hours had transpired since the police called Chicago and O.J. had made many phone calls. If you are going to accuse him this way, why didn't you ask this question of him when he was on the stand? Give the man a chance to defend himself. Why would you ignore such an obvious question unless you were afraid of the answer? According to you this is "...*monumental*"[5] testimony! A monument to what; innuendo, deception, and misdirection?

Now you are going to give us devastating testimony from Skip Taft. He said that a day after the murders, June 13th, after O.J. returned from Chicago, he saw two to three cuts on O.J.'s hands. O.J. claimed there was only one cut. If O.J. couldn't explain these two extra cuts, "...*that was the end of the road for him!*"[6] The police photographed one cut; Skip is asked if he saw two or three cuts. He responds, *"As I sit here today, I recall one cut.*"[7] You are caught up short. You re-ask this question. Skip insists that as he sits here today he saw only one cut. He is denying his own deposition testimony. Even though we have gone over this problematic hypothesis too many times, this is serious stuff. The depositions are referred to and you get in Skip's face about his need to be truthful. You and O.J.'s lawyers bark at each other.

Skip gives his explanation of why he might be confused during his prior testimony. Skip insists that his current understanding is truthful. While this is going on, I am asking myself, what's the difference? One cut or two could all be innocently explained. Time had elapsed; cuts and other answers could also be possible. Taft is an attorney and realized that if he were less that truthful the consequences would be nasty. He testified with all that in mind. Also, he could have believed as I do, the number of cuts is irrelevant unless there were corresponding cuts on the gloves. In addition, how does the assailant with the knife get cut in a 75 second double homicide? Let's cut to the chase, no cuts, and no chase, nothing for a jury to consider. Skip disgusted you with yet another unbelievable story. You score this incident as damaging to O.J. You called the witness. He didn't give you what you wanted and you are outraged. Skip didn't have to lie about the number of cuts because they didn't speak to the guilt or innocence of O.J. The cuts could have been easily explained away. He did not have to take the chance of perjuring himself. Yes, again, you used information that was not important and blew it up in your favor. Skip did look bad, no question about that. I still fail to see what this means in making O.J. look bad. Skip took the stabs from you and wouldn't back down. He was either telling the truth as he knew it now, or he felt he was helping a friend get away with paying millions of dollars. No, I spoke too soon. O.J. didn't stand to lose any money at this trial. Time has shown us that O.J. wasn't even risking money in this trial. With that out of the equation, please tell me what the motive on Skip Taft's part would be other than to tell the truth? I'll develop this in more detail later.

I have no comment on your comments regarding the testimony of the Goldman's. They brought everyone to tears. Rightfully so. Their loss was great.

Notes:

[1] Daniel Petrocelli, *Triumph of Justice*, (Crown, 1998), pg. 541

[2] Ibid, pg. 541

[3] Ibid, pg. 543

[4] Ibid, pg. 545

[5] Ibid, pg. 551

6 Ibid pg 552

7 Ibid pg 552

THIRTY-TWO
Tactics, Tactics

Breaking down the Defense

The defense calls Detective Vannatter first. They throw all the old stuff at him. Rush to Judgment, all the odd activity. Vannatter kept his cool. Thirty years as a cop he was accustomed to testifying. You believe that he handled himself well and the jury would not believe that he was a part of planting evidence. That's fine, Dan. I don't know if Vannatter did anything wrong. I don't know if it couldn't have happened without his help. He was just one of the detectives on the case. There is no way to prove that there was foul play, it just seems like some things do not make sense. You have heard all the arguments, theories, and guesses. The same problem is on your side of the case. You have stories, theories, and speculations that could be true and frankly could be just a fabrication to *move money around*. The burden in all of this is to be convincing. You promised that we would be convinced. You would remove the doubt that clouded the criminal trial. At this point I don't see how you did this with the evidence. All I have observed is lawyer tactics at their best. Not the search for truth.

Andrea Mazzola, a technician trainee, was questioned regarding the handling of the blood evidence at the crime scene. She did bungle the handling. You agree. Your assessment is *"But, so what"*?[1] What if she did handle things improperly, how did that change the results? In many ways, Dan. If the police would let rank amateur collect evidence in such a case, double homicide, high profile, they were demonstrating poor judgment in an important area. If they used poor judgment here then where else? This was such a vital part of a murder case and the experienced LAPD, after four hours of preparing to check the crime scene, turn it over to a trainee. So what? A BIG WHAT! This seems like a bad decision and would scare the hell out of me if my life were on the line.

The missing 1.5 cc of blood from the vile you want to dismiss as unimportant. If sometime in this whole proceeding you would have shown us that the blood found exceeded 1.5 cc's you would make an important point. This is a question begging to be answered, but you fail miserably. If there were more than 1.5 cc found then the jury would have to wonder where it came from. Less than 1.5 ccs and still leaves the discovery of some blood problematic. Where did the blood from the vile go? I have to believe that if you could establish that the forensics found more than 1.5 ccs you would have played it to the hilt. The fact you didn't or didn't even try to find out says you didn't want to know. If less that 1.5 cc's of O.J.'s blood was all that was found at two sites that he had been to in the past, his own residence and Nicole's, then where do you get off talking about *blood all over the place*? Tell me they found a pint of O.J.'s blood then the 1.5 ccs doesn't make a difference and I could accept your description of blood all over the place. 1.5 cc's doesn't go very far except to undermine your use of blood evidence, O.J.'s that is.

Dr. Gerdes testified at the criminal trial that the crime lab was "*...a cesspool of contamination*".[2] Your experts say the lab was just fine. Around and around with experts. You like your expert's, but not the defense's. Nothing new here. You offer as a logical explanation, *"Mistakes in procedure could not possibly explain the fact that all the test results pointed to Simpson."*[3] You can't use faulty pointers to come to a conclusion. How many other rookies were handling this material? How many people handled material that you don't know about? You can't answer that, obviously, but those are the types of questions you ask O.J. You excuse this all away because Mr. Peratis was a frail old man that just made a mistake and took less blood than he thought. Now we have frail old people handling this case. Bigots, rookies, and frail old people; don't worry though. Dan will defend you and Mr. Skilling. (Please excuse the inside joke here)

It would seem that a critical part of the detective work would be the determination of the condition of O.J. after this murder. Did he have any body wounds that would show the signs of a struggle? Any cuts? A careful examination of O.J. was in order. The record shows that all that was found by the police that day was one cut on his hand. The excuse was that's the only place they looked. *"'...I didn't look to see if there was anything else.'"*[4] What? All they looked at was one finger on O.J.'s hand. Nothing else. How preposterous. They took pictures. O.J. came in willingly. He talked to the police voluntarily. They looked at only one finger. Are you keeping a straight face here, Dan? This is way beyond dumb. Now, I am confused because you really don't need cuts on O.J.'s hands to win your case. If anything, with no cuts on the gloves, I can't see why you go to this place over and over. Yet, you need to force the point that O.J. received many cuts. The more you ask, the more I ask, "How could they have happened?" No time, subdued victims, gloved. Press on through you must.

The defense presents a passenger on the plane with O.J. to Chicago that says he looked for a Super Bowl ring on O.J.'s hands and didn't see a ring or bandage. You claim that based on where he was sitting he couldn't see O.J.'s hands. That may be true, but you must allow for the fact people move around on an airplane there could have been some opportunity for him to look at O.J.'s hands. More importantly you couldn't produce one witness, not one, Dan, who saw a cut or bandage on O.J.'s hands. Not, Kato, Park, The people who met him at the airport, ticket taker, luggage handlers, drivers, other plane passengers, receptionist at the Chicago hotel, bellman, the fellow that took O.J.'s bags to his room, autograph seekers along the way, no one, Dan, no one. It doesn't make sense if O.J. had several cuts and bled all over the place. Your argument that to have this crime take place in such a short time the initial blows by the assailant had to be lethal, this would then suggest the victims didn't have the capacity to inflict wounds.

You are feeling good at this point. The jury bought into your story and you feel the defense is losing ground. Your partner, Tom Lambert examines Dr. Gerdes, the expert corner, and challenges his credentials. He does a good job based on your description. Gerdes was exposed as not having experience in collecting evidence or validation studies. Although Gerdes did not do all the things that Lambert asked him about, I couldn't tell if these are important in making an observation that the lab was a cesspool. This seems to be something beyond the practice of collecting evidence or doing studies. I might not be a microbiologist, but I know when a men's room is filthy and not cared for. It doesn't take any special degrees to make that kind of observation. That's all I heard in his testimony. Lambert strayed beyond that and made Gerdes look incompetent. I am not qualified to comment on the import of all this so I'll use your tactic, Dan, So what?

Another expert, Dr. Baden testified that the murders took some time. This was a problem for you because you know there was only a small window if time available that could put O.J. at the crime scene and do the killings. You needed the double murder to take place in a little over a minute. Baden has done over 20,000 autopsies. He believed that Ron put up quite a struggle. He didn't have evidence that Nicole put up a struggle, although she may have. Baden testified that Ron oozed blood for 10 to 20 minutes. He was paid $100,000 for his work on the case. Plus he got to be on television. You are getting paid over $1 million and you get to be on television. Why would his testimony be any less valid than your legal work? Baden gives us very important stuff. The cut on O.J.'s hand is the type that could happen from a glass. This crime would need more than one killer to control noise or avoid escaping. Baden gives his guess as to how Ron died. Two experts with different opinions and theories, Baden says that a killer wouldn't leave a scene until he was sure both victims were dead. That makes a lot of sense. Is O.J. an expert on determining if the victims are dead? Probably not. Merely because they aren't moving is not enough to go by. How does O.J. make sure? How much time does it take for the victim to die? Baden says up to 20 minutes. He's not sure, just like Spitz was not sure they both died in 75 seconds. All of this is possible, but let's not rule out commonsense. This double murder took at least 5 to 10 minutes, according to this guesser. You take a guess. If you are over 2 minutes, let O.J. go and let's go look for the real killer. Dan still gets his money.

When O.J. explained to Baden how he received miscellaneous cuts he referred to getting his cell phone from the Bronco. You take this as an admission the phone was in the Bronco. Another nail in the coffin. We went over this too many times. I don't buy it. Baden says there are several possible scenarios. In predictable legal tactics you get him to agree that there are other possibilities. That is the problem with experts; separating the probable from the possible. You want to make the possible, probable, better than that, a fact! Volumes of mumbo-jumbo. The jury, reader and anyone else speculating on what happened should let commonsense prevail when the experts disagree. You are all contaminating our logic and making barrels of money.

Your photo expert does a good job establishing the Bruno Magli shoes on O.J. at the Buffalo/Miami football game were genuine. His credentials were better than the defense's expert. I won't walk in that shoe story again. It's been treaded on enough. You decide, jury, if O.J. was wearing these high priced loafers to kill Nicole. Or could it have been someone else, like Jason, or the several other possibilities.

You bring up the bloody socks again. The $40 dress socks under the dark sweat suit. One expert says that the blood looks like it was planted; your expert says they could have been transferred though O.J.'s perspiration. This is the same pair of socks that O.J. left for the police to find in the middle of his bedroom. Supposedly, O.J. masterfully disposed of the outfit and the knife and the Bruno Magli's, but forgot the socks. Just two problems: O.J. peeled off the tight fitting gloves and dropped them for the entire world to see and then left his socks in the open. We know that criminals make mistakes. This is why there are jails. We know they make dumb mistakes. These two mistakes are particularly conspicuous. O.J. according to Mr. P's theories didn't want to get caught. He hid evidence and created alibis; except for blood on the gloves, the hat, and the socks and all around. It was no longer the perfect crime. The crumbs if he left them would lead back to his feet. What do you do now, O.J.? Pretend you are not guilty and go off to Chicago, preventing you from cleaning up the last few pieces of evidence that might incriminate you? After making this bad decision, do you fret over the consequences of leaving incriminating bloody evidence behind? Would you fly back to L.A. or head for France where they don't extradite murderers who face capital punishment? Double murder equals capital punishment. O.J. may be arrogant, but this would be beyond the idiot level to walk into a police station without a lawyer if he committed the crimes.

You go through more blood evidence and get us caught up into how much EDTA can be found in a sample before it is rendered useless. Experts again speculate and one side says one thing and the other side says the opposite. All paid for their testimony. No wonder this judge doesn't like these expert witnesses. Your expert, an FBI specialist was not allowed to testify because members of his lab were being questioned regarding bad lab work. Shucks. You find another expert to stand in for him. This is too confusing for this reader. It is impossible to know which expert to believe. Or more likely they are all correct because you direct specific non-pointed question that merely add up to speculation. They all have the ability to say, "*I am not sure or It is possible.*", with authority. All this information is useless to me.

During the testimony that day you get news that O.J. was awarded custody of his children. This is an important point. Would a judge give over two children to someone she considered a murderer? She must have thought long and hard over this one. In the case of a judge deciding on custody it can be argued that this is one of the most impressive statements from the legal system. A white, educated woman trained in the law and duty-bound to protect the children, says O.J. should have custody. No jury selection problems here. Just a responsible person making a decision that O.J. was not a danger. I wonder how Fred Goldman took this news. You rightfully check the score. O.J. – Two; Opposition - Zero. No matter what the verdict is in your trial, O.J. is still ahead on legal points.

Notes:

[1] Daniel Petrocelli, *Triumph of Justice*, (Crown, 1998), pg.565

[2] Ibid, pg. 566

[3] Ibid, pg. 567

4 Ibid pg 566

THIRTY-THREE

Oh, No! More Shoes

More Ugly Ass Shoes

You get a two-week Christmas break. During this time you find more photos that show O.J. wearing shoes that look like the Bruno's. You are thrilled. No way can O.J. talk his way out of these photos. Despite this, O.J. still insists that he does not remember owning or wearing these shoes. I have given you many reasons these photos are not helpful to your case. It is clear to you now that O.J could be mistaken, forgetful, or lying. Any of these do not help you, however. The lying part might link into the Jason possibility or a police planting theory, but you didn't ask Jason where he was that night or if he ever wore his daddy's shoes. Your obvious failure to seek out this truth damns the whole shoe theory in my mind. You only want to deal with this out of your manufactured context. This is one of the seven vile sins of your legal tactics. You narrow the scope of your questions to be certain that the only answer you can be given is the one favorable to your position. You are getting a lot of mileage out of the shoes. O.J.'s denial in the face of the picture is making him look very bad.

O.J.'s lawyer reminds the jury that this crime has a major question,

"On June 12, 1994, did you, with the children in the house, upstairs in their bedroom, asleep, murder your wife – ex-wife – and leave her body where the kids would find it?" "'No,' he swore." "Absolutely not?"[1]

You are finished with O.J. What you are saying to this reader is after all of this testimony there are only two things you have to add to the evidence presented at the criminal trial: the shoes and the phone call from Paula where she tells O.J. they are finished. These two things do not a new trial make. In my mind, they are not incriminating. Even when added to the other evidence it does not produce a convincing case.

Notes:

[1] Daniel Petrocelli, *Triumph of Justice*, (Crown, 1998), pg. 594

THIRTY-FOUR

Bluster at the Highest Level

Close Strong

Arnelle Simpson testified that she told her dad two people were killed, Nicole being one. This speaks against your theory that when O.J. told the passenger on the way from Chicago to L.A. that his wife and another person were killed, there was no way for him to know that. Of course, you accuse Arnelle of lying.

Now time for rebuttals. You feel you have put on the perfect case. You thought there was a risk involved by putting on a rebuttal, but you needed to get one more shot at O.J. wearing those shoes at the Buffalo/Miami game. With the door open you would, "...*destroy the last vestiges of the defense case.*"[1] In closing arguments, you would "...*arm the jury with this ammunition*"[2]. I draw this quote because I love your murder metaphors; guns, ammunition, destroy. That killer lawyer instinct takes another 2 ½ days of rebuttal putting more billable hours on top of your perfect case. This consists of mainly more photo verification and bloody sock analysis.

You rest your case. Baker rests. We rest, except for your closing arguments. No new arguments, just a rehash of the old. More lawyer storytelling. The lawyers jockey for position in telling the story. They all want a chance up at bat and they all feel they have a specialty to contribute. They all want to share the spotlight. You work that all out.

How do you *attack*? With "*an all out assault on his celebrity, his image, his credibility.*"[3] Then you review all the *facts*. The media is surrounding you for post-verdict interviews. You will be a celeb. Four days of organizing your arguments. You had "...*felt a rage of my own. I had to find an acceptable way, short of using a knife, to get it out.*"[4] You are getting yourself pumped up for this legal Super Bowl.

You walk through the tumultuous mob scene to the courthouse. It was wild. Before you start your arguments you make some motions to insure that your client gets paid in the event of a verdict in his behalf. Isn't this a bit late in the game to bring this up? You were very worried up front as to how you were going to get paid. Now it occurs to you that you need to address your client's needs. As it turns out you didn't deal with this properly.

You tell your version of what happened the night of the murders and pour on the emotional factors of a double homicide of two young people. You raise two points that are figments of your rich imagination. First you have the victim during this fast killing, tearing off O.J.'s glove. That is very hard to imagine being real. Tight fitting glove, if it fit at all, being removed by the victim during the assault that takes only 60 seconds. The victim also gets close enough to take off O.J.'s knit hat. That's also hard to visualize. You also claim that they scratched O.J. yet no forensic evidence verifies that. It's your story. I have a lot of trouble picturing these events happening under the specific circumstances you portray. You bring these thoughts to a shout, "'...that there is a killer in the courtroom'"[5] and point to O.J. This is the stuff movies are made of counselor. You pat yourself on the back for your great performance. You wanted the jury to know that you were working from "...absolute certainty"[6] A show of ultimate confidence. You didn't have to go that far, but in the world of smoke and mirrors I can see that this is good strategy. Impressive, all this confidence as you go on to criticize O.J.'s lawyer and O.J. for not challenging your arguments. They did, Mr. P., you are just fooling the jury in the most contemptible way with this tactic. He answered all your questions as truthfully as he was able. You are claiming he didn't. This is a favorite and diabolical lawyer trick. The witness answers all the questions and the opposing lawyer says, *See he didn't answer any of the questions.* Poor jury, unfortunately it works too well, too often. This is very difficult for a jury to deal with. Great lawyering! Moves a lot of money around and is a sad, sad, cancer in the legal system. You try to establish that O.J. lied and lied often. Dan, I walked carefully through your book and the best I could come up with is one possible lie and a lot of so whats? The possible lie is retrieving the call from Paula and the *so what* is everything about the shoes. You felt in command of the courtroom. Powerful stuff, controlling the process. The jury is buying into your story. You can feel it. The Daniel Petrocelli Magic Show continues as you try to dispel any other cause of the murders by offering the least probable. How about some of the good theories, Dan?

The blood found is O.J.'s and no one is disputing that. How did the few little drops get there? Let's avoid the possibility of foul play. You said that's absurd, anyways. Your explanation as to how the bloody glove got on to O.J.'s property is because it had O.J.'s blood on it, so it must have come from Bundy. Listen to yourself. We have not forgotten about the 1.5 cc of missing blood that O.J. volunteered. Also, the blood is analyzed in the laboratory, not at the crime scene. Let's not forget how bungled this whole evidence was handled. You are asking questions of the jury and the entire implication is that it must be clear that O.J. was wearing those gloves. Clear to you, but not to me. You reminded the jury that there was blood dripped all over O.J.'s house. All over the house is not what was found, just on two suspicious socks.

Now you accuse O.J. of successfully hiding the cuts from the detectives. You show a picture that indicates another cut. Therefore, there should have been two cuts on the glove. The more cuts on O.J. the more cuts you need on the gloves and around we go. And then you want us to believe these murders happened in "*no time.*"[7] Please, Dan, how can you say that with a straight face? There is too little time and you know it. No reasonable person should accept the probability of all these events to have taken place in the few minutes you claim. With all the people giving you the time frame when event occurred, did you discover if they all had their timepieces synchronized? Get six people in a room and check their watches. Will they all be on the same time? That is a problem. Therefore, you will have error on top of error in the estimation game. You are trying to make this like an Olympic time trial murder event starting with a stopwatch and ending at a precise time which everyone is in agreement with. We all know that time estimations do not happen that way. There is too much room for error and miscalculation especially with Kato. I'm not sure he knows what day it is. With all this chance for error, you have the audacity to say there was plenty of time.

You ask the jury for justice and to find O.J. guilty. There's that Justice concept again. Don't forget the money, man. You want him to pay for the misery he has caused. You play a video showing Ronald Goldman at his Bar Mitzvah as a touching way to end.

Notes:

[1] Daniel Petrocelli, *Triumph of Justice*, (Crown, 1998), pg. 596

[2] Ibid, pg. 596

[3] Ibid, pg. 596

4 Ibid pg 600

5 Ibid pg 602

6 Ibid pg. 603

7 Ibid pg. 79

THIRTY-FIVE
Money Moved Around

Duty Performed or Duty Violated

O.J.'s lawyer, Baker now gives his closing arguments. Your sense of the presentation is that he had lost his fight. You point out that he agrees O.J. might have picked up Paula's message. He is making the point that this evidence is an inconsequential *so what*. How damaging would it have been for O.J. to admit picking up that message? It might have been bad news, but would this drive a man over the top enough to kill his ex-wife? It wouldn't appear so. There was no good motive to lie. Without a good motive, I repeat, so what and why?

You close with a quote from Daniel Webster and ask the jury for justice. We are all done. Eloquence, ranting, innuendo, posturing at its 1.2 million best. You are proud of your work. At the top of your game.

THIRTY-SIX

No Way

Responsibility

The judge gives instructions to the jury. A point that might go unnoticed is that the jury is not being asked if they think that O.J. murdered Nicole. *Only that he battered her.* This is not what the public's impression is over the verdict. The Goldmans want us to believe that they spoke to an act of murder. It would follow that if he battered her that evening he would also be the killer, but that wasn't what the jury was asked to rule upon. So Fred, you are the only one who will benefit (if you can get any money from O.J.) from the wrongful death aspect of this trial. Seems like another strange quirky part of law.

The jury deliberates and comes in with a unanimous decision. O.J. must pay for the death of Ron and the battering of Nicole. Mr. Petrocelli, your story prevailed. Good work except for one very important issue, the money your client didn't get.

THIRTY-SEVEN
Justice Defeated

The Pursuit of Justice

Mr. Petrocelli, you got yours and you could have proudly accounted for it in this book. Show us some accountability by itemizing the time and expenses and the refund or over-runs due, if any. Here we are 11 years later and no one has received any money except the lawyers. No wonder you wanted all your money up front. A good lawyer would probably know that his client would not get anything. How up front were you with Fred on this little detail? It is in this fact that the real story can be told.

O.J. was advised by his lawyers on how to protect his assets in the event he should lose this case. He followed their instructions. O.J. had little to no risk of losing any money with this case. Let that thought sink in deeply. Hardly any risk of losing money. He could have tried to settle with you or just forfeited. A forfeit would give an award to the plaintiffs just like the jury trial did; only in this case the judge would make the award. O.J. could argue that he would get better treatment from a judge than from a loaded jury. If there were no monetary risks, why would O.J. go to all the trouble of testifying if he were guilty? Better said, he would only agree to testify if he were innocent. As an innocent man there was no risk at all. In his heart he knows that he is innocent. He would believe going in that a jury would see this. His lawyer would have warned him, despite his innocence he could be made to look guilty. This is a cliché about jury trials. O.J. made the

313

decision to risk a bad verdict and testify in a case that he could have avoided. It was just money. O.J. had everything to gain and nothing to lose by not testifying. The only motive that makes sense is that O.J. knew he did not commit these murders as you insist he did.

We will probably never know, but what we have discovered is how lawyers can abuse the justice system and then brag about it openly. They can lie and admit to it. They can be bigots and abuse their clients. They make a whole lot of money doing all these things. I call this an evil in our society and it should be excised. Watch out misguided lawyers of America!

THIRTY-EIGHT

Summations

Summation of the evidence presented in your book:

1. <u>**Motive**</u>: You claim that O.J. had a bad day at golf, was rejected by Paula, and embarrassed by the totality of his problems with Nicole. On this day, the sum of these problems brought O.J. to a rage that drove him to premeditate a murder of his ex-wife and then kill an innocent bystander. I think that Nicole was constantly giving O.J. problems. The variable offered to account for O.J.'s murderous attitude was Paula's rejection, not being invited to a post recital dinner and a bad golf morning. He was continually on and off with Paula. So the convergence of a message from Paula and bad golf does not lead me to believe that this would drive him to murder. Breaking it down this way, it sounds foolish. These three small problems were more than O.J. could handle in one day leading to murder being the only relief. I can't accept that motive.

2. <u>**Counter-motive**</u>: There were too many reasons for O.J. to not commit these crimes. He enjoyed wealth, was an adored superstar, Hall of Fame athlete, had easy access to most everything he wanted. He had just made a date with a Playboy model. He had four children, two very young. There is a very high probability of getting caught committing a knife murder. His children were present at the scene of the crime. Only in

the heat of an argument would this make sense. Not under the premeditated hypothesis you present.

3. **Opportunity:** Anyway you cut it, this timeline doesn't work. I believe this was one of the most important factors influencing the jury in the first trial. You insisted with the help of your paid expert, that this all could have happened in the few minutes available. You do little to persuade us that here was sufficient time to murder, get back to the house, clean up and meet the driver in 20 minutes. As one of your weakest points you argue that it is possible, but fails badly in the realm of the probable. The lack of time advocates the lack of a premeditated motive. Surely, the time restraints of June 12th speak against him choosing that evening. Ronald Goldman arriving on the scene would have also ruined this opportunity. Logic will show that even if O.J. had planned the murder, if Ron was there, he probably would have passed. If he showed up after O.J. killed Nicole, he would probably be alive today. If he showed up while O.J. was in the act, most probably she would still be alive today and O.J. would be in jail. A plan needs to have the elements occurring correctly. Many a crime has been aborted because new unexpected elements have been introduced causing the perpetrator to pass. According to your timeline, there was no logical opportunity on June 12th for O.J. to commit these murders.

4. **Physical Evidence:**

    a. The knit cap as evidence presents many questions. Why would someone wear a knit cap in summer in LA? It is not a disguise that would work with Nicole, if anything it would make her concerned. Is it possible that a policeman who entered O.J.'s property without warrant stuffed a knit hat in his pocket, which he later dropped on the crime scene? Since we often see criminals in movies wearing knit hats this would be a logical choice for a plant. Nor would this have been a difficult task. All you need is sufficient motive and this case is ripe with motive for tampering and planting. Those associated in the apprehension of a high profile murderer can look forward to a career advancement and admission in the Police Hall of Fame. This is especially compelling because O.J. was a natural suspect. No one wants an unsolved murder.

b. The leather gloves are a challenge when you try to connect them to O.J. They were tight fitting, if they fit at all. With the crime taking place as quickly as you require, visualizing how and when the gloves came off presents a dilemma. Did the victims pull them off in the 60 seconds you say it took for this crime to be committed? Why would O.J. remove one of the gloves and carelessly drop it beside the body and then remove the other and drop it in his yard? This scenario just doesn't make sense. Cuts on O.J.'s hand, but not on the gloves. You carefully avoid connecting these dots. If he cut his hand in the commission of these crimes and was wearing the gloves there would have to be cuts on the gloves.

c. Shoe prints, size 12, slightly pigeon-toed found at the murder scene. This fits O.J.'s footprint description, but does it also fit Jason's or any of Nicole's lovers? He looks like he could be a size 12 and may be slightly pigeon-toed like daddy. You don't give us enough here, but maybe.

d. The Bruno Magli's have traveled far. There are still questions. Are these the type of shoes O.J. would wear with a sweat suit? Could Jason have worn them? Where are they? Where are all the murder clothes? In the time frame that you outline you give us no compelling theory as to how O.J. would have disposed of the murder clothes. It is highly unlikely that he would just drop them off along the way. They would have been too easy for the police to find. Even the best of friends would not likely risk being an accessory to a murder by disposing of them for him. And the strange combination of a sweat suit, dress socks, and Bruno Magli's along with a knit hat does not add up to a likely outfit even for a murderer. I believe that the shoes were either planted at the scene or worn by another, possibly Jason, if they were indeed O.J.'s shoes. Least likely, but not out of the question in this high rent district where Bruno Magli's reside, it could have been the footwear of another. Perhaps the fellow that caused Nicole to become pregnant or one of her other lovers, but you allow in your trial no other possibility other than O.J. You believe that he would leave all this incriminating evidence at his home and the crime scene and then fly to Chicago and when returning visit the police station for voluntary questioning. Are you crazy?

e. Simpson's Bronco contained small amounts of O.J.'s blood and Ron and Nicole's blood. O.J.'s blood in small quantities would be expected since it was his vehicle. The amount of Ron's and Nicole's blood was definitely too small considering the type of knife murder that took place. The lack of a considerable amount of blood makes me suspicious. There were easy opportunities for planting a smear here and there. Remember the chap that impounded the vehicle did not see any blood. The blood was found months later. Your convenient explanation is that he was wrong. Since there was not enough blood to make a bloody difference we have to wonder about police mischief.

f. The drops of blood found on Simpson's driveway, up his stairs, into his bedroom and bathroom offer several questions. Too often you exaggerate. How many drops were there? How do you know when they got there? Was it when he returned from Chicago with a bad cut on his hand? I need more information including specific locations. If you did the research, you wouldn't keep it from us, would you? This is the kind of information that I thought you would deliver. You promised us convincing evidence. Now if you could have produced a cut on the hand matching a cut on the glove, boy, that would have been something. Without this kind of concrete evidence what you offer is nothing, but bad logic, gross suppositions and a fairy tale. With all your bluster and rhetoric, we see you talking the talk, but not walking the walk. With all the forensics magic at your disposal what you give us is guess work. You can't even show us that the blood found exceeds the 1.5 cc's missing from the vile. All of the blood evidence adds up to more reasonable doubt.

g. O.J. had several cuts all over his hands and yet we have no evidence that there was any O.J. tissue found under the nails of Nicole or Ron. Since you are silent on this subject, we have to conclude this is another of your gross exaggerations. The best of the LAPD took pictures and found only one cut and perhaps another. You need O.J.'s lawyer and friend to give you evidence of more cuts which he doesn't deliver under the threat of perjury. How does an assailant in a 60 second murder get all these cuts you are alluding to? O.J. as a golf fanatic probably gets cuts all the time. Now that you have made me conscious of getting cuts I find them frequently without benefit of their origination. Most times I could only give you a good guess.

h. Lastly are the cotton fibers from a dark sweat suit found at the crime scene and Simpson's home and Bronco carpet fibers found at the crime scene? You have not established that the murderer was wearing a sweat suit. No one saw them. The only clue you can offer is Park testimony regarding *like someone wearing a sweat suit crossing O.J.'s property.* Since this was at night, how reliable would this be? Park's couldn't have known from his vantage point what kind of fabric the suit was made of. Since the murder clothes were never found all of this is supposition. There are too many alternative explanations to suggest one possibility as being a fact. O.J. had been on the property many times before so we can't establish when these fibers got there. If Jason was driving the Bronco then O.J. could be totally out of the picture. This case has too many circumstances to provide concrete evidence leading to guilt.

This is your list Mr. P. Add them all up and you get a few maybes and a whole lot of unanswered questions. This is the same problem that occurred at the criminal trial. Yes, O.J. had to be considered a suspect. There were many incriminating facts: abuse, blood, and constant conflict screamed out guilt, but once you look closely at the tangible facts they just don't add up. Many things were very wrong with no reasonable explanations offered except foul play on the part of the police. You don't give us any reason to truly eliminate the possibility of tampering, planting, and contamination of evidence.

You had a good chance to win this case because of the highly pitched emotional fever it provoked which you used to the hilt. There are many people today that still believe without a doubt that O.J. is the killer and they will not be swayed. If you succeed in getting enough of these on your hand picked jury, you win. This was a highly unusual case in that the bias was deep and widespread. You could feed off this and you did while Fred is still waiting at the empty trough. Did you clue him in to the fact that it was highly unlikely he would see any money? You knew and that was why you wanted your fees up front. O.J.'s lawyers had made him judgment proof. Now after 11 years we all know that just the lawyers got paid. This seems to me another miscarriage of justice that has been made possible by the influence and proclivity of lawyers acting in their own interests.

THIRTY-NINE

Reasons

The reasons it does not make sense that O.J. premeditated this murder:

1. **The bad choice of a knife as a murder weapon.** The results are uncertain. The knife may drop. You may not find a lethal target. It's very personal. Blood leaves lots of potential incriminating evidence. A knife is a ridiculous weapon in the hands of an untrained killer. There is much risk of causing noise that would wake the children and attract witnesses especially in the setting that the murder took place. Making a movie does not produce a skilled knife user. In a premeditated scenario, a knife would not be the weapon of choice.

2. <u>**Planning the murder of his ex-wife while his children were present in the house and most probably still awake does not fit the past conduct of O.J.**</u> There is no evidence that he would be capable of premeditating such cruel abuse against his children.

3. <u>**Going to McDonald's to create an alibi for pulling off this murder is just silly.**</u> There is no reasonable explanation why he would introduce a side trip with that many variables under the circumstances the tight timeline required.

4. <u>**Evidence left behind speaks to a spontaneous murder rather than a deliberate murder.**</u> In a rage anything is likely: A nearby

weapon, an uncontrollable urge to action, reason is abandoned and details are ignored. This would fit a scenario where gloves are left on the crime scene, socks left in the bedroom, and lots of blood leaving trails of clues pointing to the identity of the killer.

The lack of evidence, circumstantial and otherwise, that O.J. perpetrated these crimes:

1. Blood, blood, blood everywhere. This was your constant description yet you never show us evidence that there was more than 1.5 cc's of blood in totality. That is a problem. If events had proceeded according to your description, there should have been a lot more blood in the Bronco alone. All over the place does not equate with a smear here and there. These small smears smear the police department more than O.J. If we had more blood evidence then we could imagine O.J. coming home dripping blood and seeking an alternative entrance onto his property to avoid being seen by the driver waiting in his driveway. Over the wall, as you suggest, would mean blood on the wall and from the wall to the place where the *thumps* were heard. Or did he take off the clothes and scale the wall naked? In the time frame you offer this is unlikely. Where is all this blood? Nicole lost almost all of her blood and Ron was stabbed over 50 times. There were pools of blood at the crime scene yet you give us little blood evidence found at O.J.'s residence or in the Bronco. A drop here and there would not support this favored scenario.

2. Your conclusion that O.J. washed the bloody clothing in his washing machine during a four-minute trip from the lawn to his bedroom to change clothes. If this gives him time to wash up, dress, and meet the driver then he is traveling at warp speed. In reality this only meets the requirements of warped logic.

3. If the cuts were perpetrated during the commission of the crimes why does no one see them on his way to Chicago? No one observes blood on O.J.'s hand, not Kato, the driver, hotel

employes, baggage handlers, or anyone who might have come in contact with him during his flight or hotel check-in. The next day many people see his bloody hand. You offer us no explanation.

4. What reasons would he have to return to L.A. rather than fleeing? In Chicago, a guilty O.J. would have realized that he left too much evidence pointing to his culpability. This would be the time to *get out of Dodge*. A trip to France or another equally friendly country without extradition would make sense. If fleeing were not an option, then a wall of lawyers with plausible explanations to minimize the damage would have been the best strategy. A plea of temporary insanity, a self-defense set up, or any story that would appeal to the mercy of the public and the courts was an alternative. Merely returning to L.A. and innocently presenting himself to the police is not the way a guilty person with unlimited resources would act.

5. The bizarre episode on the L.A. freeway does not speak to fleeing or to a real attempt at suicide. This topped the scales of *I don't believe what I just saw*. Millions of people will never forget O.J. and Al Cowlings' crawling along the freeway wondering what was going to happen. Only to return home to the arms of friends, family, Jason included, and the police. No one saw a chase, except you, counselor. What we saw was a slow speed drive that led to a dead-end in his driveway.

6. The criminal case was filled with experts, money, and drama, hundreds of reporters, analysts, lawyers, criminal experts, forensic experts, and a myriad of witnesses and a year of unmatched speculation. Lines were drawn and emotions ran high. The jury saw and were told much. They all knew they were participating in something really extraordinary. The pressure to be fair and just must have been enormous. The lawyers on both sides eloquently reminded them of their duty. They would be the first to make sure a killer didn't walk. They would not want to risk being second-guessed afterwards for not deliberating carefully. Yet these twelve could not unanimously convict. Our jury system has its weaknesses. Guilty people go

free and innocent people are convicted. These imperfections are sad. This jury was given every opportunity to convict O.J. It is hard to believe that his charm and reputation as an athlete could override convincing evidence of his guilt. I will side with the criminal trial jury's conclusion. Someday we may find out how unbiased this conclusion really is.

7. **O.J. did not have to testify in this case.** He was not risking a loss of money by not testifying. The only risk that he took was that he would be found the cause of Ronald Goldman's death and as the batterer of Nicole. If he were indeed guilty what would motivate him to take this unnecessary risk. Only an innocent man would offer himself up to additional scrutiny considering twelve previous jurors came up with a conclusion of not guilty. He knows in his heart that he is innocent and no guilty verdict could change that. A guilty person would not risk being exposed to real evidence supporting his guilt. Only an innocent person would know there could be no real evidence pointing to his guilt.

8. If O.J. knew who the killer was he would not be taking any risk and in some obtuse way would be defending the guilty person. It is not an unreasonable for a father to protect a child. That is the reason I have pushed the Jason theory very hard. *I hope I made it very clear earlier that I have no reason to believe that Jason is the killer. I don't know who caused the deaths of Nicole and Ronald.* The reason I raise a theory that was known by Mr. Petrocelli and his team is to underscore the evil in our system. The police, the lawyers, and the government had a solemn obligation to track down every possible suspect and to create a plausible theory leading to the arrest and conviction of the murderer(s). Because they committed so early in the process to O.J. being the only one with motive and capability to be the killer they were stuck with their position. The slightest admission of other possible suspects with motivations to kill these victims would appear to contradict their conviction. It is somewhat strange the word *conviction* comes to mind here. Those in the business of profiting from crime bought into this story and wouldn't budge. This is an injustice to every person

in America who pays these people's salary directly or indirectly. Prosecutors, detectives, police, and all sundry supporting cast members too often use the system for their own selfish means. In this case for money and fame, but also for other advantages, salary increases, prestige, to name a few. I am aware of too many instances that justice is used as a playground for avaricious players. This minor part of our justice system causes terrible damage. Innocent people are convicted and killers roam the streets. By not asking Jason where he was that night, not checking thoroughly into Faye's drug contacts, not interviewing each and everyone of Nicole's known lovers, not looking for neighborhood foul play, the many options that were possible in this case, the real killer(s) were let off the hook and the critical time was spent fabricating evidence instead of following new leads. If O.J. were the killer he should pay. The government did their level best to convict. There was not enough convincing evidence even with their manipulations to find this man guilty.

9. (My look at point # 8) This next point is I believe the pivotal reason for the writing of this book. As I repeat throughout this text, there is a substantial amount of inconclusive evidence that O.J. committed these crimes. The whole exercise of bringing O.J. to justice could be described as a deflection from the true guilt being placed upon the incompetence of the LAPD from the beginning of this investigation. This set in motion a cover-up throughout the whole system. They were convinced was the only reasonable suspect. This fixed conviction in their minds led them away from evaluating the evidence in a manner open-minded enough to uncover the true murderer. Instead of searching and understanding the clues in a broadminded way, they masterminded the evidence to support their theory. What this amounted to was loss of critical time to find clues leading to the arrest of the real perpetrator(s). This is the true crime that this whole story tells us. True justice is irrevocably lost. In crimes, critical evidence is overlooked in favor of evidence supporting our cherished beliefs including racism, gender bias, and all other manner of separatist issues.

This civil suit was a travesty. It is counter-intuitive that O.J. should have to go through another trial after being found not guilty. It would seem reasonable that before a judge permitted another trial, the plaintiff should have to show clear and convincing new evidence that and additional trial is warranted. Mr. P. didn't even have the shoe pictures at the time this trial began. The new evidence of the Paula message is irrelevant as far as bringing additional information that could convict. The only possible way that Mr. P could win was by picking a sympathetic jury and out-lawyering his opponents, which includes being a more convincing storyteller. This should not have warranted a civil trial that uses the American resources in such a flagrant and irresponsible way.

Our next chapter in this legal adventure will be an invitation for our readers to get involved. First, you will be asked to vote as if you were a juror on possible scenarios. You will be asked to submit experiences of being abused by lawyers. Finally, you will be challenged to recommend improvements to how justice can truly be served in our wonderful United States of America.

FORTY

Murder Scenarios

If O.J. were the killer, how the crimes happened:

Based on all that I learned from the criminal trial and the reading of *The Triumph of Justice* I couldn't convict O.J. of committing the double homicide. I don't rule out that it is possible, but it is neither probable, nor likely that he committed these crimes. All the theories and the evidence cause me to imagine what happened on the evening of June 12th. What was going through O.J.'s mind if he were planning to kill his ex-wife? By imagining how he planned and executed the crimes I might be able to conclude whether or not he was guilty.

There seems to be three major possibilities as to how O.J. would have killed Nicole and Ron.

1. Nicole is killed first and Ron comes upon the scene and becomes the second victim.

2. O.J. kills Ron first and then kills Nicole. (This was the FBI expert's theory.)

3. O.J. catches Ron and Nicole together and knocks out Nicole then kills Ron.

Let's see where these theories take us:

THE EVENING OF JUNE 13, 1994

O.J. just returns to his house after having a burger with Kato. It is about 9:35 pm at least according to Kato's watch. O.J. goes to his bedroom to change into an outfit to carryout his plan to kill Nicole. He has had it with her and there is no other way to end the torment that she has been giving him, but to kill her.

Now we enter O.J.'s mind and thought process: "What do I wear? Sweat suit, yep, freedom of movement. There is a problem though. It is the summer and it is warm out. I have put my sweat suits away. Also, a sweat suit is a bit baggy and Nicole may grab on to it during a struggle. Better wear something tight fitting, but the sweat suit still seems like a better choice. Socks, which pair should I wear? Sweat socks or a pair of my over-the-calf business socks. What am I thinking? Why would I even consider wearing business socks with a sweat suit? I am going to be wearing sneakers with my sweat suit and those business socks just don't work with sneakers."

You can see that we have two problems already. A sweat suit mid-summer is not the best outfit, but it can work. The choice of business socks doesn't make any sense. We need an explanation here, Mr. P. I'm stuck. Second, I don't select wearing a pair of sneakers with my sweat suit. That is highly unusual, but maybe there is a better choice. Walking shoes, climbing shoes? How many pair of shoes do I have in my closet? I wish Mr. P had let us know this fact. The more footwear in the closet, the less likely he would select the Bruno's.

"I will pass on the sneakers and slip on an expensive pair of loafers. This will confuse everyone. A pair of expensive loafers with a sweat suit makes a perfect murder outfit. Let me check the time." I estimate 9:50 pm. "Let's get going Juice; my airport driver will be looking for me at about 10:45. Let me see what else do I need? Oh, a knit cap." What is O.J. thinking, it is June and warm out, why does he need a knit cap? Does he want to look like a criminal when Nicole sees him? This would make her suspicious. This killer is going to make a fashion statement; expensive sweat suit, loafers, business socks and now a knit cap. Can't be a real killer without a knit cap, I guess.

"There is something I must consider. After I kill Nicole with this knife, this outfit is going to have her blood on it so I am going to need a way to get rid of this evidence. Oh, the knife also. I will need to clean-up, get dressed again and be ready for my driver in less than an hour."

"Let me think. How do I get rid of the evidence? Time is my enemy now. If I can't get rid of all this stuff, I'm a goner. This is an unbelievably dumb murder plan. I can't just throw away the stuff; the police are going to be looking everywhere. On the way to the airport is not good. Too many people around watching me; everyone knows O.J. Maybe one of my friends will get rid of the evidence. Let's see whom I can ask. Al, Skip, 'Skunkhead'? What should I ask them to do? Should I call them now and get them ready? They are probably not going to like this idea to help me murder my ex-wife. Who can I ask that is such a good friend that they will agree to hide the evidence? Damn, how do I get rid of the bloody clothes, shoes, hat, and knife without help? Beats me; seems like a knife murder with all the blood has too many problems; back to the drawing board." At this point O.J. would realize that he has many serious problems and would change his plan, but we must push on to complete Mr. P's story.

"I am going to wear this strange outfit and I really can't think of how I am going to dispose of the stuff, but wait a minute. When I attack Nicole where are the kids? It's not 10 o'clock yet and they may still be up. How do I do this and not get them involved? This is a tough one. Nicole may get a chance to scream and struggle. This could frighten the kids and bring them downstairs to find me killing their mother. That would not be a good thing. Possible, yes. Probable, yes. Think a bit faster here the clock is ticking. Just like in a football game. You have to watch the clock and plan your game around available time. How do I avoid the kids? It's a problem, but Mr. P wants me to go ahead anyway."

"Now, let's go over how I can kill Nicole with a knife. I am going to ring the bell and ask to see her. She is going to wonder why I am at her house as we just spoke a half-hour ago and I will be surprising her. She knows I am going off to Chicago and will be tight on time. What good reason would bring me over late at night under these circumstances? I wish I needed something for the trip and just asked to come by to pick it up. She comes down the stairs with whatever that is and I stab her totally by surprise." This could be an interesting theory, but there is no evidence that Nicole had anything for O.J. and she just made plans to have her mother's glasses delivered by Ron.

Without a reason for Nicole to be expecting O.J. it becomes very difficult to picture how O.J. could get in a good position to kill her with a knife. Nicole was killed from behind. That means O.J. would have to have a plan to get behind Nicole. That's very tricky. You can't ask Nicole to turn around, that's too suspicious. I can't imagine how O.J. would believe he could kill Nicole with a knife and not get caught. Too many things could go wrong: screaming, fighting for her life, and running--something a person would normally do when attacked by a killer with a knife. A gun would be a whole different matter. Surprise is a powerful ally in a gun murder. A silencer, a few shots and it's all over. No bloody clothes to hide, no noise, not disturbing the children, just a gun to hide. That's not easy either, but certainly less complicated. Committing a perfect crime is very difficult these days, unless you are in the business of murder. Using a knife is about the most ridiculous choice.

Again, this would normally be a stopping point for O.J. as it is too risky and too dangerous. Since Mr. P has the murders taking place about 10:30-10:40, O.J. has 40 minutes to drive to Nicole's and think this all over. Another problem here, O.J. is time squeezed because of the appointment with his airport driver. We have him killing in the next half an hour. During this time what could O.J. be doing and thinking? He has time to think over his plan and determine the risks to himself. He has time to think over alternatives to getting rid of Nicole. Since he is on this tight time schedule, it would be similar to a quarterback, wasting precious minutes during a two-minute drill. O.J. would be screaming at him, "Let's get going. We don't have any time." One of the theories you throw out is O.J. sitting in the Bronco across from Nicole's during this time and when he saw Ron come upon the scene, he went into the final stages of the rage and carried out his plan, but now including Ron as a victim.

Let's take a step back in this visual. We will imagine O.J. now back at his house. He is dressed, with weapon and ready to go to Bundy to kill Nicole. Does he take the Bronco or the Bentley? The big problem with both of these vehicles is they are easily recognizable as being owned by O.J. if parked near Nicole's home. This is a neighborhood of walkers, joggers, and lots of eyes and ears. Taking either vehicle would be dangerous; too likely someone will see and become a witness. As it turns out no one positively identified the Bronco. That is strange to me considering all the traffic in that neighborhood. O.J. needs to make another difficult decision. "If I take the Bronco and anyone else sees it, I am toast." This would be another place that the plan would stop. The factors are clearly too dangerous if one wants to commit the perfect crime. "Mr. P insists that I choose the Bronco and of course I bring my cell phone. I can't leave that behind." If O.J. gets a call during all of this there is no problem answering the phone?

Now O.J. is driving to Bundy in his Bronco. This could be at about 9:50 according to Mr. P's timeline. The drive is about 5 minutes that brings up another big problem. If the murders took place in 40 to 50 minutes from now, O.J. can't just go park near Nicole's and sit around. This gives too much opportunity to be noticed. This also blows a hole in the FBI's theory that O.J. was sitting across from Nicole's wondering what he should do. Being in this neighborhood for all that time would surely have gotten him identified; bad planning with his conspicuous white Bronco. There are two other reasonable alternatives: He stayed in his house until about 10:30 or he just drove around. The driving around theory seems weak. If we think about him burning all this time knowing he has a deadline and a knife murder to commit, that also makes no sense. Any athlete, especially a football player is very conscious of time. They have been under the pressure of a clock their entire sports career. I wouldn't be surprised if O.J. could tell you with surprising closeness how long two minutes are. In Mr. P's story he wastes a precious half hour. If he were going to commit a knife murder and put his life on the line, it wouldn't be reasonable for him to wait. He has to meet a driver after he cleans up and gets ready for his trip. Mr. P gives us this time problem and no explanation.

Whatever would have happened during this time is speculative. It is now 10:40ish and O.J. makes his move toward Nicole's home. He rings the bell. Nicole asks on the intercom, "Who is it?"

"It's me, Nicky, come on down."

"O.J. it's late and I just put the kids to bed. Go home."

"No I really need to talk to you. Please come down for a minute."

"Okay, let me put something on, I'll be right there. Are you sure this can't wait. Aren't you going to Chicago in a few minutes?"

"That's right, but I need to talk to you."

She would probably become suspicious and have told him to call her on his cell phone, but we will do it your way, Mr. P.

Nicole comes down the stairs and gets to the door. She looks through the peephole and there is O.J. What a sight with a sweat suit and knit cap. She wonders what is going on. This is the middle of summer. He is supposed to be going on a trip in a few minutes. Very strange, but he is odd at times. She opens the door.

"What do you want, O.J.?"

We now have to imagine what happens next. O.J. can't just come at her with a knife. He has to shoot for vital organs. With a knife in his hand, he spins her around, catching her by surprise and begins to stab her. She tries to get free. O.J. must have gotten one hand over her mouth so she can't yell. With the free hand he continues to stab her. Somehow with one free hand he manages to draw the knife across her throat and nearly severs her head. With my eyes closed, I am trying to picture this attack and struggle. It doesn't work, Mr. P. Nicole falls to the ground and O.J. turns to leave when he sees Ron come upon him. Oh, shit, Ron says, "Hey, hey, hey!" O.J. has to attack Ron because he is now a witness to this murder. They are face to face and O.J. lunges at Ron with the bloody knife. This would mean there would be some of Nicole's blood on Ron's knife wounds. I don't remember any forensics along this line though it seems important. Why the silence? This is very big when you think about it carefully. If either victim has none of the other victim's blood in their wounds then it had to be more than one knife and logically more than one assailant, especially if it took about a minute to perpetrate. What about that one, Mr. P? The fact that we are still guessing as to which one was murdered first is by default evidence that ones blood was not found on the other. There must have been more than one knife and therefore more than one assailant. Ignoring this elementary possibility adds to your unwillingness to examine alternative. I did read elsewhere there were small amounts of Nicole's blood on Ron, but this still doesn't add up.

After going through your book to learn why O.J. was the killer I am left with the same feeling after the criminal trial. It might have been possible for O.J. to commit this terrible crime, but the evidence doesn't prove guilt. The absence of elementary police work makes me suspicious of the entire process. This murder begged for thorough investigation of all possibilities and I don't see that this was done. Justice is the victim when there is a failure to examine all the evidence. My journey through Mr. Petrocelli's book gave me the opportunity to pound on how lawyers are abusing the justice system. This is not new to the public, but when it is presented in the way that _Triumph of Justice_ confesses, it was too compelling an opportunity to express my feelings on the subject.

Years have gone by and again O.J. writing a book that got the public angry reopens the case. Mr. Simpson's actions after this murder have not endeared him to the public. He has fallen from grace. I can't restore that, but I can't convict either.

NOT ENOUGH TIME
NO CUT ON GLOVE
NO NOISE
NO TRANSFER OF BLOOD BETWEEN VICTIMS
   UNLIKELY
A POLICE OFFICERS PLEADING THE 5TH RE:
   EVIDENCE
LOOKS LIKE IT WOULD TAKE MORE THAN ONE
   KILLER
NO WEAPONS OR CLOTHES FOUND
NO CLEAR CUT EVIDENCE
NO REASONABLE EXPLANATION OF WHY HE WOULD
   BECOME A KILLER
NO NEW INFORMATION SINCE THE CRIMINAL TRIAL

No, Mr. Petrocelli you did not convince me he was **_indeed the killer_**. You did expose how lawyers conduct themselves in the pursuit of money. Not a pretty picture when the goal is supposed to be the discovery of **Truth.** This case raised strong emotions and it is hard for people to change attitudes or conclusions, but this terrible crime can have a long lasting benefit if we see the weaknesses in the system and are moved to want changes.

THE END
TO CREATE A BEGINNING

APPENDIX

JURY VOTING CARD

1. I believe O.J. Simpson murdered Ronald Goldman and Nicole Simpson.

   Yes____   No____   Possible, but not Probable_____

2. I believe the police tampered with the evidence.

   Yes____   No____   Probable _____

3. I could not convict because:
   a. The blood evidence was contaminated. _____
   b. There wasn't enough time for O.J. to have killed two people. _____
   c. Spousal Abuse and a bad day does not present enough of a motive._____
   d. The evidence was not convincing. _____
   e. The theory of how the murders took place didn't make sense. _____
   f. The police failed to check other possibilities._____
   g. Other._____

4. My theory of the crimes.

    a. A bad drug deal or collection   _____

    b. Jason   _____

    c. Former Nicole boyfriend   _____

    d. Kato   _____

    e. Hired Killers   _____

    f. Other criminals   _____

    g. Enemy of O.J.   _____

    h. Enemy of Nicole or Faye   _____

    i. O.J. and someone else   _____

a. Other _____

5. If you could convict, what where the reasons?

Scale 1-10 , 10 *most likely*

o   a. History of spousal abuse.   _____

o   The blood evidence.   _____

o   O.J.'s conduct after the murders.   _____

o   No other likely suspect.   _____

o   O.J.'s testimony   _____

o   The totality of the circumstantial evidence.   _____

o   Other _____

1. Are you:

   Caucasian,   Afro-American   Hispanic

              Oriental   Other

2. Was Mr. Petrocelli truly interested in finding "Justice"?

   True   False

3. Is Mr. Petrocelli a racist?   True   False

4. Did this case and the criminal case represent the evils in our legal system?

   True   False

5. Any additional comments.

THE BLARE OF SILENCE

Often in life more is said in silence. The silence in many critical aspects of the O.J. Simpson trial blares out that justice was not served.

A double homicide demands that the police and the prosecution use every means at their disposal to find the killers. This did not happen in the O.J. Simpson case. Why not? Obvious suspects were not pursued. Logical suspects weren't tracked down. Too much silence. The fact that there was no noise during the commission of these crimes screamed out that it probably took more than one person to subdue the victims and control the noise. Why weren't some of Nicole's lovers suspects? Especially, the chap that caused Nicole to have an abortion. Since Nicole had an active sexual life it would seem that a rejected lover might be a suspect. We, the public, heard nothing about eliminating other possibilities that led to the murders. The silence is deafening.

Despite the circumstantial evidence pointing to O.J., he was entitled to have other suspects interviewed with the same focus placed on him. Those following the case put alternative possibilities forward. They were obvious, yet the police and the prosecution were singularly committed to getting O.J. The suspicion falls on the system because it is a conspicuous *rush to judgment*.

The public is aware of the financial rewards and the celebrity that comes with such a high profile case. Because of this there is an obligation on the part of the justice system to make it clear that a citizen is being treated fairly. This did not happen in the O.J. Simpson case. Because of the incredible coverage, the message the prosecution gave out is one of victory at all costs. O.J. was too big a quarry not to shoot down. O.J. was to be one of the prosecutorial trophies of the century. The jury didn't agree. But, the public based on what Mr. Petrocelli reveals in his book has convicted him. And finally, what we ended up with is the Lady of Justice getting her throat slit. An ugly picture, yes, but undeniably true. Shame, Shame for the silence.

A LETTER TO THE KIDS

During the writing of this book I began to realize that I would be affecting people in a way that was not intended. I thought that on one hand explaining to the world that your father was not responsible for the deaths is something you already knew, but didn't need to be reminded. Things are said about your mother that is not flattering. Too many in the world came to their conclusions about how the crimes took place without understanding what happened and that has to hurt. I do open the door for law enforcement to look for the killer. I don't know where that's going to take them,
but the whole subject will be stirred up again. That's not good, but unavoidable.

This book evolved with more than one theme. The first is to recommend that before people conclude how a crime took place, they should have sufficient facts. Also, attorneys instigate much of the problem and I call one on it, but he is one of many. Finally the justice system too often gets caught up in achieving a desired, even understandable result rather than pursuing the truth. All of these are harmful to our nation. Hopefully some day there will be a chorus speaking out against this serious problem.

I truly hope this all has a positive result. If not, please understand that I do regret any negative outcome.

A LETTER TO FRED GOLDMAN

I guess this book could enrage you. You have been convinced of O.J.'s guilt and I'm saying there is reasonable doubt. What is important is the real killers are apprehended. To the extent that I stir up interest and the police look into the logical possibilities, it will be better than having the crime unsolved. Yes, Fred you may think you solved this murder, but the legal system disagreed.

As far as Daniel Petrocelli is concerned, he should have told you from the beginning that O.J.'s lawyers probably have him judgment-proofed. The chances of you getting money from the case were problematic. That's why Daniel didn't want to take the case on contingency or pro bono. Those unflattering observations I have made regarding the lawyers that have carried the business of winning at the expense of justice and the clients should hit home with you. Whatever my writings may do to stir this murder up once again, I'll be expecting a reaction from you. My wish is to see Justice have victory here.

A LETTER TO THE BROWNS

The entire episode of the murder of your daughter is a nightmare no one should have to endure. Writing this book brought me to places that were uncomfortable, but I was being led by the writings of Mr. Petrocelli. He didn't paint your daughter in a good light. Many assumptions are being made and very few facts are there to support them. If the real killer is still on the loose, then the police have an obligation to continue to solve this murder.

The single concept for me was to try to discover what was reasonable to have taken place. Many acted poorly during this whole ordeal. Let's hope that the real killer is found.

A LETTER TO MR. DANIEL PETROCELLI, ESQ.

I had a choice of how to write the critique of your book and the way you handled the O.J. Simpson's case. Although it can argued that the ills of society are best fixed through kindness, love, compassion, empathy and friendship, I didn't use any of these laudable ways to communicate my upset with your abuse of the justice system. You are a victim also. You were seduced by the rewards that come from being a lawyer who will do all that is necessary to win, even at the expense of abandoning the truth. Your confession of this weakness in your own hand reveals that you are not unaware of the way you fight for victory. If your book promised to show how a lawyer could successfully win, even if the evidence and logic are not on his side, then fine. But, you made an important claim to the contrary. You claimed that *Justice* was the prime objective. This distinction drew the line I tried to follow throughout your book. Did Mr. Petrocelli stay faithful to the truth, and even at the expense of losing the case? Or did you employ tactics to deceive, manipulate and engineer a victory?

Daniel, you let me down. You let your client down, and you let the American public down. My attack on your tactics however, is only metaphorical. All you did was give me an example of how many lawyers practice the art of winning. The reason that this is something to write about is that the practice is pervasive and costing the American public dearly. Not only in the cost of goods and services, but also in the sacred trust they should have in the judicial system.

If those who read my book understand that Mr. Daniel Petrocelli, Esq. stands for a group of lawyers abusing the legal system, then this writing is more than showing O.J. was a victim, it is a protest against those who use the system for personal gain rather than seeking Justice.

ACKNOWLEDGEMENTS

If you feel that this reading experience brought you more than the price of the book you can thank those that helped make it happen. Since I knew that the premise would be highly controversial, I sought the opinions and help of anyone that would spend time discussing the subject. Several friends were generous with their time, criticism and help. Judges, lawyers, criminal psychologist, former prosecutors, drug dealers, and just regular folks gave me additional insight into the reasoning behind the opinions regarding O.J's role in these murders. Of course to Mr. Petrocelli for providing a map to the more reasonable truth, despite his intention to do otherwise.

Friends poured over the manuscript for typos and silly mistakes. Winston, Hector, Billy, Bill, Joseph, gave important insights. Denise Foley helped jumpstart the journey and the challenge of getting the book into your hands was tackled by Julie Feuerstein. The constant encouragement from Bart kept the boat afloat. And most importantly, JR, that found and cured zillion mistakes, gave the love, and encouragement to make a dream of getting this message across a reality. Thank you.

Printed in the United States
100845LV00003B/162/A